THE ESSENTIALS OF
FORMAL AXIOLOGY

Rem B. Edwards

University Press of America,® Inc.
Lanham · Boulder · New York · Toronto · Plymouth, UK

Copyright © 2010 by
University Press of America,® Inc.
4501 Forbes Boulevard
Suite 200
Lanham, Maryland 20706
UPA Acquisitions Department (301) 459-3366

Estover Road
Plymouth PL6 7PY
United Kingdom

Library of Congress Control Number: 2010932648
ISBN: 978-0-7618-5290-2 (paperback : alk. paper)
eISBN: 978-0-7618-5291-9

CONTENTS

Contents

PREFACE

The value theory presented in this book was originally developed by a very distinguished 20th Century Philosopher, Robert S. Hartman. You can learn more about him and his ideas in the philosophical parts of each chapter of this book. What this book presents is based squarely on his work and on later critical and constructive reflections upon it. There are at least two ways of talking about his theory of value: first, in plain English that almost anyone should be able to understand, second, in somewhat more technical philosophical language. In *The Essentials of Formal Axiology*, these approaches will be separated from one another as much as possible in the first two chapters, though never completely. This book is designed both to introduce axiological thinking in the simplest possible way to those who have little or no exposure to it, and to explain the specifics of formal axiology to those who already have some familiarity with value theory in general. The first part of Chapters One and Two will largely be a non-technical explanation of key axiological concepts. Later in those chapters, a "Philosophical Exposition" will be given to further enrich the reader's understanding. Each Philosophical Exposition will explain relevant topics as clearly and simply as possible, but some philosophical language will be introduced and further developed along the way. In succeeding chapters, beginning with Chapter Three, the easy-to-understand language, though present, will not be separated from the Philosophical Expositions because by then readers should be familiar and comfortable enough with philosophical language and with thinking hard about issues of value and valuation.

Let's begin with the word "axiology." This is a technical word already, but it can be explained in a relatively non-technical way. "Axiology" means "value theory." Value theory deals with topics that concern us all—questions of good and evil, right and wrong, beauty and ugliness, reasonableness and unreasonableness, correctness and incorrectness. These value words are familiar to all. Yes, there are theories, about human values, just as there are theories about many other things like atoms, human nature, gravity, and the origin of our universe. Theories about values exist in such abundance that you will not have time to learn about them all. This book will try to save you a lot of time and trouble by focusing on the one value theory that seems to its author (and many others) to work best—a good value theory about goodness itself. It is called "Formal Axiology." Just how well it works, how much sense it makes, and how helpful it is, you must finally judge for yourself, but studying and thinking about what is explained in this book should help. Eventually, you may want to look elsewhere at other theories of value. This is only a beginning, not the last word!

The approach to values presented in this book is called "Formal Axiology." Just what is "formal" about it will be explained in greater depth in following chapters. For the time being, try to understand that things happen in patterns, and formal axiology attempts to show us the general or formal patterns into which human values and valuations fall. Road maps show roadway patterns that might lead to where we want to go. Formal axiology will identify the patterns involved in *what* we value (value-objects) and *how* we value (valuations or evaluations). Since knowledge is power, understanding what and how we do and should value should empower us to live better lives, which is something that all of us want very much to do.

The major objectives of this book are:

1) to explain formal axiology and some of its applications,

2) to provide a *critical* introduction to axiology that faces both its strengths and its limitations,

3) to advance formal axiology beyond where Hartman left it by suggesting and developing ways of overcoming its original limitations. Hartman himself expected this to happen. I hope that he would be pleased with what readers will find in this book,

4) to advocate the adoption of and to encourage further developments and applications of formal axiology.

I thank the Robert S. Hartman Institute and the heirs of Jan Hartman for permission to quote from Hartman's *The Structure of Value* and his other published and unpublished writings. Short quotes from his journal articles should fall within "fair use."

This book is dedicated to the loyal Officers and Board Members of the Robert S. Hartman Institute and our Iberoamerican Branch in Mexico who work so hard and faithfully without pay to make Hartman's work available to the world.

Rem B. Edwards
Lindsay Young Professor of Philosophy, Emeritus
The University of Tennessee, Knoxville, TN
May, 2010

Chapter One

THE FORM OF THE GOOD

Tying to explain values to people is like trying to explain water to fish. We are swamped in values all the time—like fish in water. Every wakeful moment, we are valuing something, and that something is a value-object. Consciousness is wakeful processing and evaluation of values, so we can't escape values as long as we are alive and alert. We are involved with values every moment of our lives, but, like fish valuing water, we usually just take them for granted and do not pay special attention to them. When fish are out of water, *then* they take notice, but by then it may be too late! We need to pay attention to our values before it is too late, while we are still in the swamp! All of us want to live valuable lives, good lives, meaningful lives; and knowing what to value as well as how we value can really make a difference. If you want to be a good student, a good parent, a good worker, a good lover, or a good anything, there are certain things that you need to know, like the meaning of "good," and how to apply it. So also with living a good life.

To explain values (value-objects), we have to begin somewhere, but where we begin will not be exactly where we will end. To begin, let's say that values are things that interest us, or things that we want. This is really not the best definition of "value," but it will get us started. Notice that some of our interests or desires are positive and some are negative. We are interested in warming ourselves by the fire on a cold winter's night, but we don't want to burn our hands in the process. We want to be popular and have friends, but we don't want to alienate people and end up friendless. We want to find someone to love who in turn will love, understand, and be loyal to us, but we do not want to be loveless, misunderstood, and friendless. All of these things are values, though for some purposes we may want to call the negative ones "disvalues." The preceding Preface said that value theory deals with good and evil, right and wrong. Broadly understood, good and evil, right and wrong are all values, some positive, some negative. We make value judgments about them.

Good things come by degrees, so degrees of goodness also count as values, broadly conceived. We have lots of value words for degrees of goodness such as "fair," "average," "poor," and "no good" or "worthless." All of these are "values."

Yes, "value" has a very broad meaning that includes degrees and negatives as well as positives, but much of the time we give "value" a narrower meaning and treat it as the same thing as "good." A valuable thing is a good thing; a bad thing is a disvalue—an evil, something wrong, worthless, ugly, hurtful, irrational, or tasteless. Often, "value" just means the same thing as "good," so if we can figure out what "good" means, we will know what "value" in this positive sense usually means.

1. What "Good" Means

We are conscious of, interested in, attracted to or repelled by *something* all the time we are awake. Our interests are often felt as wants or desires, attractions or revulsions. If we want an apple, we have to know what "apple" means. If we want a new car, we have to know what "new" and "car" mean. If we want to text-message, we have to know what "text-message" means. So it is with "good." If we want goodness, we have to know what "good" means. If we don't know what we are seeking, we will never find it, or if we do we will not recognize it. This book should help you to understand the goodness you seek and how to find it.

This is where the trouble starts. Maybe nobody knows what "good" means. Or maybe we all know, but nobody can explain it. Maybe "good" is so basic that it cannot be analyzed or defined. Or maybe "good" just means something else like "enjoyable," "desired," "liked," or "preferred." Maybe it just means "Hurrah," nothing more. Philosophical thinkers have tried all of these approaches to understanding the meaning of "good." For one reason or another, all these have been blind alleys. This book will make a very long story very short and try to give you something that really will work.

In formal axiology, "good" just means "concept fulfillment." This may seem mysterious at first, but it can be explained in language that you can understand. Once you get it, you can use this knowledge to become a better judge of values and disvalues and to live a more fulfilling life. "Concept fulfillment" is "The Form of the Good" that Philosophers have sought since the time of Plato. Here what this means.

Suppose you want to buy a new car; of course, you want to get a good one. You soon realize that you will be able to tell the difference between good ones, not-so-good ones, and very bad ones, only if you learn a lot about the new cars now being sold. Buying a new car is a big deal. It calls for an investment of thought, time, and effort. Most people don't shell out their money for something that complicated and expensive on a whim or on the spur of the moment. They do a lot of research and give it a lot of thought before they buy, so that is what you now begin to do. You may read a lot about cars, talk to many people about them, try to find out what your family members want, and even consult consumer magazines or internet sites for information about them. You realize that you will never get a good car unless you know what to look for, so you try to develop some expertise in judging cars, and you may call on some experts to help you. You want to do more than just "kick the tires;" you realize that you need to know what you are doing—or else! As you learn more and more about the makes and models that are available, you begin to get a clearer picture of what you really want, and you learn to make comparisons. You discover that some cars have the features you want and others do not. Gradually, you begin to get a pretty good idea about what you are looking for, and you learn which makes and models fulfill your expectations and which do not. You realize that you might not be able to get absolutely everything that you want, that you might have to make some compromises and settle for a fairly decent car instead of a perfectly good one.

Still, you want the best car you can get for your money. You want a really good one if you can get it. Now, think for a moment about what you have been doing while trying to find a good car. You gradually clarified in your own mind what you want, that is, what a good car for you would be like; and you learned enough about what is available on the market to realize that some auto makes and models fulfill your hopes, desires, and expectations much better than others. If you are really lucky, you have found the perfect car of your dreams, the one that has everything! You will then likely enjoy owning and driving it.

The one that "has everything" that it is supposed to have would be a really good one, so think a little bit more about this "everything." Having everything means measuring up, meeting your expectations, fulfilling your standards or criteria. Well, that is exactly the same thing as, "Good means concept fulfillment." Step one in finding a good car was to clarify and formulate your standards or criteria for "good car." You may have done this only in your own mind or thoughts, or you may have written them down in a list. Just clarifying what you want probably took a good bit of time and effort. Once you have done this, that is your concept of a good car. Given that concept, the next or second step was to examine, measure, and get information about the available alternatives. Step three was applying your concept to what was actually available. You try to find the particular car that has everything that you are looking for; if and when you do, you have found your good car. A formal pattern underlies all of this, and it applies across the board to all forms of goodness, not just to cars. "X is good" means that "X fulfills its concept," or "X fulfills the standards or criteria applied to it." "X is good" means that X has everything, that is, it has *all* relevant good-making features or properties.

People have different tastes in cars, so any two individuals might have different standards, criteria, or concepts of what a car is supposed to be. Yet, when they find the one that meets their standards, they have found a good one. The Form of the Good is universal and objective; its application is relational, subjective, and depends on people and their circumstances. Consider these two concepts of "good car," and note that the elements that make up the standards or criteria partly overlap (between 8 and 13 below):

CAR A
1. large enough for a family
   (a family sedan)
2. automatic transmission
3. smooth quite ride
4. gas efficient
5. standard equipment sound system
6. four doors
7. large trunk space
8. safe tires
9. reliable, needing few repairs
10. comfortable seats
11. safety features like seat belts,
    air bags, strong bumpers
12. air conditioning
13. affordable price

Car B
1. small and cozy for only two
   (a small sports car)
2. straight shift
3. stiff noisy ride
4. even more gas efficient
5. special powerful sound system
6. two doors
7. small trunk space
8. safe tires
9. reliable, needing few repairs
10. comfortable seats
11. safety features like seat belts,
    air bags, strong bumpers
12. air conditioning
13. affordable price

Most people buying cars will consider more than these thirteen things; they will have a richer idea or concept of what a good one is supposed to be like. Once they know what they are looking for (once they have their concept of a "good X"), they can then do some knowledgeable shopping. They can then apply their standards or criteria to particular cases or cars. They may want to know if some particular car, for example, their own car, is a good one, or they may want to compare the cars for which they are shopping. Either way, they will need a concept of a good car. They will also need to gain some knowledge of actual cars to see what they are like. They can use the Form of the Good to make comparisons and well-informed shopping decision. If they are lucky, they will own, or they will find, a real car that matches their expectations, one that fulfills their concept, criteria, or standards—a good one.

Note carefully that the process of formulating a list of criteria to be fulfilled by any good thing, including cars, need not be a purely individual or solitary enterprise. Identifying relevant good-making properties can be, and often should be, a collective or social enterprise. When buying a new family car, for instance, everyone in the family should have a say-so about the good-making properties they want, and some participants may have to make compromises. All of us can usually benefit from the value insights and perspectives of others, no matter what we are evaluating, but when all is said and done, after every relevant person has had an input, the Form of the Good is concept fulfillment, even if sometimes we have to settle for what is a bit less than the absolute best.

This should be enough to give you the right idea about what "good" means. A good anything has all the features that our ideal for it says that it ought to have, that it would be best for it to have. Good is concept or standard fulfillment. The *conceptual elements* or intensions in our concept-to-be-fulfilled (1 through 13 in the above examples) can be called "*ideal* good-making features" or in more technical language, "good-making predicates." The *realities or extensions* that correspond to them are "good-making properties." Predicates and intensions are the "concept" elements in "concept fulfillment." Properties and extensions are the "fulfillment" elements in "concept fulfillment." Good-making properties are the attributes by virtue of which a thing is good *because* it fulfills its ideal good-making predicates. To find a good car, we must locate one that *actually has* the good-making features or properties called for by our ideal. "Good" just means "concept, criteria, or standard fulfillment." Good things match or fulfill their ideal standards. As Hartman said, "In terms of modern axiological philosophy it [good] means that the thing is good if it has its good-making properties" (Hartman, 2002, 210). This seems simple and obvious enough once we understand it, but took Philosophers over 2000 years to get there! Robert S. Hartman said it first!

We can become much more efficient evaluators of goodness and degrees thereof if we master the Form of the Good and learn to apply it whenever we make value judgments. Without realizing what they are doing, consumer magazines and internet websites practice applied axiology all the time. They list the good-making features of products or services being considered; then, they identify particular products or services offered by various manufacturers or providers. Finally, they tell us which products or services measure up to the relevant standards, and by what degrees. Consumer products are not the only things that can be assessed using the axiological Form of the Good. The goodness of *anything* can be assessed this way—a good worker, a good employer, a good parent, a good child, a good friend, a morally good person, a good self, a good religion, a good belief-system, anything whatsoever. We can and often do debate and disagree about which good-making features are appropriate for each of these; but to make an informed decision about what is good, we always have to use the axiological Form of the Good. This usually takes some time, thought, and effort, but it works!

Thus, to be an effective judge of the value or goodness of anything, we must:

1. Have *a relevant idea or ideal*, the elements of which are "good-making features or predicates."
2. Examine or inspect *the things* to which this ideal applies.
3. Learn which of these things best *match or correspond* with the ideal, which ones actually have the relevant "good-making properties."
4. Judge which particular one best fulfills the ideal when making comparisons.

Having done all of these things, we can then act accordingly and reasonably. We can make well informed practical decisions and ethical decisions. Maybe more than one thing completely fulfills our ideal. Then it does't matter which we pick. Anything that has everything will do.

EXERCISE: Using the following FORM OF THE GOOD, try to assess the goodness of several things in which you are interested.

GOOD-MAKING FEATURES ACTUAL FEATURES
1. _____ 1. _____
2. _____ 2. _____
3. _____ 3. _____
4. _____ 4. _____
5. _____ 5. _____
6. Extend as far as needed. 6. Extend as far as needed.

Note that "good" itself does not belong anywhere inside these lists. As explained next, "good" belongs to the total set or list of good-making features, not within the set. Good consists in the completeness of the list or the set.

2. Degrees of Goodness

Good involves completeness; good things have *all* of the good-making features that we want or expect them to have. Their actual properties perfectly match all of their ideal properties. Their good-making features are all there. *Good means actually having a complete set of ideal good-making features or properties.*

Sometimes, we have to settle for things that are less than good, or good only by degrees. We don't always end up with a perfect car, or a perfectly good anything else. We have many words for things that are less than perfect or ideal, words like "fair," "average," "poor," and "no good" or "worthless." Our houses, jobs, co-workers, vacations, or whatever, may be only fair, average, poor, or no-good. All these words signify degrees of goodness that fall short of the ideal by gradations. *Good* things have *all* their ideal attributes; *fair* ones have *most* of them; *average* things are *so-so*; *poor* ones lack *more than half* of their ideal features; *no-good* or *worthless* things *hardly count* at all. Hartman acknowledged that in ordinary language we have many words to mark these distinctions.

> While "good," "fair," "bad," and "no good" are the basic value terms, there are a great number of equivalents....Such linguistic axiological quantifiers are "excellent," "perfect," "fine," and so on for *good*; "so-so," "not bad," "o.k.," and so forth for *fair*; "poor," "not good," "inferior," "deficient," and so forth for *bad*; "rotten," "lousy," "miserable," and so on for *no good* (Hartman, 1957, 205).

It is not just the *number* of good-making features that matter. Their importance or quality also counts, so we may have to go even deeper to decide how to rank them. Ranking will be discussed more later, but we can easily see that some good-making features count more heavily than others. To some people, the color of a car (not mentioned in the list above) is very important, but to others it is secondary to other good-making features, like those that are noted above. Ranking may be just a matter of personal interests and tastes, but often there is a large consensus about rankings. People recognized as "experts" on any topic are the custodians of agreed-upon features and rankings. Each of us can be an expert about only a few things, so we often just have to trust or rely upon the authorities.

To understand how some features can be more important than others, consider our own bodies. Some of our body parts are much more important to us than others. Our "vital organs" are absolutely indispensable. Without brains, hearts, kidneys and such, we just can't make it, though modern medical miracles can provide us with interim substitutes for them (except brains). However inconvenient, we can also get along without "non-vital" body parts, even without substitutes. Can you think of a few? For almost everything, some good-making features are more important or valuable than others. To show or see that, we may just have to apply or re-apply the Form of the Good more carefully and thoroughly. We may have to apply it to each kind good-making property as well as to some total set of them. For example a good car has good brakes, but what are our criteria for identifying good brakes? A healthy person has a good heart, but what are our criteria for having a good heart?

What features should a really good human body have? How about a fair body? How about an average body, or a poor one? How about one that is no good at all (e.g., a dead one)? The familiar distinction between "vital" versus "non-vital" organs and body parts tells us something about degrees of importance. If some things are not there, or do not work right, we would still have a pretty fair body (as most of us do). Without even a few more significant features, we might still have an average body. When really essential organs and structures go, then we are left with poor or no-good bodies. We are left with poor health, or with no health at all (dead, or almost so). [Compare Hartman's somewhat technical discussion of the different body parts of a horse (Hartman, 1967, 195-197)].

The Form of the Good can be applied to anything of value and to degrees of goodness. Some jobs, for example, may be better than others by degrees, and this goes for just about anything—employers, workers, places to live, vacation spots, athletic teams, pension plans, governments, plumbers, politicians, preachers—anything. "Better" just means "having more good-making features or properties." "Worse" means "having fewer good-making features or properties. "Best" means having more than all the others; "worst" means having less than all the others. By degrees, things are less and less good as they lack more and more good-making attributes, some perhaps more essential than others. By degrees, things get better and better as they have more and more good-making features. The "more" or "less" here can be both qualitative and quantitative. "More vital organs" is qualitatively as well as quantitatively more significant than just "more organs in general."

3. The Meaning of "Bad"

We can have bad things at least three ways, by lacking good-making properties, by having bad-making properties, and by having undesirable combinations of properties.

A. One way to have bad things was just illustrated and explained. *Some bad things just lack good-making features.* Many past thinkers identified "bad" or "evil" with "privation," that is, with lacking good-making properties. Often, this is an adequate account of badness, but sometimes lack-of-goodness only indicates neutrality. Privation is not always the whole story.

B. Maybe some properties are just bad to start with, and *some bad things just have bad-making properties.* Maybe there is a "Form of the Bad" that corresponds to the "Form of the Good," though Hartman and other axiologists have not previously said so. "Bad" or "evil" could also be "concept fulfillment." Some bad things seem to have bad-making features or properties, not just to lack good-making properties, though they are likely to do that too. Hartman implicitly acknowledged this when he used the "bad-making properties" phrase in explaining the position of another philosopher (Hartman, 2002, 111); but "bad-making properties" needs more explanation.

In some instances, badness, evil, or "sin," as the theologians would say, has real power and reality in itself; and, despite Hartman, it is not mere privation of goodness or the clash of good-making properties. This is fairly obvious when we look at morally bad people. Hitler, for example, was not a bad man simply because he *lacked* love, kindness, peacefulness, and intelligence, though he did lack them. No, he was a bad man because he *possessed* demonic power, hatred, malice, viciousness, cruelty, malevolent cunning, etc. Most theologians say that sin is something very real and powerful in itself, not a mere lack of goodness, though it is that, too. Plato, who held that evil is privation, also said that being is power. He did not seem to notice that some evils have great being and power. The hurtful dispositions that we usually call "vices" are not mere privations. They are real and powerful inner forces or manifestations of evil that actually exist. They are just bad to start with. Some bad-making features really exist as such and are not just privations of being or goodness. Most moral vices involve very real and potent bad-making feelings and very real and hurtful destructive actions. Cruelty, malice, hatred, envy, injustice, and the like involve much more than just not acting for the good or being so motivated; they involve effectively acting for evil and being so motivated. So we really need a distinction between fulfilling "positive" or good-making properties and "negative" or bad-making properties. Both "good"and "bad" can involve "concept fulfillment."

Many non-moral properties are also just bad from the outset. They are more than just privations because they have a very real and powerful existence and presence. Excruciating suffering and pain are the most obvious examples of this. These are not just privations of pleasant or neutral feelings. They are overwhelmingly potent bad or undesirable feelings in themselves that really exist. Anyone in, or who has been in, great pain knows that pain has a terrible reality of its own and is not mere privation of pleasure, of being, or of any other good-making properties. Privation could just be neutrality, not badness. Badness often goes far beyond mere lack or absence of goodness.

All of us also know how to distinguish between "positive" and "negative" feelings or emotional states. When we are in negative emotional states, we are sure that there is something real and forceful (it is tempting to say "positive," but "potent" might be a better word) about them. They are not mere states of deficiency, not just non-being. It isn't that something really good is *lacking*; it is that something really bad and potent is *present*. Examples of inherently bad-making but very real feelings are those involved in depression, sadness, despair, loneliness, jealousy, boredom, and many other terrible "states of mind." Such emotional states are often called "mental pains." Mental pains are very real and powerful. They are not mere privations.

The upshot is, although bad *can* be just the absence of good-making properties, the worst kinds of badness are usually *more than this*. The worst kinds of evil have a power and reality of their own, an inherently bad presence and actuality. Just as some properties are inherently good-making, so some are inherently bad-making, and we can conceptualize each. If so, then bad things as well as good things can involve concept fulfillment. There is a Form of the Bad, as well as a Form of the Good, and either can be fulfilled. In this sense, perfectly bad things would *have* all relevant bad-making properties, not just lack good ones. For example, a person who is perfectly bad morally would both have every conceivable vice and lack every conceivable virtue. Most bad people are just bad by degrees, not absolutely, just as are most good people good by degrees. For that, we can be thankful!

So, bad-making features, like good-making features, can be fulfilled by degrees. We can apply a ranking system of "good," "fair," "average," "poor," and "no-good" to degrees of goodness. We could also develop and use words for degrees of badness. For example, ranging from worst to neutral, we might have a ranking system like "terrible," "grave," "alarming," "troublesome," and "indifferent." Ordinary language may not be very precise in discriminating degrees of badness.

C. A third form of badness also needs to be recognized, *undesirable value combinations*. For this, we will need a technical name. In axiological theory, this form of badness is called a "transposition." Transpositions result when two positive values combine with one another in negative or undesirable ways to bring about a bad state of affairs, a new and undesirable whole, *a bad value combination*. For example, two perfectly good cars can crash into one another to produce a good wreck, which is terrible for the cars because it diminishes their good-making properties as cars. Good wrecks produce bad cars. Intelligence can be combined with explosives to produce smart bombs or roadside bombs. Good feelings can be combined with bad ideas to produce propaganda or misleading advertising. We will return to "transpositions" or bad value combinations later after discussing positive "compositions," which are value combinations that enhance or increase value.

In sum, bad can be:

A. absence of good making features, or

B. presence of bad-making features, or

C. combinations of otherwise good things that diminish or destroy value.

4. Philosophical Exposition

All the important things explained thus far can be re-expressed in technical philosophical language that can be made readily intelligible. The last part of these first two chapters will involve philosophical conversations with Robert S. Hartman, the creator of Formal Axiology. These philosophical expositions will further enrich your understanding, but they will also involve technical philosophical words or concepts.

Robert S. Hartman was influenced by many of his predecessors. He, too, stood on the shoulders of giants. One person especially had a tremendous influence on him—the British philosopher G. E. Moore, who lived from 1873 until 1958. Alfred North Whitehead said that "All philosophy is a footnote to Plato." It would also be true to say that "All 20th Century value theory was a footnote to G. E. Moore." Moore was a Platonist of sorts who, like Plato, sought the Form of the Good in an ethereal realm out of this world, so Whitehead's pronouncement still holds. Moore's most influential book, *Principia Ethica*, was first published in 1903, near the beginning of the 20th century. Almost every later value theorist tried to come to terms with Moore, as did Hartman. But how did Hartman do it?

A. G. E. Moore and the Meaning of "Good"

G. E. Moore posed his famous "Three Questions of Ethics," slightly paraphrased.
1. "What is *meant* by 'good'?" (Moore, 1903, 37)
2. "What *things* are good?" (77)
3. "What *ought we to do?*" (146)

The second and third questions will be discussed later, but right now, we are interested only in Moore's first question. First, let's be clear that the meaning of "good" isn't just an issue for ethics. Today, this would be called a question of "metaethics," which deals with the meaning of ethical concepts and with methods that can be used to justify ethical judgments. Also, "good," once defined, does not belong exclusively to the domain of ethics or moral conduct. It is an *axiological* word that extends *far beyond ethics*. As Hartman indicated, "What Moore calls "Ethica" should really be called "Axiologica" for Moore endeavored to find not what is moral good but what is "good in general" (*Principia Ethica*, p. 4)" (Hartman, 1967, 335, n. 6). Accounts of morally good people and good deeds belong to ethics, but non-moral things can also be good—good sex, good apple pie, good ideas, good cars, good rain—almost endlessly. "Good" belongs to axiology, the general theory of value, which includes ethics, but extends far beyond it.

Note that "good" is a word or a concept. Words have meanings, and Moore was after its meaning. He thought that we could make no progress in "ethics" or value theory (axiology) until we first understand its meaning, for "good" is, Moore thought, the central concept of ethics or value theory.

So, how did Moore define "good"? Oddly, he insisted that it could not be defined! He did not deny that we could *give synonyms* for it like "desirable," "valuable," or "worthwhile;" but he was very skeptical about using other words to define or analyze the meaning of "good." Some words will not work at all, he insisted, especially descriptive words like "pleasant" or "desired," words that name what he called "natural properties." Such definitions commit what he called the "naturalistic fallacy."

Moore thought that goodness is *a non-natural* property (like those in Plato's "realm of ideas"). The word "good" *refers* to *something,* but what? It refers to a quality, but not a natural or descriptive quality, Moore held. It refers to a kind of "other worldly" quality, to something very much like Plato's Form of the Good, to something not of this world, to something "non-natural." According to Moore, "good" cannot be defined either *by giving natural property synonyms* or by *using a more complicated set of descriptive words.* Why not? Using natural properties commits the naturalistic fallacy. And using more complicated sets of words won't work either, Moore insisted, because, "good" is *a simple* concept, like "yellow." It has no simpler parts; there are no simpler words for it or to explain it. Either you know what it is, or you don't. Like the concept of "yellow," the meaning of "good" is *"unanalyzable,"* according to Moore. We know perfectly well what it means, but we can't break it down or analyze it into simpler parts. Good is good, just as yellow is yellow, and that's that. We can name and point to *good things,* just as we can point to yellow things, but we cannot define either "good" or "yellow" by breaking them down into simpler concepts. "Good," Moore contended, is *a simple, unanalyzable, indefinable, non-natural concept or property.* This "other worldly form" sticks to some things in this world—good things, but it does not stick to other things—neutral or bad things. We know it when we "see" it, experience it, or intuit it; but we can't define it, according to Moore.

As Moore knew, many philosophers tried hard and often to define "good," but such attempts usually commit what he called the "naturalistic fallacy"—the fallacy of identifying "good" with some natural, empirical, or descriptive property or properties. Such definitions attempt to define something that cannot be defined, and they confuse answers to the second question of ethics (or axiology) with answers to the first. People often believe mistakenly that they are defining "good" when they are really only saying that some particular kind of thing is good. For example:

1. Some (but not all) *hedonists* contend that "good" is synonymous with "pleasure" or "pleasant." (Correspondingly, "evil"just means "pain" or "painful" to them.)
2. *Desire theorists* contend that "good" means "any object of desire," or "desire fulfillment."
3. *Interest theorists* contend that "good" means "any object of interest," or perhaps "interest fulfillment."

Yes, pleasures, desire fulfillment, and interest fulfillment are good things; but that is not what "good" means. In Moore's view, such "naturalistic" definitions of "good" either (1) try to define the indefinable, or they (2) confuse the *meaning* of the non-natural quality of "good" with some natural or empirical quality like pleasure, desire, preference, or interest, (i.e., with some *thing* that is good). Natural qualities are those that can be experienced with our five external senses, or with internal self-awareness or introspection. (We can't *sense* pleasures, desires, emotions, and interests with our five "external" senses, but we definitely can experience them internally or introspectively.)

Perhaps the quality to which the word "good" refers is known by something like a rational intuition, but it cannot be sensed or felt. Asking whether desires, objects of desire, interest, preferences, etc., are really good makes perfectly good sense, so "good'" cannot be identical with them in meaning, Moore argued. Whether they are good is an "open question," but it would not be if their meanings were identical. "Is getting what you want really good?" is not a meaningless or self-answering question like, "Is getting what you want getting what you want?" But it would be if their meanings were the same, Moore contended.

Moore believed that he could answer his second question, "What things are good?" but not his first, "What does 'good' mean?" Here is the gist of his own answer to his *second* question, "What things are good?"

> By far the most valuable things, which we know or can imagine, are certain states of consciousness, which may be roughly described as *the pleasures of human intercourse and the enjoyment of beautiful objects.* No one, probably, who has asked himself the question, has ever doubted that personal affection and the appreciation of what is beautiful in Art or Nature, are good in themselves (italics added) (Moore, 1903,188).

"Good," Moore insisted, has some kind of real connection with natural properties like "the pleasures of human intercourse" and "the enjoyment of beautiful objects," but it is not identical with them in *meaning.* These are *good things;* their natural properties make them good; but they are NOT *the meaning or definition of "good" itself.* Moore puzzled over the connection between "good" and "good-making natural properties" for the rest of his life, but he never figured it out. To him it remained an unresolved mystery. Robert S. Hartman figured it out!

B. Hartman's Formal Definition of "Good": The Axiom of Axiology

Robert S. Hartman agreed with much that Moore said about defining "good." He agreed:

1. that "good" is not identical in meaning with any single or any complex set of natural qualities or properties, and

2. that "good" is intimately related to the natural qualities or properties of *good things* (like enjoying human intimacy and beauty in nature and art).

Hartman profoundly disagreed with G. E. Moore on two other issues. He insisted:

1. that "good" *can* be defined (Hartman, 1967, 120, 131, 338 n. 13), and
2. how natural properties are related to "good" can be explained and is no mystery (133-136).

Hartman agreed with Moore that "good" cannot be defined *naturalistically* in terms of merely descriptive or empirical concepts or properties. As Hartman explained it, the naturalistic fallacy is "Any attempt to define value in general by specific kinds of value—ontological, teleological, epistemological, etc., as perfection, purpose, function, knowledge, God, pleasure, self-realization, preference" (Hartman, 1967, 100). Nevertheless, "good" can be defined *formally*, and G. E. Moore completely overlooked this possibility (131).

A *formal* definition would capture The Form of the Good—the general logical pattern inherent in all intelligible uses of "good." There is something to Plato's "Form of the Good" after all, but Hartman makes sense of it without having to locate it in some transcendent otherworldly "realm of forms." The Form of the Good is a logical or conceptual form, not an other-worldly metaphysical form. It is located within the very world in which we live and think. Hartman was the very first philosopher to "see" the form of the good very clearly. You will not find his definition anywhere in the history of ethics or in value theory before Hartman, even though once expressed, it seems so obvious. The meaning of "good" or "value" *can* be expressed in words; it can be defined, formally, as "concept (or standard fulfillment," as previously explained.

Discovering and articulating the Form of the Good was not easy or instantaneous. Hartman set out to find the general form or pattern that all meaningful uses of "good" have in common. This was no simple or easy quest. He wrestled long and mightily with the problem. One day, after years of reflection, the answer came to him in a revealing (not a blinding) flash of insight. Here is how Hartman described his quest and its resolution or disclosure:

> The nature of goodness itself could only be approached, I decided, through analysis of the *word* "good."
>
> I spent several years thinking about that word. Whenever I read or heard it, I noted its use. In the *Oxford English Dictionary*, I found 135 uses and in Grimm's *Dictionary of the German Language*, 528 quarto columns. Eventually I had collected thousands of samples, by which time [1948] I had left Wooster to teach philosophy at the Ohio State University at Columbus.
>
> Now what had all these uses in common? I spent most of my sabbatical time in 1949 trying to wring the answer from my piles and piles of evidence. Finally, on the afternoon of the day before Christmas, as I was putting a book back onto a shelf in my study, it suddenly hit me, out of the blue, and I knew I had it (Hartman, 1994, 51-52).

So what was it that hit him? *Good is concept fulfillment!* That formal definition is the basic axiom of axiology! Good things are the ones that fulfill the standards, criteria, or conceptual ideals or norms that we apply to them. This means that good things have *all* the properties that they are supposed to have, that they exemplify all the properties called for by the idealized conceptual standards that we apply to them. Their extensions (referents) exist in one to one correspondence with their intensions (ideas or concepts). Their actual properties match their ideal predicates. Of course, for less than good things, those that are only fair, average, poor, or bad, the correspondence of actual properties with ideal predicates is less than one to one, by degrees. Here is how Hartman explained it.

> Value ... is defined as a formal relation, namely, the correspondence between the properties possessed by a subject and the predicates contained in the intension of the subject's concept (Hartman, 1967, 154).

> Let us define anything as good (or valuable) if it is what or as it is supposed to be (Hartman, 1991b, 13).

> To measure value by meaning means, then, to use meaning as a measuring rod which fits the thing and from which the number of the value of the thing can be read off. Meaning as logical intension, or as a set of predicates, is, precisely, such a standard of measuring. Just as the units of the meter are the centimeters, so the units of an intension are the predicates it contains. This set of predicates is compared with the set of properties actually possessed by the thing; and the thing has *value* in the degree that the set of its properties corresponds to the set of predicates in its intension; just as the thing has *length* in the degree that the units of length it possesses correspond to the centimeters contained in the measure of its length, the meter (Hartman, 2006, 28).

Review again the Form of the Good as explained in Section 1. Remember that it can be applied to absolutely anything. Once you have mastered it, you will know how to evaluate *anything* rationally. No matter what you are evaluating, to determine rationally if it is any good, you must first be clear about the good-making predicates that make up your relevant conceptual standard or norm; then you must somehow experience or get to know the thing or reality being valued; then you must compare the thing with its norms to see how it measures up. If it matches, it is good.

Hartman's axiom of axiology, the Form of the Good, *also explains how natural properties are related to "good."* G. E. Moore never figured this out (Hartman, 1967, 133-136). We have words for natural properties; we call them "predicates;" for example, the predicate "pleasure" refers to the property, pleasure. Hartman says that a "predicate" is "the name of a property" (Hartman, 1961, 389, n. 2). Sets of natural predicates compose our ideal standards or criteria; good things have the corresponding natural properties. Natural properties are "good-making properties" precisely because they correspond to and are called for by the ideal conceptual predicates by which goodness is measured. "Good" is the one-to-one correspondence between a set of ideal good-making predicates and a matching set of descriptive good-making properties. Good things are meaningful, that is, they fulfill their ideal meanings. Not-so-good things are less meaningful, less fulfilling.

C. "Good" vs. "Value"

Hartman did not always treat "good" and "value" as synonyms, so he did not always identify the meaning of "good" with his most logically basic principle. He usually did, but in a few places, he introduced another very abstruse definition of "value" that is quite different from the definition of "good" as just explained. He occasionally compared the meaning of "value" with Bertrand Russell's definition of "number." Here is how he did it.

> According to Russell, a number is the class (extension) of classes (extensions) similar to a given class (extension). There also ought to be a concept which is defined as "the set of intensions similar to a given intension." This is the concept of a value (Hartman 1967, 17-18. See also 51-52, 105, 325, n.47).

Hartman's explanation of what this means is almost as incomprehensible as his original statement of it, but consider the following explanation.

Note first that we have many value words—good, fair, average, poor, no-good, bad, evil, disvalue, and so on. In the next chapter, we will see that there are many kinds of goodness or positive value, intrinsic, extrinsic, and systemic. "Good" is just one value word among many, "bad" is another value word, so we need a more inclusive word to cover "good" and *all* these other value words. "Value" seems to fill the bill, or at least Hartman so specified. Thus, occasionally, Hartman defined "value" differently from how he defined "good." "Good" is "concept fulfillment"; but "value" is "the set of intensions similar to a given intension."

Well, what did Hartman mean by "the set of intensions similar to a given intension"? All value words like good, fair, average, poor, no-good, bad, evil, disvalue, and so on are used many times in ordinary conversation and thinking. Every time one of them, "fair," for example, is used, its meaning is "similar" to what it means all the rest of the time in other contexts or applications. So it is with all such value words. On Tuesday, we may call a variety of things "fair" or "good," but their meaning is still "similar to" what they mean on Wednesday or Thursday. That is, their meaning-form on Tuesday is in one to one correspondence with their meaning-form on Wednesday, Thursday, or any other day of the week.

Hartman could have saved us a lot of headaches if had just said that each value word has the same formal meaning every time we use it, and that "value" is our most inclusive word that covers all other value words.

Hartman made only occasional uses of the preceding distinction between "value" and "good," (Hartman, 1967, 149); usually he just identified the two.

Axiologists today may disagree about how important or helpful this distinction is. Clearly, "good" as "concept fulfillment" is what Hartman understood to be the basic axiom of axiology, and most of the time he treated both "valuable" or "value" and "good" as synonyms. So do most axiologists today.

D. Intensional and Extensional Properties

All good things fulfill the norms, criteria, or standards that we apply to them. They are what they are supposed to be. But what is the difference between "good things" and "standards"?

Standards or criteria of goodness are conceptual in nature. They are inten-- sional meanings. Standards consist of sets of ideas or thoughts, specifically ideas about how things are supposed to be, beliefs about what desirable things are supposed to be like. They consist of sets of ideal predicates, technically, of positive normative intensions or concepts. Usually these are the names of natural properties, so the relation between "good" and natural properties is intimate but not identical. Hartman thus solved the problem that G. E. Moore never solved. Natural properties enter into and largely make up our value ideals or standards; they are "good-making" without being goodness itself.

Except for good ideas, *good things* are not conceptual in nature. They are the realities, the extensional meanings, mostly natural objects and processes, to which we apply our standards or criteria. They are the extensions that fulfill our intensions, that is, our conceptually formulated expectations. When the actual properties of good things match up with our ideal predicates, they fulfill our conceptual norms; they fulfill their concepts. Their extensions, extensive meanings, or referents correspond to or correlate with our intensions, our conceptual ideals and meanings, the words by which we name them.

"Good" thus involves meanings, both connotative and denotative. In this technical sense, "good" or "value" is *meaning*. Hartman defined "concept" as "a mental content having both an intension and an extension" (Hartman, 1967, 31). In his own words, "A concept is a mental content having a 'double aperture.' On the one hand it has meaning or intension, on the other reference or extension. The intension is a set of words or symbols, the extension a set of items, concrete or abstract" (31). Both intensions and extensions are meanings, connotative and denotative. Intensions are just words, or thoughts expressed in words. Most words refer to something beyond themselves; they function as signs of or mental tokens for realities. Extensions are the realities or objects to which our words or thoughts (intensions) refer. Intensions are thoughts like "trees" and "rocks." Extensions are the real trees and rocks to which these words point—their referents. We are now familiar with Hartman's distinction between "predicates" (thoughts) and "properties" (the referents of predicates). Predicates are intensions; properties are extensions.

When anything is good, its extensional meanings (properties) exists in one to one correspondence with its ideal intensional meanings (predicates). We often say that a "good life" is a "meaningful life." The properties of good things exist in one-to-one correspondence with the positive predicates (meanings) contained in our standards, criteria, or normative concepts. That is the meaning of "good." That is the Form of the Good.

As explained earlier, concept fulfillment can be a matter of degrees, which is why some desirable things are only fair, average, poor, or no-good. For less than good things, the correspondence of actual properties with ideal predicates is, by degrees, less than one to one. As Hartman himself put it, "A thing is *good* if it has *all* its intensional properties, *fair* if it has more intensional properties than it lacks, *bad* if it lacks more than it has, and *no good* if it lacks most of the intensional properties" (Hartman, 1967, 210-212; see also 160-162).

In one sense, "good" is not a property of good things at all. It is a logical or formal property of the total set of their properties—namely, their *completeness.* In this sense, "good" applies only to *conceptual sets*, not to *things of value* as such (Hartman, 1967, ix, 13). However, the objects to which we apply our standards can also be complete in their correspondence with our standards, so in a secondary sense, "good" does apply to good things. Good things have in themselves all the properties that they are supposed to have, the properties that match up completely with our ideal expectations for them.

E. Definitional and Expositional Properties

In some discussions, Hartman distinguished between two kinds of predicates/ properties—definitional and expositional—only the second of which is relevant to a thing's goodness (Hartman, 1967, 178-179, 187-188, 195-199). From the outset, we must recognize that the line between expositional and definitional properties is not absolutely sharp. Both depend on human selection, and sometimes we select as definitional properties those that might be classified as expositional in other contexts, and vice versa. According to Hartman, "The exact line where an exposition becomes a definition is not ascertainable, precisely for the reason that the thing is an empirical and not a systemic one. Exposition and definition, however, are easily discernible in practice" (195).

In practice, *definitional* properties just tell what something is, not whether it is good or bad. To be classified as a certain kind of thing, any X has to have its defining characteristics. For example, being a "car" means being "a self-moving vehicle on wheels used for passenger transportation." In this definition, the concept "car" is placed within a more inclusive or generic class concept, that of "vehicles," and some of their parts or functions are given in order to distinguish "cars" from other "vehicles." Cars are "self-moving," which makes them different from horse-drawn buggies. Cars have "wheels," which differentiates them from self-propelled boats. Their primary function is "passenger transportation," which distinguishes them from self-moving trucks on wheels. To be a car at all, an object must have these properties; it must be:

1. a vehicle
2. on wheels
3. self-moving
4. used for passenger transportation

However, just being a car does not tell us whether something is a *good* car. A car that has *only* the defining characteristics of a car would not be much of a car! Nothing that exists outside of our minds has *only* definitional properties. As Hartman often explained to his students, "Suppose I give you my car keys and ask you to the parking lot and get my car for me. You then ask me, 'Which one is it,' and I reply, 'The good one.' Well, you will never be able to find my car!" So it is with everything that we try to evaluate. Any good X, must have the defining properties of X just to be classified as an X; but its *goodness* depends on many more properties than those given in its definition, and we have to know what these are to determine its worth. Hartman called these the "expositional" properties; all good-making properties are expositional properties. He wrote that "The definitional properties must in all cases be fulfilled; the value differentiations adhere to the expositional properties exclusively" (Hartman, 1967, 178). Strictly speaking, "good" is not *definition* fulfillment; it is *exposition* fulfillment; "'good' means fulfillment, by the subject, of the exposition of the predicate" (179).

To explain, though our tastes in cars may differ, as we saw in describing "CAR A" and "CAR B" in section 1, any good car must have many *good-making properties in addition to its definitional properties*. Note that the defining properties of "car" above were not even mentioned in either of these "A" or "B" lists of good-making properties. Goodness turns solely on expositional properties. Only expositional properties count as the good-making properties of good things. However, definitional properties are not "value-free." We judge them to be of great importance in naming things and assigning them to classes; but once something gets classified, exposition takes over.

Where do we get our norms, criteria, or standards for judging positive worth, our lists of good-making predicates, like those above? The answer is, they come from many sources. Some of the most obvious are:

cultural conventions,
value-laden languages,
our parents and peers,
religious institutions and authorities,
trend, fashion, or style moguls,
arbitrary choices,
informed choices,
human nature,
conscience, value intuitions.

Obviously, people can and do disagree about which particular items count as good-making predicates/properties. For example, if Democrats and Republicans were to make up lists of the desirable properties of a "good President," or if fundamentalistic Christians and Moslems were to make up lists of the desirable properties of a "good religion," their lists would not have exactly the same contents, though they might partly overlap. Particular items within a standard set can be much debated. Agreement is often reached, but in highly controversial cases, complete consensus is unlikely. Real people can have very honest disagreements about what counts as a good-making predicate or property, and some hard thinking may be required to get anywhere close to the bottom of such disagreements. When all is said and done, people often just have to agree to disagree—and there is nothing that axiology can do about that. In *applying* Hartman's *axiom*, large elements of value relativity can and do enter. Hartman was well aware of this. He wrote that "The axiom of value is *objective*. It is valid for every rational being whatever....But its application is *subjective*" (Hartman, 1967, 110). If we do not agree on the norms, or if we apply them incorrectly, or if we are mistaken about the actual properties of objects being evaluated, then our value judgments will not agree (110-111). To illustrate disagreement about norms, Hartman asked us to consider

> The three judges and the three final contestants in a poodle show. Which poodle would get the prize and be the best? There are here not three poodles but six, the three actual poodles and one poodle each in the minds of each judge, which for him constitutes the ideal poodle or the definition [exposition] of poodle....That poodle will get a judge's vote which most closely resembles the ideal poodle in the judge's head (Hartman, 1952, 8).

In Chapters Three and Four, we will return to "objective in theory but subjective in application," but do not become an ethical relativist too quickly! There may be some universally valid norms or values that practically everyone accepts, at least in their more rational and reflective moments. Chapter Four on "Ethics and Other Applications" shows that formal axiology can identify and verify a few universally valid norms. These will not simply follow logically from the axiom of axiology, but the axiom can be applied to them once they are made available.

The distinction between definitional and expositional properties has a bearing on the much discussed and debated "fact–value" or "is–ought" distinction. Hartman regarded this distinction as "obsolete" because all facts contain values and all values contain facts. They are just two sides of the same coin. How so? Hartman defined "fact" as "anything that is," having the property of "being" (Hartman, 1967, 96). But how do we decide what something "is"? As he further explained,

> Our perception cuts out of the undifferentiated chaos of properties a certain set for differentiation into thinghood. This set is the set of properties Kant called Description. It must be differentiated down to the minimum set of descriptive properties, Definition (218).

Facts are thus less than complete sets of descriptive properties selected to represent particular beings or thinghood; but facts are not valuationally neutral. They are noticed, evaluated, picked out, chosen, and emphasized for their importance. "Thus, the factual set of descriptive properties is a fixation of one set of the variety of valuative sets. It is the fixation of a most important, indeed, the most important such set: the set that makes order out of the chaos of property combinations" (218). A thing's definition or facticity is fixed by the evaluative process of judging and selecting which properties are sufficiently important and typical (i.e., valuable) to serve for identification and communication purposes. Once defined, a thing's "totality of descriptive properties is not lost" (21). This totality includes both its definitional and expositional properties; its complete set of evaluative/descriptive set of properties. Facticity is a sub-set of a thing's total set of evaluative properties selected for identification and communication, and expositional properties are the sub-set of a thing's total properties that functions as good-making. Facts are just "typical" constellations of definitional properties (261) included within a thing's total set of properties. Thus, every "is" (a normatively selected factual set) belongs to an "ought" (an all inclusive normative set), and every ought contains descriptive properties functioning definitionally, typically, or expositionally. "*Value properties are sets of descriptive properties*" (209). Describing is one way of valuing.

F. "Better" and "Best"

Hartman did not explicitly discuss the threefold "good, better, best" scheme of ranking with which most of us are familiar. In this commonplace ranking scheme, "good" corresponds with Hartman's "average," "better" with Hartman's "fair," and "best" with Hartman's "good." The words are different, but the logic is the same. However, Hartman did give formal definitions of "better, and "worse."

> "Richer in properties" is the definition of "better," "poorer in qualities" is the definition of "worse" (Hartman, 1967, 114).

> *X is a better C than y* means that *x* has more expositional properties of *C* than *y* and is therefore "more of" a C than *y*. "Better than," in other words, relates two members of the same class, the first of which has more of the class properties than the second.... *Y is worse than x* means that *y* has fewer expositional properties than *x* (Hartman, 1967, 162-163).

The "class properties" mentioned above are the expositional, not the definitional, properties. To be a "C" at all, two things being so classified and compared must exhibit all relevant definitional properties; they differ only in the degree to which they exhibit relevant good-making expositional properties.

Hartman defined "better" and "worse," but he did not define "best" and "worst" in *The Structure of Value*. However, he did define "best"and "worst" as follows in his earlier article on "Value Propositions."

> *X is the best C* means that x is the one and only C that has the maximum of expositional properties of C, and *x is the worst C* means that x is the one and only C hat has the minimum of expositional properties of C—which does not have to mean that x is no good. The worst C may be a fair one (Hartman, 1957, 208).

In addition to what Hartman noticed, bad things as well as good things can fulfill concepts, so the distinction between "good-making" and "bad-making" properties needs to be added to Hartman's definitions of "better" and "worse." "Good-making properties" are the "expositional properties" that good things must exemplify. Thus, "better" *should be defined* as "richer in good-making properties," not just as "richer in properties." If one thing is richer in bad-making properties (e.g., pain, cruelty, or hatred) than another, it is worse, not better. "Worse" could be defined as "poorer in good-making properties," though it may also be understood as "richer in bad-making properties."

Hartman's definition of "best" can be reworded to mean "having more good-making properties than anything else in its class of comparison," and "worst" can be reworded as "having fewer good-making (or more bad-making) properties than anything else in its class of comparison." Recognizing that bad things as well as good things can fulfill concepts goes beyond Hartman, who formally recognized evil only as privation. Badness or evil is not always just a lack of good properties, or a conflict of good properties, though it can be; it is often the presence of bad-making properties, as previously explained. Hartman never realized that "worst" might in some instances mean "having *more* properties (bad-making ones) than anything else in its class of comparison."

We judge to be best that which most fulfills our expectations, where these have been formulated and expressed conceptually in a coherent set of standards. We can't simply equate "best" with "most preferred," even if preferences ultimately undergird our choices of the elements that compose our standards. Sometimes we prefer sweet, sometimes sour, sometimes the combination of the two, as in a lemon pie; but we know that some lemon pies are better than others. The set of "good making" elements in our standard for "good lemon pie" might be:

A. An appropriate degree of sweetness
B. An appropriate degree of sourness
C. A distinctive "lemony" taste
D. A creamy texture
E. Served cold.

Now, suppose we have slices from three different lemon pies before us, and we are asked to judge if one if them is a good or the best lemon pie. We taste all three (element C. above), and we find that

Pie # 1 is just right in all five respects.
Pie # 2 is too sweet, and it has not been cooled, but it is otherwise OK.
Pie # 3 is not sour enough; it tastes like grapefruit or orange rather than lemon; and it has a grainy texture.

Applying our good-making criteria to these three pies, we find that they are fulfilled or satisfied to varying degrees, so we judge on rational grounds that the first is the best one, the second is pretty fair, and the third is only average or poor. Degrees of value depend on degrees of standard-fulfillment. "Good" is complete standard fulfillment, and "fair," "average," "poor," and "no-good" or "bad" indicate declining quantitative or qualitative degrees of fulfillment. When making comparisons, the best one is the one highest in this scale. It may not always be completely good; it may just be the best of the lot at hand.

How can we tell that some things are better than others? We must have a formula with these ingredients: 1) A conceptually expressed set of standards or expectations ("good-making predicates"), 2) one or more objects to which the set is applied, and 3) a perceptual examination or test of the objects to see how well their actual properties measure up. Comparison takes account of both resemblances and differences.

If we cannot directly experience the things we wish to compare, we may have to get our information about them second hand. In much of life we have to rely on the experiences of other people, though often we can check things out for ourselves. In any case, where things are being compared, the one that most measures up is the best, though more than one in any given set may do this. All students in a class might be "A" students.

Preferences ultimately underlie adopting elements A through E in the set we use for judging lemon pies, for example, but the process of valuing involves much more than just preferring, feeling, or emoting. It involves having cognitive or rational sets of good-making predicates (the elements in the concepts or standards to be fulfilled), and experientially testing objects to see how well they measure up to these standards.

G. Comparing Apples, Oranges, and Devils

"You can't compare apples and oranges." How many times have we heard that one! Yet, this truism is not true! Why not?

Things can be classified in practically innumerable ways. Each classification or word in our language bears its own definitional and expositional properties, its own good-making criteria. For example, an "athlete" can also be classified as a "baseball player," a "catcher," a "hitter," a "runner," a "professional," a "star," an "amateur," and in many other ways. Specific good-making criteria go hand in hand with every such classification, and any given thing may be good in one classification and bad in another. As Hartman explained,

> Anything which under one concept is good because it fulfills the concept may under another concept be bad because it does not fulfill that concept. Thus, as Spinoza observed, "a good ruin is a bad house, and a good house is a bad ruin" (Hartman, 1967, 111; see also Hartman, 1991b, 22).

When we hear that apples and oranges can't be compared, we need to know how they are being classified. We can't compare apples with oranges as "apples," or oranges with apples as "oranges." Some classifications do not fit, but others might. Things that cannot be compared at one level of abstraction, that is under one set of concepts, can be compared if they both fall under a more general or inclusive concept that bears its own good-making properties. So it is with apples and oranges; they are both "fruit," and as fruits they can be compared with respect to their similarities and differences. We can ask and intelligibly answer, "Are apples better fruits than oranges?" The answer may be, "No," but the comparison can be made. The answer may involve, "It all depends," but the comparison can be made, as next explained.

One dictionary definition of "fruit" is, "the edible pulpy reproductive body of a seed plant." Given this *definition*, both apples and oranges are fruits. The chief good-making or *expositional* property of fruit is sweetness; there may be others, but for simplicity, we will focus on this one. Sweetness cannot be a defining property of "fruit" because many fruits are not sweet—especially in their "green" stages, and both green and ripe ones must be included under the definitional rubric of "fruit." Even a bitter or sour green fruit is a fruit.

Given the axiological concept of "better than," the question, "Are apples better than oranges?" means: "Do apples have more good-making expositional fruit-properties than oranges?" If sweetness is the principle expositional good-making property of "fruit," the question becomes, "Are apples sweeter than oranges?" This is where "It all depends" comes in. Are we comparing green apples with ripe oranges, green apples with ripe apples, green oranges with ripe apples, equally ripe apples and oranges, one variety of applies with another variety of oranges, or what? Maybe it all depends on the particular variety of apple or orange at hand, or where and how they are grown, or how early in their development they are picked. Varieties are additional classifications with their own good-making properties. Even if inexact, comparisons of fruits (in sweetness, etc.) can be made; *so we can compare apples and oranges.* It all depends on how they are being classified, which properties count good-making, and which classes, sub-classes, or particulars are being compared with respect to their good-making properties.

Emphasizing "good" as a broad axiological word, not just an ethical word, Hartman was asked in one of his classes if there could be such a thing as a "good Devil." He replied that no Devil could be a "morally good Devil"; that would be a contradiction in terms since "Devils" are by definition grossly immoral. However, the concept of a "morally good Devil" is quite different from the concept of a "good Devil." "Devil" as Devil has its own set of good-making criteria, and by those criteria, Devils can be compared with respect to their being "good Devils." Some Devils might be better as Devils than others. (Compare Hartman's discussion of "good murderer, 1967, 125.)

To elaborate, let's assume that Satan and Beelzebub are two different Devils. In most ways, they are similar, but in a few ways, they differ. Both manifest every conceivable vice, but Satan exemplifies them to a much higher degree than Beelzebub. For instance, Satan tortures his victims with fiendish delight, but Beelzebub is a little bit soft-hearted or squeamish and, though he tortures his victims, he does so with much less enthusiasm, relish, and pleasure. If "fiendish intensity and delight" are axiological (but not moral) good-making properties of a "good Devil," a Devil who really is a Devil, then Satan would be *a better Devil qua Devil* than Beelzebub. Beelzebub has fewer (less intense) bad-making properties, than Satan. Just as we can compare apples and oranges, so we can compare the axiological worth of Devils, now that we understand "good," "bad," "better," and "worse" as defined within axiology. Good Devils as Devils would still be morally bad.

H. "Good" and "Good For"

We should not confuse "good" with being "good for." Hartman thought that many people, philosophers included, are at times very confused about this. He wrote, "In formal axiology, "good" and "good for" must be strictly distinguished" (Hartman, 2002, 175. See his most detailed discussion in Hartman, 1967, 163). *Something that is good, that fulfills its concept completely, may or may not be very good for something else.* For example, a good apple may be very good for a person's health, and a good book may be very good for a person's mental development. However, *a good thing that fulfills its own concept may also be very bad for something else.* Being bad for something else means that it does not fulfill, may be incompatible with, and may diminish the well being of that other thing, as measured by its own ideal concept. A good that fulfills its own concept may be a bad-making property in relation to or in combination with something else, some other reality. Being "bad for" involves value combinations that diminish or destroy goodness.

We have already seen that a single thing may be good when judged under one concept but bad when judged under another concept. Our hypothetical Satan is good when judged under the concept of "devil" but bad when judged under the concepts of "moral," "kind," "compassionate," and "loving," because Satan just does not fulfill those concepts. The same is true of a human murderer who is good when judged solely under the concept of "murderer" but bad when judged under concepts like those that identify Satan as bad. Being "good for" or "bad for" are not like judging *one single thing* or reality under *two different and logically independent concepts or predicates* like "devil" and "moral."

According to Hartman, "good for" or "bad for" involve *two different realities,* *x* and *y,* to which *a single predicate or intension* applies. Their concepts are somehow logically intertwined; they have what Hartman called "overlapping intensions" (Hartman, 1967, 163; 2002, 332).

Some examples may help. Part of the very concept of a "good devil" is that he "tortures his victims with fiendish delight," and, as indicated above, Satan does this, so Satan is a good devil, but he is a morally bad individual who does things that are bad for others. In that respect, he is representative of all torturers. Once we start considering Satan's victims, however, we are taking two realities, *x* and *y,* not just one, into account. "Good for" involves *two different realities* and at least *one* *"overlapping" concept or predicate.* What *Satan* does to his *victims* (e.g., inflict pain) is not good for his victims. Satan inflicts excruciating pain upon his victims, so pain becomes an integral part of their very being. "Pain" is the overlapping concept or intension, something that Satan inflicts on others as a "good" devil, but this property of experienced pain becomes a very bad, undesirable, integral, and inescapable part of his victims' own present reality. Excruciating pain is not *good* *for* Satan's victims. It does not fulfill the concept of what is good for them. Excruciating pain is not a good-making property for those who suffer it, though it is for devils who inflict it. It diminishes and definitely does not enhance the well-being of those being tortured. "Inflicting pain" is not a "good-for-making" predicate. Excruciating pain is a bad-making property in and for those who suffer, a property that diminishes their well-being. It is bad for, not good for, those who experience it. Satan's inflicting pain is good for Satan judged as a devil, but it is not good for his victims judged as victims.

Quite apart from hypothetical devils, "pain" considered as such can be fulfilled by degrees. Some pains are worse than others. Degrees of pain are actually measured by medical professionals by asking patients to judge their present pains on a scale of 1 to 10, where 1 is just a mild irritation and 10 is the most excruciating suffering imaginable. Judged axiologically, pains as pains could be "poor" as "2s", "average" as "5s", "fair" as "8s" and "good" as "10s." Pains at level "10" would be "pains that really are pains." All degrees of pain would be inherently bad for those who suffer, however, so a good pain would be inherently bad for suffering patients, even if, like the pain of a beneficial operation, it is a "necessary evil" for achieving other health related goals. Looking at it another way, a bad pain as pain (that is, a not very intense and prolonged "1") is better for sufferers than a good pain (that is, a very intense and prolonged "10"). "Bad" pains are "good for" or "better for." "Good" pains are "bad for" or "worse for." In this, there is no paradox once we realize that "good" and "good for" are very different axiological concepts that should not be confused with one another.

Injuries and diseases can also be rated or ranked according to degrees of fulfilling their own concepts, versus degrees of fulfilling or diminishing the ideal self-concepts of real people who are injured or diseased. A good disease or injury can be very bad for real people, so, once more, "good" and "good for" are very different axiological concepts. A severe injury like a broken jaw suffered in a boxing match is very bad for the injured fighter, though it may have been an integral part of a good fight, as fights go, and the pains thereof may be good pains, as pains go. "Good" diseases or injuries as such are "bad for" patients; "bad" diseases or injuries as such are "better for" patients. As explained in later discussions, many of the things that philosophers have championed as "intrinsically good" or good in themselves (e.g., pleasures and knowledge) are really best conceived as only "good for" us.

Armed now with the Form of the Good and its derivative value forms, you are now in a position to make rational value judgments about almost anything, even Devils, murderers, pains, injuries, and diseases—and how they affect people! Yet, a few important distinctions still need to be made and explained in the following chapters.

Chapter Two

WHAT THINGS ARE GOOD AND BETTER?

Now that we understand the Form of the Good, we can begin to work with it and apply it. What things are good? The answer is very simple. Almost anything can be good, but not all in the same way. This calls for a lot of explaining.

You probably doubt almost immediately that almost anything can be good. Aren't some things bad? Yes, but just as almost anything can be good, so almost anything can be bad, but not all in the same way.

Because almost anything can be good or bad, we need a very general theory of value, something much broader than a theory of ethics, which is only a theory of moral good and evil, right and wrong. "Good" and "bad" are not just moral or ethical words, concepts, or categories. If you doubt that almost anything or anyone can be *morally* good, you are right. Cruelty, malice, hatred, selfishness, and indifference to suffering are morally bad, but "good" and "bad" do not just apply within morality. To see this, try the following exercise. First, write down all the letters of the alphabet. Then, write down at least one good thing that starts with each letter of the alphabet. Make your own list, and give more than one example for each letter if you wish. Here is an illustration of how this might work.

a. good alphabet

b. good baseball

c. good Child

d. good definition

e. good emerald

f. good Father

g. good graph

h. good hotrod

i. good I

j. good judgement

k. good knife

l. good Lover

m. good measurement

n. good nuts

o. good One-and-only

p. good proposition

q. good quilt

r. good Reverend

s. good statement

t. good toy

u. good Uncle   x. good Xmas
v. good variable   y. good yardstick
w. good water   z. good zinc

After making your own list, ask yourself if everything in your list might not also be bad under some circumstances. Probably so! In Chapter One, you learned how to tell the difference between the good ones and the bad ones. The good ones fulfill expectations, standards, ideals, criteria; the bad ones don't, or they have distinctive bad-making properties. Try to see that ideals or standards of goodness apply to every item in your own list, as well as to the list above. Try to think of what some of these standards might be, and consider whether different people might choose or use different criteria. You may want to play around with such thoughts for a while before going any further.

When you are ready for the next step, ask yourself if you see any general patterns of goodness that apply to items in your own list, or to list above. Here are a few clues. A certain order was deliberately imposed on the list above from the very outset. *Every third item above falls into the same general pattern, and each of these patterns exemplifies a different kind of goodness or value.* Your own list may not illustrate this order, at least not in such an orderly way, but you may find this order or pattern in your own list as soon as you learn to recognize it.

The next task is to learn to recognize and explain the threefold orderliness into which good things or values tend to fall.

1. Three Kinds of Good Things or Values

What things are good? There are different kinds of goodness, so no wholesale answer will work. Every third item in the above list of good things falls into one of three groups, each of which is a different kind of positive value or goodness.

Group 1 consists of items a, d, g, j, m, p, s, v, and y.

Group 2 consists of items b, e, h, k, n, q, t, w, and z.

Group 3 consists of items c, f, i, l, o, r, u and x.

To be classified together as the same basic kind of value, every third item must have something in common. Can you identify what is common to them? If not, here are a few clues.

Everything in Group 1 is primarily a thought, an idea, à concept, a word, something mental, verbal, or conceptual, even when expressed in print or on paper. Alphabets, definitions, graphs, judgments, measurements, propositions, statements, variables, and yardsticks are mental constructs. Most of them are fairly simple, but we use or apply them all the time to make much more complicated mental concepts. Out of such simple ideas, we make vastly complex systems of philosophy, law, theology, history, mathematics, logic, physics, chemistry, biology, and all the formal, social, and natural sciences. Even if we are not professional scientists, we probably took some such courses in high school or college. Our society values conceptual things so highly that it requires us to be exposed to them as we grow up, like it or not. And most of us learn to like it, to one degree or another.

Out of the relatively simple things in Group 1, we construct all of our beliefs, some better developed and organized than others. We have beliefs about ourselves, other people, our jobs, our businesses, our country, our world, our God—about far more than we can consciously say. All of these beliefs are constructed out of simple things like alphabets, definitions, judgments, or statements, and all of them are mental or conceptual in nature. Life itself is conceptually meaningful to us because we have ideas, notions, symbols, statements, beliefs, doctrines, and convictions. And we have good-making *conceptual* criteria for what counts as a good life.

This is leading up to something, namely, that mental realities or ideas are very important or valuable to us. They constitute one very fundamental kind of value. For the moment, we are trying to avoid philosophical words, but sometimes they are illuminating, helpful, and needed. Let's call the sort of things represented in Group 1 *"systemic values" or "systemic value-objects."* Not everyone who considers human values realizes how much special significance we attach to thoughts and beliefs. Many thinkers do not recognize this as a distinctive realm of human values, but, following Robert S. Hartman, we will do so.

Everything in Group 2 is an object, process, or activity in the physical, material, sensory world. We are acquainted with them because we can sense them with our so-called "external senses." We can see, hear, smell, taste, or touch them. They are the stuff of everyday life and experience—baseballs, emeralds, hotrods, knives, nuts, quilts, toys, water, and zinc. These familiar objects are representative of everything in our common everyday world of sensory experiences. Without them, life would not be very much fun; without them we would not even exist at all. Without physical resources, the basic "necessities of life" like food, drink, air, water, fire, earth, sunshine, and our own bodies, we would not exist at all. When we are significantly deprived of them, we suffer and eventually die. We spend a very large part of our lives "working for a living," but that means doing things that will give us the physical resources we need to survive and flourish. Mere survival is not the whole story; we can also work for fun things, or just for the fun of it.

Work can be drudgery, but if we are lucky, work can be enjoyable and self-fulfilling. "Work" here is an example of everything that we do with and for our bodies; but there are innumerable other examples of bodily activities, such as playing and giving. Like earth, air, fire, and water, our bodies and physical activities are objects and processes that exist and are experienced in the physical world. We have access to them through our external senses as well as through our immediate awareness of embodiment and time. We work and act not just to get basic physical necessities; we work and act to get things that will make life easier, more comfortable, more fun, more enjoyable, more worthwhile, more fulfilling, more meaningful, more benevolent—things like blankets, hotrods, emeralds, knives, nuts, quilts and "things" in general. We work for "luxuries" as well as for "necessities."

Our stores are full of such things, and so are our houses, closets, garages, and garbage dumps. We highly value physical things and strive for a "higher standard of living," materially understood. Often, we overvalue or undervalue such things.

Let's call things in Group 2 *"extrinsic values"* or *"extrinsic value-objects."* Extrinsic goods are usually defined as "useful things." We tend to value them precisely because they are useful or instrumental in leading to something beyond themselves. Almost everything in our familiar sensory world, almost every physical object and action, is useful for something, either immediately or later on—either actually or potentially. Let's call them "things" for short. Things in the world are extrinsic values, good because they are actually or potentially useful. We normally want money because we can spend it to get other things. So it is with all extrinsic goods; we want them not *for their own sake* but because they do something *for us.* "Mere things" have no mind, consciousness, or awareness of their own, so they are not intrinsically good. They are also not just thoughts in our heads, so they are not systemic goods. They exist in themselves or outside of consciousness, but they are not of value in, of, to, and for themselves. They are of value because they are useful to people, who are ends in themselves, who are of value in, of, to, and for themselves. Ideas and people can be useful, too, but that is not their primary reality or value significance. More will be said later about this complication, but all value-objects can be evaluated *as if* they were some other kind of value.

Everything in Group 3 is a person or a conscious being. We have many ways of talking about persons; we use many words that apply to persons, but mainly we use proper names and personal pronouns. Children, Fathers, I(s), Lovers, our One-and-only(s), Reverends, and Uncles also apply to people. By extension or analogy, some words that apply to people may apply also to animals, even if people are their primary referents. Think for a moment about people who have special significance for us. All of the person-connoting words in Group 3 are capitalized to indicate that we are not just talking about *classes* of Children, Fathers, Lovers, etc., in general. The emphasis in this list is on particular persons who happen to be children, fathers, lovers, etc. Of course, "X-mas" is not a person, but what can you do when "X" comes up for something intrinsic? Christmas is of great significance to many people because it is a time of and for much interpersonal intimacy and affection. "X-mas" may be about as close as we can come with an "X" symbol for something intrinsic, but admittedly this is a metaphorical stretch!

Let's call the things in Group 3 *"intrinsic values"* or *"intrinsic value-objects."* We value ideas, we value things, and we value people and other conscious beings like animals and God. Ideas have systemic worth; they are conceptual. Things have extrinsic worth; they are useful. Conscious beings have intrinsic worth; they are ends in themselves, valuable as such, good in, of, for, and to themselves. Ideas and things are good because they immensely enrich or enhance the lives and experiences of people, but why are people good? The buck stops here! We are valuable for our own sakes; we deserve to exist and have a right to exist for our own sakes. We are final ends, not mere means and not mere abstractions. Ideas and formalities exist for us, not us for ideas and formalities. Things exist for us, not us for things. People and other conscious beings have a special kind of value that other realities do not have, but what is so special about people? The "Philosophical Exposition" part of this chapter will go deeper into this.

Here is a summary of what has been said thus far.

Answering "What things are good?" requires distinguishing between three different kinds of value or goodness, systemic, extrinsic, and intrinsic.

1) *Systemic value-objects are mental constructs or concepts.* Given this understanding of the nature of systemic values, we can further ask, "What particular things or kinds of things are systemically good?" Instances noted thus far are alphabets, definitions, graphs, judgments, measurements, propositions, statements, variables, and yardsticks. More general instances are such things as languages, words, ideas, thoughts, beliefs, doctrines, and commonsense, mathematical, logical, scientific, philosophical, or theological belief systems. Some people mistakenly think that ideas are ends in themselves.

2) *Extrinsic value-objects are actually or potentially useful objects, processes, or activities within our everyday public sensory world.* Given this understanding of the nature of extrinsic values, we can further ask, "What particular things or kinds of things are extrinsically good?" Instances noted thus far are: baseballs, emeralds, hotrods, knives, nuts, quilts, toys, water, and zinc. More general instances are all useful material objects, processes, and human actions, the primary significance of which is their actual or potential utility. We value such things because we can use them to achieve ends, purposes, goals, and objectives beyond themselves. Some people mistakenly think that things are ends in themselves.

3) *Intrinsic value-objects are ends in themselves, properly so. They are of value for their own sakes, of value in, of, to, and for themselves.* Given this understanding of "intrinsic values, " we can further ask, "What particular beings or kinds of beings are intrinsically good?" Examples given thus far are unique individual persons. Capitalized words for them indicated individuals, not general classes of Children, Fathers, I(s), Lovers, our One-and-only(s), Reverends, and Uncles. We use proper names and personal pronouns to talk about unique persons. Other unrepeatable realities that significantly resemble unique human persons could also intrinsically be good—like God, and individual animals. These complications will not be addressed in this book except in the section on "Other Applications" near the end of Chapter Four. The emphasis here will be on unique human persons.

2. Applying the Form of the Good to Good Things

Chapter One explained the Form of the Good, namely, concept or standard fulfillment. Now we must ask how this applies to the three kinds of value just identified. Good is the fulfillment of our positive ideals or standards. Good things have all the good-making features or properties that our ideals of goodness say that supposed to have. Fair, average, poor, and bad things fail by degrees to have all the good-making features that our ideals say that they are supposed to have. How does this work, given the distinctions between systemic values, extrinsic values, and intrinsic values? We need at least three different kinds of standards.

A. Systemically Good Things

Systemic fulfillment or goodness requires that language, concepts, ideas, thoughts, and beliefs have the properties that they are supposed to have. So what properties are they supposed to have? Surprisingly, some of them are supposed to have just the very properties or features that we give them when we think them!

If some of our ideas are just supposed to be exactly what and as they are, nothing more, then there is no difference in such cases between the features that they have and the features that they ought to have. In such instances, there are no *degrees* of systemic value fulfillment. Very often this is true, particularly with respect to what we might call "pure intellectual constructs" like those of mathematics and logic. Consider a simple example. A "circle" is, by definition "a closed plane curve consisting of all points equidistant from a point within it, the center" (Hartman, 1991b, 18). Technically, the concept of "circle," and "good circle," turn out to be identical. If a two-dimensional figure is not a closed curved line, or if all its parts are not equally distant from its center, then it just is not a circle. It might be an oval or a triangle, but it is not a circle. Strictly or technically speaking, a circle always has all the features that it is supposed to have; otherwise, it just isn't a circle. So it is all with all pure intellectual constructs.

According to Hartman, "Only with constructive concepts can one be absolutely certain that they contain all that their object does, for these constructs come about together with, and actually are, their object. They possess *complete* precision, for they are creations of the human mind itself rather than abstractions" (Hartman, 1967, 81). The features that they have are exactly the same as the properties that they are supposed to have. They can't go wrong or fall short. Thus, there are no degrees of systemic concept fulfillment, at least not with respect to pure conceptual constructs. Strictly speaking, there are no fair, average, poor, or bad circles. With circles, it's all or nothing. About conceptual constructs, Hartman explained,

> These things cannot *be* unless they are what the concept—or rather the system of relations of which it is a term—defines. Hence the corresponding things cannot fail to fulfill their concept for unless they do so they are no such things....The values connected with systemic concepts, therefore, can only be synthetic being or not being, complete fulfillment or complete nonfulfillment, perfection or nonperfection (Hartman, 1967, 194).

Speaking less strictly, however, there can be degrees of approximation to systemic perfection in the empirical world. None of the circles, lines, and points that we see or draw are perfect mathematical circles, lines, or points, technically speaking; but in everyday discourse we still correctly call them circles, lines, or points because they closely approximate the ideal. Our use of language is not always as rigid as required by pure intellectual constructs. Pure intellectual constructs may actually grow out of their ordinary meanings by processes of "extensive abstraction" that progressively eliminate non-essentials until only the bare essentials remain (Hartman, 1967, 89-90). Real lines have both length and width; mathematical lines eliminate width and have only length without width. Real points have size, shape, and position; mathematical points get rid of the size and shape and leave only position. Pure intellectual constructs refer only to themselves and always have exactly the properties we give to them. They cannot fail to fulfill their concepts because their extensions are identical with their intensions. They are either perfect or non-existent.

However, most of our words or concepts are not pure intellectual constructs that exist only in our minds; yet, they too are systemic value-objects. Most of our words are not mere words about words, or thoughts that refer only to themselves. All concepts exist in our minds, but most of them refer to other or extra-mental realities, not just to themselves. "Impure" concepts that refer or point beyond themselves have good making features that can be fulfilled by degrees. For example, we all know perfectly well that there are good and not-so-good definitions, and most definitions are not just about themselves. We have logical ideals or expectations that good definitions must fulfill, and we know from experience that definitions can often be improved. Since good definitions have many good making properties, they can differ in degrees of adequacy. We can apply the Form of the Good to different kinds of *definitions*, as follows.

GOOD MAKING PREDICATES FOR CONVENTIONAL DEFINITIONS	GOOD MAKING PREDICATES FOR THEORETICAL DEFINITIONS
1. capture socially prevailing meanings	1. create or construct new theoretical meanings
2. include everything normally included in the definition	2. include everything that the theory requires
3. exclude everything normally excluded	3. exclude everything the theory requires
4. use words with clear meanings	4. use words with clear meanings
5. contain no vague or ambiguous concepts	5. contain no vague or ambiguous concepts

The fifth criterion is fulfilled more easily by theoretical constructs than by words in ordinary language. Yet, words in ordinary language are systemic value objects.

Consider another instance of fulfilling these criteria by degrees. "Car" might be defined as "a self-moving vehicle on wheels." The three defining predicates are:

1. self-moving
2. vehicle
3. on wheels

For many practical purposes this definition might work perfectly well, but it could be improved. It includes too much; it fails to exemplify the third and first good-making properties above; it includes trucks as well as cars, so it does not adequately capture its socially prevailing meaning. Still, we might count it as a fair definition of a car; but we could make it more precise and conventional by adding one more defining predicate,

4. used primarily for passenger transportation.

We often find ourselves groping for better definitions, and we often work in practice with definitions that are only fair to middling.

Consider another case where ideas can be adequate by degrees. We know how to distinguish by degrees between good or bad, better or worse, belief systems, whether they be commonsense, scientific, philosophical, psychological, theological, economic, or whatever. Consider the following.

GOOD-MAKING PREDICATES
FOR RATIONAL BELIEF SYSTEMS

They:

1. are logically consistent
2. are confirmed by experience
3. are not refuted by experience
4. cover everything intended
5. do not cover too much
6. have the simplest possible number of explanatory principles or entities
7. have explanatory power
8. are elegant or beautiful
9. are fruitful for future research and discovery
10. make reliable predictions
11. can be applied in daily living
12. bring about intersubjective agreement

Try applying the above criteria to any belief system you like, and you will see that some are better (more rational) than others by degrees. Additional or different good-making criteria or standards for rational belief systems may be relevant; but, clearly enough, some systemic values (concepts) can fulfill their standards by degrees. Not all systemic value-objects are like pure conceptual constructs, where it's all or nothing. Consider again the simple systemic values listed at the beginning of this chapter (items a, d, g, j, m, p, s, v, and y). What would a good alphabet, definition, graph, judgment, measurement, proposition, statement, variable, or yardstick be like? We could develop sets of good-making features for each of these that would apply by degrees to particular examples. Once we learn to formulate and apply relevant rational standards to ideas, even if not "all or nothing," we know how to apply the Form of the Good to systemic value-objects. This can be done by degrees as well as in totality.

B. Extrinsically Good Things

Extrinsic ideal fulfillment or goodness requires that *things* that we can observe in our everyday world of public space-time have the properties that they are supposed to have. So, what properties are *things* supposed to have? This can only be answered on a case-by-case or class-by-class basis. In Chapter One, cars of different kinds served as examples of this. No matter what special kind of car you want, there is a Form of the Good for it.

Being a capable extrinsic valuer has a lot of practical significance—we might even say "cash value." We can definitely improve our skills as practical evaluators. Almost all the things we do, experience, use, shop for, buy, or sell in everyday life have extrinsic value. All of them can be evaluated case by case, item by item, class by class, product by product, in terms of concept or standard fulfillment.

Consumer magazines usually give unbiased advice about what to buy, once we know what product or service we want. They can even help us to decide what to want. Advertising can tell us about useful and interesting things, but we know that advertising is highly prejudiced (biased) and does not give us very much relevant or detailed information. To get more dependable information, we may have to rely on the judgments and past experiences of friends and acquaintances. We may ask others about the relevant good-making features of various consumer products and services. Of course, we may also make uninformed choices on the basis of whims, but these usually do not turn out very well. Being shrewd and practical persons means making well informed comparisons of and decisions about the things of the world. Having sound practical judgment involves knowing and applying the Form of the Good to things, processes, and actions within our common sensory world.

In addition to extrinsically good *material things*, we must also consider another class of extrinsic goods—*our own actions and social roles*. Our own bodies and what we do with them are extrinsic values, although they can be taken up into the realm of the intrinsic as integral aspects of our unique total reality and goodness. When we consider ethics in Chapter Four, will think about how our bodies and what we do with them can be morally useful. But, for the moment, let's just think about our bodies and actions as practically useful in mainly non-moral ways.

Very often, especially on the job, we have to evaluate people with respect to their usefulness. This is often called "social worth," which means "social usefulness" or "usefulness to others." This kind of extrinsic worth applies to the behaviors associated with all the social roles we play in everyday life. When people are in certain roles, certain behaviors or actions are expected of them. Norms or expectations are built into systemic role-concepts; and the behaviors that fulfill them are extrinsically good. We judge the extrinsic social worth of ourselves and other people by how well we or they fulfill relevant role-expectations.

Do people actually have the good-making properties of particular roles they play? Often, but not always. By applying the Form of the Good to them, we can distinguish between good, fair, average, poor, and nearly worthless athletes in general and baseball players, pitchers, catchers, infielders, and outfielders in particular. Coaches, recruiters, and fans know what behaviors to look for in players, and athletes in particular positions know what is expected of them. They understand the good-making behavioral properties of their special athletic roles; they have criteria or standards that they apply to themselves in their roles. No matter what the game is, the top coaches, recruiters, players, and fans understand what to look for; and they know it when they see it.

By applying the Form of the Good to them, employers and employees can be and often are graded for social worth, ranging from good to bad, from better to worse. Workers know how to tell the difference between better and worse bosses, managers, and employers. Bosses, managers, and employers know how to tell the difference between better and worse workers. "Job Performance Evaluations" just apply the Form of the Good to the actions of workers, managers, and CEOs, etc., in the workplace. Included are the actions through which they express their feelings and attitudes, as well as their special job performance skills. Extrinsic standards of goodness or social usefulness are applied to people when hiring, firing, training, promoting, or demoting. Which behavioral standards or predicate/properties are relevant depends on particular social roles in particular workplace environments.

Knowing how to judge the usefulness of others also applies to more personal social roles. Using capital letters earlier, Children, Fathers, Is, Lovers, our One-and-onlys, Reverends, and Uncles were identified as belonging to Group 3, things that are intrinsically good. But using only lower case letters for them, we could be considering them as belonging to Group 2, that is, we could be considering them only as members of general classes of useful children, fathers, lovers, etc.

People can be evaluated in many different ways, extrinsically, systemically, or intrinsically. Any good can be evaluated as if it were some other kind of good. Nothing is morally wrong with evaluating people extrinsically so long as usefulness is compatible with and does not overlook or violate their inherent or intrinsic individual worth. Sometimes we do relate to people as extrinsic values, as representatives or instances of particular social or practical roles. We have broad ideal expectations for both impersonal roles like "carpenter" or "policeman" and more intimate social roles like "husband," "wife," "son," and "daughter." When children learn the meaning of social-role words, they learn about these expectations. The "ought" of these roles is built into their "is." People who are good at being socially useful fulfill their social role expectations completely; others do so only by degrees. Try writing out some good-making criteria for a few practical social roles, perhaps those identified above. Then dare to apply them to someone you know, or to yourself.

One way to tell whether people are being evaluated for themselves as individuals, that is, for their own unique intrinsic worth, or only for their extrinsic social or practical useful, is this. If they are *replaceable without loss of value*, they are being evaluated only for their extrinsic (or systemic) goodness. If they are not replaceable without loss, they are likely being evaluated for their unique intrinsic goodness. If, Joe, Bill, and Jack can readily replace one another as good punters, painters, preachers, or parents, they are being valued only as extrinsic goods, only as good-of-a-kind, only as good examples of some general class of valuable-because-useful things. Only when they are valued as irreplaceable in their uniqueness are they being reckoned as intrinsically good.

C. Intrinsically Good Things

Intrinsic ideal fulfillment or goodness requires that unique individual persons have all the properties that they are supposed to have as unique individual persons. So what properties are they supposed to have? This, too, must be answered on a case-by-case basis, but here "case-by-case" means "person-by-person" rather than "class-by-class."

How do we tell whether any unique person has all the properties he or she is supposed to have? What are the good-making properties of unique individual persons? If concepts that express ideals are required, they must be ideals that apply to unique persons, but whose or what concepts should be used?

The obvious place to start is with the ideals that unique persons set for themselves. Every human being has a "concept of self," sometimes called a "self-image" or a "self-ideal." Self-deals or self-expectations are integral parts of our self-knowledge, and by them we measure our own self-worth. The pronouns "I" or "my" will be used to illustrate this, but this will be a universal "I" or "my" that applies to every reader, and the details will vary from person to person.

I have a concept of myself that includes knowing who I was in the past, who I am at the moment, and who I aspire to be in the days ahead. Most of my descriptive properties have been lost to conscious memory. I have forgotten almost everything that there is to know about my past self. Looking forward, my self-ideals belong to the "who I aspire to be" part of my self-concept. My self-ideals may vary somewhat from day to day or year to year, but some of them are relatively enduring or constant aspects of my character. Who I aspire to be can never be exactly the same as who you or anyone else aspires to be, for we are all unique individuals.

Who I was and who I am now—my given reality—sets limits on who I can realistically aspire to be in the future. I can't be just anything or anyone, for there are some things I definitely cannot choose to be, some things I am not and never will be qualified to be. Human potentials are always finite. I need to know my limitations as well as my strengths. I know that I will never be a great mathematician, but I can at least do basic arithmetic. I will never be a famous astronomer, but I can still learn a lot about the stars. I can never be a professional football player, but I can understand and appreciate the game and the players. I cannot play all games, but I can play and enjoy some. I cannot hold an endless number of jobs, but I might have several different jobs during my lifetime and be very good at them. I cannot marry an endless number of spouses, but I can love, enjoy, and do my best for my One-and-only. I cannot have an endless number of children, but, if I have any at all, I can try my best to be a good parent to each of them. I cannot think an endless number of thoughts, but I will learn all I can, make well informed decisions, and try to be a reasonable and knowledgeable person. Our self-ideals can be realistic without being overly restrictive, self-defeating, or cynical. Very often, though, we can surprise ourselves if we give it a try, so we should also be on guard against having excessively narrow and shortsighted self-expectations! We don't want to underestimate or overestimate ourselves.

I aspire to develop and use my own unique personal interests and talents, and I hope that they will help me to make my way in the world. Many things that interest other people do not interest me; other people have special talents that I do not have; I have many physical and mental limitations. Yet, I also have many very worthwhile physical, mental, and social strengths. I have my own special interests, talents, projects, and responsibilities, and I want to realize or actualize my own special self. Some of my own personal projects and responsibilities are very significant to me, and I want to bring them to fruition. To do any of this, I realize that I have to know myself. I also have to play the hand that I have been dealt, a hand that nobody else has, and so very much depends on how well I play it.

I understand and accept my very concrete life situation. I have definite parents, a definite upbringing, a definite family history, a definite spouse, and definite children, friends, co-workers, and employers or employees, with whom I have specific personal relations, and toward whom I have special obligations or responsibilities. I have my own unique station in life and its duties. I have personal relations, interests, projects, and obligations that nobody else has, at least not in exactly the way that I have them. I cherish and aspire to sustain these relations, to actualize my projects, and fulfill my unique personal obligations to everyone in my life. I aspire to be true to my situation and its duties, to be faithful to my own people, and to fulfill my own personal responsibilities. These aspirations are integral parts of my self-concept, my self-ideal. They are integral aspects of who I am and aspire to be.

I also aspire to be a happy person and to avoid as many of life's tragedies as I can. I want to have a positive outlook on life and to be as free as I can be from self-doubt, self-conflict, irrationality, anxiety, depression, guilt, anger, and other debilitating emotions. I know that my life will not be trouble-free, but I don't want it to be more trouble than it is worth. I aspire to make "good living" and to live "the good life" as I understand it. I want to prosper and be successful, but not to the point of being greedy or having to cheat, deceive, or exploit other people. I want to live in harmony with other significant people in my life.

Much of what I aspire to be has to do with my morality and with the still small voice of my own conscience within. I aspire to be a morally good person, even though I know that not everyone does. I aspire to be a spiritual person, though I know that not everyone does. I aspire to be a truthful and honest person in a world where dishonesty is the "norm" (statistically normal). I do not want to be hurtful or brutal, though others do. I do not want to be exactly like everyone else. I aspire to be a brave person, but not rash and foolhardy. I hope to be a kind and considerate person, even if I sometimes come across to others as aloof and distant. I aspire to overcome my aloofness and all my other personal shortcomings. I want to grow morally and spiritually. I aspire to be a helpful and loving person, though I know that I still have a long way to go. I aspire to contribute positively to my society, to help it become an even better society, to leave it better than I found it. I aspire to love and serve God faithfully. My moral and spiritual ideals are very detailed and complicated—too much so to spell it all out here—but you see what I mean. I will not go much further in detailing my moral, spiritual, and personal aspirations because by now you get it. Now you see what is meant by having and fulfilling my own concept of myself as a unique human being. You understand now that my self-concept includes self-ideals, self-expectations, and self-aspirations, both moral and non-moral, but hopefully not immoral!

In a nutshell, I aspire to be an authentic person, a person of integrity. I want to be true to myself, faithful to the standards of personal worth that I set for myself. I aspire to be a good person, a good *me*. Now, what is *your* concept of yourself?

This explains and illustrates what is involved in having and fulfilling the conceptual ideals that I set for myself, my self-concept. More will be said about this later in the section on "Philosophical Exposition."

3. Ranking and Combining Good Things

At this point, we understand that there are at least three very different basic kinds of valuable things, systemic, extrinsic, and intrinsic.

• *Systemically good things* are concepts valued or regarded as concepts.

Examples are: ideas, beliefs, belief-systems like those of science, theology, or philosophy, laws, rules and regulations, rituals, logic, mathematics, and formalities of every kind.

• *Extrinsically good things* are useful activities, processes, and things or objects in our common sensory world.

Examples are: cars, boats, trains, tools, machines, houses, property, natural processes like digestion, weather, and growth, and human actions.

• *Intrinsically good things* are ends in themselves, desirable or valuable for their own sakes (Hartman, 1967, 140).

Examples are: unique individual persons, God, and animals in the full richness of all their properties.

The Form of the Good can be applied to each of the above kinds or dimensions of goodness. Each dimension of goodness, and each good thing within it, have relevant good-making criteria or characteristics. These have to be spelled out on a case-by-case, class by class, person by person basis. Different people may have and apply different criteria in all dimensions of value. This is the main reason why axiology is absolute only in theory but relative or subjective in application.

Each of these three kinds of value and their combinations must be ranked with respect to their relative priority. Good things like those above can be combined with one another in many ways to produce new value-wholes, some of which are of greater value than their parts, some lesser, some unchanged.

A. Ranking Good Things: The Hierarchy of Value

We recognize distinctive kinds and degrees of value, so we need some value priorities. Some good things seem better than others. Maybe some good things deserve much more of our time and attention than others. Maybe some good things will enrich ourselves and the people we really care about more than others. We need to set some priorities, to decided what comes first in our lives, what comes second, what comes third, what comes last. Can axiology help us to do this? Yes. Working with the three basic forms or dimensions of value considered thus far, ask yourself these questions, remembering that here the word "things" covers physical objects, processes, and actions.

Do *ideas* about things or people have more value, or less value, than the *things* or *people* themselves? Do real things have more value or less value than real people? After careful consideration, perhaps you will be able to see intuitively that the following ranking of the three basic kinds or dimension of positive value is correct.

People have more value than either things as such or ideas as such.
Things have more value than mere ideas about them.
Ideas have great value, but less than the things and people that they signify.

If you accept the above value judgments, you have affirmed the basic axiological Hierarchy of Value. On a more theoretical level, this Hierarchy of Value says:

Intrinsic goods have more worth than extrinsic goods, which in turn have more worth than systemic goods.

Expressed at a more practical or applied level, this means:

People are more valuable than things, and things are more valuable than mere ideas about people or things.

If you learn nothing else from the study of axiology, you should at least learn this much. If you take this Hierarchy of Value to heart and put it into practice, it will transform your whole life! Later we will explore some philosophical complications.

B. Combining Good Things

Instances of the three basic kinds of value can be combined in many ways to produce new value-wholes, some of which are of equal, greater, or lesser worth than their parts. Some combinations enhance or add value. Axiologists have a special word for such positive value combinations, "compositions." This is the technical word for good things combined with one another in positive value-enhancing ways. Some value combinations diminish or destroy value. Axiologists call negative value combinations "transpositions," the technical word for otherwise good things combined in value diminishing or destructive ways. Some value combinations make no difference at all, and we do not have a technical axiological word for that, though they are usually treated as compositions if they do not diminish overall value.

Pairs of the three most basic kinds of value can be combined with one another in only eighteen ways, as illustrated below. In the *formulas*, which below are given first in complete words, the value on the left is modified positively or negatively by the value on the right. In the *examples*, the items that modify are on the left, and the modified items are on the right. The language just flows more smoothly that way. The first nine below are positive, arranged from best to least good; the last nine are negative, arranged from least bad to worst, in accord with the Hierarchy of Value.

1. An intrinsic value enhanced by an intrinsic value. *Example*: A person loving another person.
2. An intrinsic value enhanced by an extrinsic value. *Example*: A gift to a person.
3. An intrinsic value enhanced by a systemic value. *Example*: A nice thought about a person.
4. An extrinsic value enhanced by an intrinsic value. *Example*: A person devoted to an antique object.
5. An extrinsic value enhanced by an extrinsic value. *Example*: A tire on a car.
6. An extrinsic value enhanced by a systemic value. *Example*: The thought of a machine.
7. A systemic value enhanced by an intrinsic value. *Example*: A person's devotion to a belief.
8. A systemic value enhanced by an extrinsic value. *Example*: Buying a creative idea.

9. A systemic value enhanced by a systemic value. *Example*: A premise supporting a conclusion.

10. A systemic value diminished by a systemic value. *Example*: One thought that contradicts another.

11. A systemic value diminished by an extrinsic value. *Example*: Burning a book (the book's ideas).

12. A systemic value diminished by an intrinsic value. *Example*: A person's hatred of a doctrine.

13. An extrinsic value diminished by a systemic value. *Example*: Negative thoughts about the weather.

14. An extrinsic value diminished by an extrinsic value. *Example*: A nail flattening a tire.

15. An extrinsic value diminished by an intrinsic value. *Example*: A person wrecking a car.

16. An intrinsic value diminished by a systemic value. *Example*: An unfavorable thought about a person.

17. An intrinsic value diminished by an extrinsic value. *Example*: Water drowning a person.

18. An intrinsic value diminished by an intrinsic value. *Example*: A person murdering another person.

The eighteen value/disvalue combinations above are arranged, ranked, or prioritized according to the axiological Hierarchy of Value. The first three positive combinations illustrate the most valuable kind of value, intrinsic values that are enhanced in turn by intrinsic, extrinsic, and systemic values. The next three (4-6) illustrate the second most valuable kind, extrinsic values that are enhanced by intrinsic, extrinsic, and systemic values. The last three positive combinations (7-9) illustrate the third most valuable kind, systemic values enhanced in turn by intrinsic, extrinsic, and systemic values. The last nine negative value combinations follow the reverse order with respect to value diminishment. Systemic diminishment is less bad than extrinsic diminishment, which is less bad than intrinsic diminishment. (In the Hartman Value Profile, at least two items are out of logical order).

In all the preceding examples, objects of value are combined with one another in pairs; but value combinations can be much more complicated, and in the real world, they usually are. Objects having systemic, extrinsic, and intrinsic value can be combined with one another in innumerable ways, that is, in value combination strings of indefinite length. Consider just one illustration:

A person murdering another person by drowning him in water because of an unfavorable thought about him.

Value combinations can get very complicated, and keeping track of them can be very hard. For this reason, formal axiologists, beginning with Robert S. Hartman, aspire to develop a formal or mathematical way to calculate the results of value combinations. The formal calculus of value will be discussed later, but let's admit for now that a lot of work still remains to be done on it.

The goodness or badness of value combinations cannot be determined simply by just "adding up" the good-making properties of each component. Value combinations are new value wholes, so new sets of good-making properties usually have to be worked out for them. For example, we have separate and distinct sets of good-making criteria for "good milk," "good peach," and "good freeze," but they don't necessarily add up to the criteria we need for "good peach ice cream." A long string of good ideas does not necessarily add up to a good book. A collection of good violinists, cellists, trumpeters, and flutists doesn't necessarily add up to a good orchestra. A set of good acts doesn't necessarily add up to a good play. New sets of good-making properties are usually required to evaluate new axiological wholes, new value combinations. Value combinations have their own distinctive good-making predicates/properties, but this calls for more philosophical explanation.

4. Philosophical Exposition

Chapter One explained Robert S. Hartman's definition of "good," here called the "Form of the Good." The present chapter deals with the three distinct kinds of goodness or value that he recognized—systemic, extrinsic and intrinsic—and with their combinations. "What things are good?" must be construed in at least three ways: "What things are systemically good?" "What things are extrinsically good?" And "What things are intrinsically good?" Systemic goods are concepts or ideas. Extrinsic goods are useful objects, processes, and actions in our common perceptual world of space-time. Intrinsic goods are persons, ends in themselves, beings valuable for their own sake (Hartman, 1967, 140). Many examples of these were given already. Now, we will consider all of this philosophically.

A. Deriving the Three Dimensions of Value

Robert S. Hartman knew that many philosophers before him distinguished between extrinsic and intrinsic values. To this common twofold philosophical distinction, he added the third, systemic values. Systemic values were there all along, but Hartman was the first to recognize them as a third distinct kind of goodness. As he put it, "The whole realm of what we call *systemic value* is new to value theory" (Hartman, 1967, 330, n. 29; 295).

Hartman often called the three basic kinds of value "value dimensions." He wrote, "Systemic value, extrinsic value, and intrinsic value are the three value dimensions" (Hartman, 1967, 114). About these three basic kinds or dimensions of goodness, some important philosophical questions must be asked, such as: How do we know that there are only three? How did Hartman arrive at these three?

First, how do we know that there are only three kinds or dimensions of positive value? We don't, but Hartman certainly made great start. He concentrated on these three, and so do most axiologists today. If you can do better, that is, if you can identify additional fundamental kinds of value, more power to you! There is nothing to stop you from trying! Just do it! However, these three do seem to cover most of the ground. The most obvious difficulty with finding additional dimensions of value is that the candidates are likely to be only sub-divisions of these three basics. For example, we could divide extrinsic values into efficient and less efficient means to ends—but they would still just be extrinsic values; or we could try to make strong distinctions between degrees of the inherent worth of people, God, and animals; but they are all ends in themselves, valuable for their own sakes.

Second, how did Hartman arrive at these three value dimensions? The Philosopher G. E. Moore understood "What things are good?" to be about intrinsic goodness (things valuable for their own sake). Hartman knew well that extrinsic goodness (being useful as a means to ends) had also been much discussed previously. Extrinsic values, Hartman believed, are useful sensory things, processes, or actions existing in our public world of space-time. Hartman just adopted these two kinds of goodness, intrinsic and extrinsic, from the philosophical tradition. To these he creatively added the third, systemic goodness (conceptual values).

Clearly, the three dimensions of value are logical additions, philosophical additions, to the Form of the Good. They cannot be deduced or inferred from it. That there are three kinds of goodness, these three in particular, does not follow logically in any way from the Axiom of Axiology, the definition of "good" as "concept fulfillment." Once these three kinds of value are made available, the Form of the Good can be applied to instances of each, just as the numbers of arithmetic can be applied to oranges and apples, once available. Because they cannot be logically deduced from it, the Form of the Good itself does generate the three value dimensions. Hartman claimed that "Once the axiom is accepted, the rest of axiology follows as a logical deduction from this axiom" (Hartman, "The Science of Value: Five Lectures on Formal Axiology," unpublished, 24). This is definitely not true if he meant that the three forms of value are somehow logically contained within the axiom itself and can be deduced from it alone. From "Good is concept fulfillment," nothing else follows without *additional premises*. The three basic kinds of value are logically independent *philosophical* features of Hartmanian formal axiology, as was his application of transfinite mathematics to them. None of these fundamentals can be divorced from philosophy or simply deduced from the Axiom of value. To the extent that these are philosophically controversial or incomplete, formal axiology will be philosophically controversial or incomplete. The three dimensions of value are derived from *philosophical* reflection on how to group human values into identifiable kinds. They are *philosophical additions* to the Axiom, The Form of the Good, not simply deductions from it.

We are deeply immersed in values (or disvalues) constantly, just as fish are deeply immersed constantly in water. Values pervade human consciousness from beginning to end. Can we discover some order in our all-pervasive phenomenology or experience of values (and disvalues)? That is one thing that Philosophers do. They seek out, identify, classify, and rank the basic structures of value, among other things. Values come to us in at least three basic kinds—systemic, extrinsic, and intrinsic. Each can be either positive or negative, either valuable or disvaluable.

B. Justifying the Hierarchy of Value

Some kinds of positive value are more valuable than others. Some values should have higher priority than others. The three basic kinds of value fall into a hierarchy of worth. Viewed from the bottom up, systemic value-objects are the least valuable of the three, next comes extrinsic value-objects, and at the top comes intrinsic value-objects. Viewed from the top down, intrinsic values have more worth than extrinsic values, which in turn have more value than systemic values. In application, using "things" to mean "physical objects, processes, and actions," this means:

> *People are more valuable than things; and things are more valuable than mere ideas of things or of people.*

Why is this so? Philosophers want to know. Maybe you do too!

Notice first that the positive Hierarchy of Value involves making comparative value judgments. It involves judgements of "good," "better," and "best" (corresponding technically to Hartman's "average," "fair," and "good"). We now understand that "better" means "having more good-making properties than," and "best" means "having the most good-making properties." Hartman explicitly affirmed that the Hierarchy of Value is "connected with the application of "better" to the concept of value itself" (Hartman, 1967, 254). This means that some kinds of value are *better* than others because some *have more good-making properties* than others. Referring to three value dimensions, Hartman explained,

> They constitute a hierarchy of richness, intrinsic being richer in qualities than extrinsic value, extrinsic richer in qualities than systemic value. "Richer in qualities" is the definition of "better," "poorer in qualities" is the definition of "worse" (114).

> The hierarchy of value [is] based on the fact that, since value is defined as the fulfillment of a connotation, the more of a connotation there is to be fulfilled the higher is the value (267).

After reminding us that "better than" means "having more properties of the intension than" (257), Hartman explained:

> The more fulfillment of an intension there is, the better is the value. Since the intrinsic value fulfills a singular intension ($\aleph_1$) it fulfills more of an intension than an extrinsic value which fulfills an analytic intension ($\aleph_0$) and extrinsic value fulfills more of an intension than a systemic value which latter fulfills a synthetic

(schematic, n) rather than an analytic intension. Hence an intrinsic value is better than an extrinsic value and an extrinsic value better than a systemic one (258).

It seems that Hartman thought that sheer quantities or numbers determine the ranking of systemic, extrinsic, and intrinsic values. He appears to solve the ranking problem by assuming that: 1) systemic values have "n", (a finite number), of good-making properties, 2) extrinsic values have "$\aleph_0$", (a denumerable infinity), of good-making properties, and 3) intrinsic values have "$\aleph_1$", (a non-denumerable infinity), of good-making properties, corresponding to like-numbered sets of intensional predicates (Hartman, 1967, 112ff., 275). This progression of finite and transfinite numbers makes it easy to solve the ranking problem. *Quantitatively*, intrinsic values have the most good making properties, extrinsic values even less, and systemic values the least of all..

However, we have not yet followed Hartman into the transfinite, and we may never get that far, as section F. of this chapter explains.

Can we find some other way, some pre-systematic way, a more philosophical and less questionable way, to justify the Hierarchy of Values? Why should we accept the ranking judgment that extrinsic values are better than extrinsic values, which are better than systemic values? This question can be answered without getting into transfinite mathematics.

Without assuming any infinities, here are some philosophical considerations that support the Hierarchy of Values.

First, words, thoughts, ideas, propositions, belief systems, truths (systemic value-objects), have less value than things or people because they are only tokens or symbols that stand for and point to other realities like things, or people, or God. Things and people have more value than the words or symbols that point to them because they really do have *more* good-making properties, not just quantitatively, but *also qualitatively*. To see this intuitively, just ask yourself which you would prefer to have, the idea of a car, or a real car; the idea of a vacation, or a real vacation; the idea of (e.g., blueprint of) a house, or a real house; the idea of a lover, or a real lover; the idea of a friend, or a real friend; the idea of a child, or a real child? This could go on and on, but you get the idea. After careful consideration, you should find that you prefer the real thing over the word or symbol for it. To see intuitively that people have more worth than word combinations, ideas, or systemic values, ask yourself what you would do, choose, or prefer if you absolutely had to choose between philosophy (or any intellectual pursuit) and your spouse, or child, or best friend. Hartman made this very personal when he wrote,

> Value conflicts on this intrinsic or spiritual level can only be resolved in favor of the person. I love my wife, and I love my philosophy, and the two go nicely together, but should there be a conflict, then the person takes absolute precedence. Oddly enough, *my own philosophy has taught me the relative unimportance of my philosophy.* Suppose you are a husband who works for a

corporation. When everything is normal and there's no emergency, then there's no conflict. When the corporation has an emergency and your wife is normal, then the corporation takes precedence. When the corporation is normal and your wife has an emergency, your wife takes precedence. When both the corporation and your wife have emergencies, then there's absolutely no doubt about it from a value point of view. Your wife takes precedence (Hartman, 1994, 94).

Second, so, your wife (or spouse) takes precedence over philosophy and over your corporation (an "artificial person," a conceptual construct). But if things are more valuable than mere ideas, why are people more valuable than things? The answer is that people have many kinds of good-making properties that mere things do not have. We can identify many of these *qualitative differences*, and they clearly add up to "more than," thus "better than."

People are both quantitatively and qualitatively richer in good-making properties than mere things. For example, we have consciousness (at least intermittently—when we are not asleep or otherwise "knocked out"), but mere things never have any consciousness or awareness of their own. We can know and think, but mere things have no minds or thoughts of their own; they never know what they are doing or what or who they are. We can plan ahead and develop long range plans of life for ourselves, but mere things cannot plan ahead at all; unknowingly, they act lawfully. We have concepts of ourselves, but mere things have no concepts at all. We can act to fulfill our purposes, but mere things have no purposes of their own. We have desires and interests, but mere things have no desires and interests of their own. We can feel emotions, but mere things have no emotional life of their own. We can feel joys and sorrows, pleasures and pains, happiness and unhappiness, but mere things do not feel anything. We can love ourselves and one another, but mere things are not lovers. We have a conscience that prompts us toward good and away from evil, toward right and away from wrong, but mere things have no conscience or sense of right and wrong. We are moral beings, but mere things are amoral; they have no morality or moral sensitivity. This could go on and on, but you get the idea.

People (intrinsic value-objects) have vast quantities and qualities of good-making properties that mere things do not have. We have *more* good-making properties than mere things (extrinsic value-objects), and this "more" is both qualitatively and quantitatively superior. This "more" makes us better than mere things. That is what "better" means!

The same considerations apply to our being better than mere ideas; both qualitatively and quantitatively, intrinsic values have far more good-making properties than systemic values. Ideas also lack all of the good-making properties identified above that mere things lack. Moreover, if extrinsic values were not useful to us or to any conscious beings, they would actually have no extrinsic worth at all, for such worth just consists in their usefulness to conscious beings. Ideas also have value only for us, not "to themselves," "for themselves," "in themselves" or "in isolation" from conscious beings. Other individuated conscious beings like God and the animals also have many if not all of these intrinsic good-making properties by degrees, but that is beyond the scope of this book.

In deciding whether ideas have more value than, the same value as, or less value than the realities to which they refer, the crucial thing is to correlate specific ideas of good only with the specific good realities to which they refer. Is the idea of a person as good as a real person? Is the idea of good consequences as good as the good consequences themselves? Is the idea of a beneficial deed as good as the deed itself? Is the idea of money as good as cash in your pocket? Are moral ideals as good as actually living a moral life?

With respect to ideas, the Hierarchy of Value means that a good thing in either of the other two dimensions is better than the mere idea of it. We must clearly understand that this works for *"good"* if and only if *specific ideas are being compared only with their specific objects* with respect to their relative worth (but not when they are being compared with something else). In other words, any good reality is better than our idea of that good reality because it has more good-making properties than a mere idea of it. This has the negative corollary with respect to *"bad"* that specific bad realities in any dimension are always worse than our mere ideas of those specific bad realities because bad realities have far more bad-making properties than our mere ideas of them do.

To illustrate further, in e-mail correspondence, Don Blohowiak asks, "Does the Hierarchy of Value imply that a recidivist child molester and killer has more value than all the world's libraries and museums?" This is a great question, but it misapplies the Hierarchy of Value rule, (1) partly because it compares a bad thing with good things, instead of comparing degrees of goodness (or badness), as in the Hierarchy, but (2) mainly because it simply does not follow the rule. To follow the rule, we would have to ask: "Is a real child molester and killer worse than our idea of a child molester and killer?" and to that the answer is obviously, "Yes." And we would have to ask: "Are real libraries and museums better than mere ideas of libraries and museums?" and to that the answer is obviously, "Yes." We just have to be careful about what we are comparing—not "apples with oranges" but mere ideas of apples and oranges with real apples and oranges. A real orange is very tasty, but the mere idea of an orange is not; even the idea of tastiness is not very tasty! The same sort of questions should also be asked of many similar examples:

Is a real garbage dump worse than the mere idea of a garbage dump?

Are real instances of "freedom, equality, or human dignity, or the system of justice" better than mere ideas of such?

Is a real God more valuable than the mere idea of God?

In all instances, for the Hierarchy to work properly, specific ideas have to be correlated with their specific objects, and only with such; but, properly understood and employed, *it does work*!

Ranking things philosophically involves getting in touch with our deepest preferences or value intuitions, our most fully informed and carefully considered preferences or value insights, our consciences. Our deep and carefully considered preferences can be made conscious and explicitly expressed in something like the Hierarchy of Value. Considerations like those in the preceding paragraphs should enable us to affirm the essentials of the Hierarchy of Value: People are more valuable than things; and things are more valuable than mere ideas of things or of people. Getting in touch with our deepest value intuitions and preferences can also help us to select the good-making properties that belong within all of our ideal concepts-to-be-fulfilled.

C. Uniqueness and Human Worth

All of the above features belonging to people but not to mere things or ideas are *universal properties* or qualities that we all have in common as human beings. They belong to us by virtue of our common humanity. As such they are quite powerful and convincing as "better-making-properties"; but *they do not constitute our full individuality or uniqueness.* With one another we share capacities for consciousness, thinking, planning, conceiving of ourselves, acting purposefully, feeling emotions, feeling pleasures, loving, being conscientious, being moral, etc. Precisely because these properties are universally human, *they alone* cannot mark our identity or worth as individuals. Hartman wanted to move beyond our common humanity and show that our intrinsic worth is tied somehow to our being absolutely unique, but this would seem to require additional good-making properties. What sense can we make of this?

Immanuel Kant said that we should respect *humanity* within ourselves as an end in itself. This is only a small part of the story, Hartman thought. Humanity is something very abstract that we have in common with other people, and there is nothing unique about it, even if its defining properties are distinctively human, which is doubtful. If we value only our common and/or distinctive humanity, we still do not value our unique individuality. When Kant explained what he meant by valuing humanity—"respecting persons"—it turns out that he had in mind valuing only the moral law within us—something purely systemic—which falls very far short of both the fullness of our common humanity and our distinctive personal individuality. As he said, "Respect for a person is properly only respect for the law (of honesty, etc) of which he gives us an example" (Kant, 1949, 19, n. 3). Valuing rationality, self-consciousness, activity, experience, or valuation in general are not the same as valuing concretely existing, unique, self-conscious, holistic centers of such properties. Individual persons have far more good-making properties than mere "humanity," commonly shared.

Try a thought experiment. First, think of many things that you have in common with all other people. Humanity, whatever that is, is indeed an important part of who you are, but not the whole of it. The moral mandates of deepest-level conscience, and our most profound rational intuitions, seem to spring from our common humanity or human nature, but there is a lot more to us as unique persons than that.

Next, try to think of some things that are true of yourself as an individual but not true of anyone else in the universe. If you really put your mind to it, you can come up with many things that are true of you but of no one else in the world or universe. If nothing else, consider that no one else has exactly your set of genes, fingerprints, eye patterns, and innumerable other fine-grained physiological features and structures. No one else has ever had exactly your space-time locus, or your distinctive perspective on the universe. No one else has ever had exactly your experiences. No one else has ever made your decisions or manifested your creativity. No one else reiterates exactly your unique integration, synthesis, and configuration of properties—your total property inventory—even though you share innumerable general properties or qualities with other people. No one else has exactly your station in life and its duties. No one else has your uniquely personal combination of responsibilities, interests, and projects. As William James said, no two people (you included) ever divide up the universe between "me" and "not me" in exactly the same way (James, 1890, 289). No one else can enrich the universe with goodness in your own distinctive way. As an intrinsically valuable reality, no one else could take your place or replace you without loss.

Our uniqueness consists in the total set of properties and relations that we have and are, including how our attributes are arranged, ordered, or configured. This includes our common morality, rationality, affections, activities, and humanity, *as well as* all the concrete individuating properties and relations that belong to each of us alone. If we value ourselves, and if others value us, only for the abstract characteristics we share with others, we are in principle expendable and could be replaced by others having the same characteristics, without any overall loss of goodness or worth.

Most if not all of our systemic and extrinsic properties are repeatable; and if these alone have value, we can be replaced without loss of value by others who exemplify these same properties. Someone else can wear the numbers on our jerseys, work at our jobs, and be paid the same salary by the hour. If we are a quarterback, a center, a second baseman, or a catcher, other players can replace us as long as we are valued merely as extrinsic means to filling those positions or winning games. If we are teachers, coaches, students, engineers, or salespersons, others equally competent can replace us in such roles without loss of value—as long as we are being valued only because of the functional class properties that we share with others.

If we are a friend, a husband, a wife, or a child, other people in our lives can make new friends, wed again if we divorce or die, and have additional children; but can our "replacements" really take our place in truly intimate intrinsic human relationships? Not if others know and love us as unique human beings! When Thomas Jefferson followed Benjamin Franklin as American Ambassador to France, he was asked if he was Franklin's "replacement." He replied: "No one can replace him, sir; I am only his successor" (Mayo, 1942, 115). What a profound axiological insight!

So it is with all of us! If we die prematurely, our successors will also be unique persons; but, once lost, the value of our own unique individuality (and that of other people when they are lost) is gone and can never be replaced intrinsically. A new intrinsic relationship is never a replacement relationship. Even with new intrinsic gains, lost loved ones are still lost; and people with developed capacities for intrinsic valuation are acutely sensitive to this loss. To think that one individual person could ever replace another in an intrinsic relationship is to fail to understand the concept of "uniqueness" and to appreciate the value of unique conscious beings.

To the question, "What things or entities are intrinsically good?" Hartman answered: individual persons (not just generic humanity), as well as other unique conscious beings like God. (His position on animals was ambiguous, to say the least.) Philosophers have not always agreed with him, he acknowledged; but, he insisted, every human being is unique, and the intrinsic goodness of "persons" is tied to our uniqueness, not just to our universal or common humanity. Formal axiology, he said, affirms that

> The universal has the lowest, the unique the highest value... Formal axiology confirms the radical value reversal of existentialism, in particular Kierkegaard: its highest value is the individual, the lowest the system, with classes—of individuals or things—in the middle (Hartman, 1967, 254).

Hartman knew that many philosophers (and non-philosophers) claim that universals (repeatable properties), not individuals (unrepeatable realities), are the only entities that are intrinsically good. Hartman's answer, shared with Kierkegaard, that "Unique persons are intrinsically good," was indeed a radical reversal of philosophical tradition. Most philosophers seem to think that only universals are intrinsic goods. Universal are repeatable qualities or relations, things that can and do occur more than once; unique beings can and do occur only once. Red, green, sweet, and sour are universals. They occur over and over again. So do the universal or repeatable properties that have been championed as intrinsic goods by most philosophers over the centuries, for example: truth, beauty, goodness, knowledge, enjoyment, pleasure, happiness, the moral law, love, freedom, creativity, desire fulfillment, interest fulfillment, and so on. Few people subscribe to this entire list, so philosophers disagree somewhat about what kinds of things (entities) are valuable for their own sakes. The author of this book once subscribed to John Stuart Mill's view that universals, specifically, pleasures, qualitatively conceived, are the only things that are intrinsically good (Edwards, 1979), and he explicitly disagreed with Hartman in print about this (Edwards, 1979b, 12; Edwards. 1979a, 143). Eventually, he changed his mind, many years after Hartman's death. Why?

Taken altogether or collectively, the following *seven philosophical "pre-systematic" arguments for the superiority of individuals over universals* seem convincing. If axiology is ever to evolve into something like a science, it will need a solid philosophical foundation, from which it can never be divorced, even as it aspires to become a science.

First of all, truth, beauty, goodness, knowledge, enjoyment, pleasure, happiness, the moral law, love, freedom, creativity, desire fulfillment, interest fulfillment, and so on are indeed very good things; but they are not intrinsically good things. They are "good for" things. They are good or valuable because they enhance or enrich the lives of unique individual persons, but they are not valuable "in themselves" or "in isolation" from unique conscious persons. Why not?

G. E. Moore said explicitly what many philosophers have practiced, namely, that if we wish to find out if anything is good "in itself" we have to isolate it in experience, memory, and imagination from everything else with what it is normally associated. Then, after carefully applying this "Principle of Isolation," if we find intuitively that something all by itself is desirable in itself or for its own sake, we can reasonably proclaim it to be intrinsically good (Moore, 2003, 91-96, 187-189).

Now, let us seriously apply Moore's Principle of Isolation to all of the above universal goods. To do so, *they must be isolated from everything else with which they are normally associated, including individuated conscious awareness.* They must be considered all alone, all by themselves. They must be found to be valuable for their own sakes in and by themselves. When that is done, what results? We should be able to see intuitively that "by themselves" they have no worth at all "in themselves." Yes, they have great value to us or for us, but not just "in and by themselves." They have great value to us, in us, and for us, but they mean nothing to, in, by, or for themselves. They are intrinsic-value-(people)-enhancers, but they are not intrinsic values in isolation. They are good for, but not intrinsically good.

Actually, their value status is even more dire than this. We can never completely isolate them completely from ourselves, for we are always there thinking of them, evaluating them, and applying the Principle of Isolation to them! They cannot even exist, much less have value, "in and by themselves;" they can exist only in us or other individuated conscious beings; and they have value only in, to, and for us or other such conscious individuals like God and the animals. Robert S. Hartman well understood this, writing:

> When we ask people what they think is the main thing in their lives, we get all kinds of answers. Knowledge, love, money, success, health, but rarely the answer that existentially is the only correct one: *the main thing of my life is that I live it*, the fact that *I am*, that I was born, brought into this world. This *substance* of our existence we forget and are content with some *qualities of* this existence: money, love, success, etc. But all these are possible only under the condition that *I am*. If I am not, all these qualities and gifts are not either. Qualities *of* existence are only possible when there is existence itself. Therefore, to concentrate on qualities and forget the substance that alone can have these qualities means concentrating on the nonessential and forgetting the essential. He who lives a life that forgets existence and concentrates on not life itself but its accessories does not truly live; in the existential sense, he vegetates (Hartman, 1970, 314).

Second, individual persons have many good-making properties, like consciousness for example, that are not possessed by any of the universals that are standard philosophical candidates for being intrinsically good things. Consider just one item from the above list. "Pleasures" are often said to be intrinsically good, the only such things, according to philosophical hedonists. One problem with this claim is that "pleasures as such" have no consciousness of their own and do not even exist without or in isolation from conscious individuals. G. E. Moore thought that hedonists who affirm that "Pleasure alone is intrinsically good" were never telling the whole story about their own views. Surely, he insisted, they "have always meant by pleasure the consciousness of pleasure, though they have not been at pains to say so" (Moore, 1903, 90). The same must be said of everything in the traditional list of repeatable properties or universals that philosophers have offered as candidates for "intrinsically good things." When philosophers proclaim that such things as truth, beauty, goodness, knowledge, enjoyment, pleasure, happiness, the moral law, love, freedom, creativity, desire fulfillment, interest fulfillment, and so on, are intrinsically good, surely they mean the consciousness of such things, though they have not been at pains to say so. They are *good for* conscious individuals, not "in themselves" or "in isolation."

Third, consciousness "as such" cannot be, isolated from individuality; all consciousness is individuated consciousness. There are no examples to the contrary. There is no such thing as non-individuated "consciousness in general" or "in isolation from individuals." If you can find such a thing, produce it, and then proclaim your theory! Even mystical experiences belong to mystics. All conscious beings are unique, though not all unique beings are conscious. Consciousness can never be completely isolated from ourselves as unique individuals; individuated conscious persons are always there thinking of it, evaluating it, and applying the Principle of Isolation to it. Consciousness cannot even exist, much less have value, "by and in itself;" it can exist only *in us*; and it has value only in, to, and for us or for other conscious individuals like the animals and God.

Fourth, in addition to consciousness, individuated human beings have many highly significant good-making properties that are not possessed by any of the universals in standard philosophical accounts of intrinsically good things. In fact, they are the same properties not possessed by any extrinsic goods.

1) Truth, beauty, goodness, knowledge, enjoyment, pleasure, happiness, the moral law, love, freedom, creativity, desire fulfillment, interest fulfillment, and so on have no consciousness or awareness of their own, but we do.

2) They have no minds or thoughts of their own and never know what they are doing or what or who they are, but we do.

3) None of these universals can plan ahead, but we individuals can plan ahead and develop long range plans of life for ourselves.

4) These things have no concepts at all, not even truth; but we do. Knowledge involves concepts, but they are always our knowledge and our concepts. Concepts

have no concepts of their own. Knowledge has no existence or reality "by and in itself." As William James noted, "An idea neither is what it knows, nor knows what it is" (James, 1891, 477).

5) None of these universals have purposes of their own, but we do.

6) Desires and interests are always our desires and interests; desires and interests do not have desires and interests of their own, but we do.

7) None of these universals have an emotional life or happiness of their own, not even happiness itself, but we do.

8) None of these things are lovers, but we can love ourselves and one another. Love "in and by itself" cannot love; it cannot even exist, but we can and do.

9) None of these universal properties have a conscience of their own, not even conscience itself; but we have a conscience that prompts us toward good and away from evil.

10) None of these abstract universals are moral beings, responsible moral decision-makers, not even morality or "the moral law" itself; but we are. This differentiation could go on and on, but, once more, you get the idea.

Concrete individuated persons (intrinsic values proper) have significant quantities and qualities of good-making properties that mere universals (intrinsic values improper) in and by themselves do not have, just as we have more good-making properties than mere things (extrinsic values) in and by themselves. Because we have *more* good-making properties than mere universals, we are *better* than they, we have more value than they do, just as the Hierarchy of Value proclaims. We have them, but they do not have us!

Fifth, if such universal values (intrinsic value enhancers, properly understood) did not enrich our lives or those of any individual conscious beings, they really would have no worth at all, for their worth just consists in enriching the lives of unique conscious beings, in being *good for* us. Once again, truth, beauty, goodness, knowledge, enjoyment, pleasure, happiness, the moral law, love, freedom, creativity, desire fulfillment, interest fulfillment, and so on are very important or valuable things; but they are not valuable "in isolation" or "in and by themselves;" they are only valuable "in, for, and to us." They are good-making properties within worthwhile individual conscious lives, but without such embracing individuated realities, who cares? They are good for us, but not good in themselves. *"Good for" rather than "intrinsically good" is the proper way to think about them.*

Sixth, if we accept the standard philosophical view that such universal goods, and they alone, have intrinsic worth, what kind of value are we left with as individual persons? A familiar objection to the claim that pleasures alone have intrinsic worth is that it reduces our individual worth to merely pragmatic or extrinsic significance. It reduces us to merely useful things, extrinsic goods. Given these assumptions, unique unrepeatable persons are valuable only as receptacles for containing universal repeatable goods. The traditional view implies that we are like useful but otherwise insignificant buckets that hold precious water, but that is the only value we have. The water is the good stuff; the bucket is practically nothing, a bare extrinsic necessity. Yet, this conclusion is very hard to swallow!

"Pleasure alone is intrinsically good" is not the only assumption that reduces individual worth to extrinsic worth. Kant's deontological or formalistic "moral law" does exactly the same thing. Deontological theories take systemic laws or rules, rather than pleasures, consequences, or people, to be axiologically fundamental. Kant thought that the moral law alone has unqualified (or intrinsic) goodness.

Kant is famous for saying that we should "Respect persons as ends in themselves." He got the words right, but not the axiological reality. "Respect for a person," he explained, is "really for the law, which his example holds before us" (Kant, 1956, 81). In other words, people are valuable as containers to hold the really good stuff, the law, but only the law is of real value. "Respect for persons," for Kant, is just a roundabout way of saying "Respect for the moral law." Kant clearly rated systemic value (the law) higher than intrinsic values (concretely existing real persons with their total property inventory). For him, people are valuable as extrinsically useful buckets to hold the systemic law, but they really do not have any intrinsic worth of their own; real people as we experience them are only appearances, not realities, Kant thought. Instead of writing "intrinsic worth," Kant said that the law is "good without qualification." This was the philosophical perspective that Hartman was trying to reverse when he proclaimed, with Kierkegaard, that individuals have the highest value and systemic values the lowest. All theories claiming that only universals, no matter what kind, are intrinsically good, treat individual persons as merely extrinsic means to the actualization of those intrinsically good universals. Upon deep reflection, this is highly counterintuitive! Individual persons are much more valuable than buckets or receptacles.

Seventh, if individual persons do not have intrinsic worth, they are replaceable without loss of worth by something else, but can we in good conscience accept this conclusion? For holding water, pleasure, or the moral law within, one non-leaky bucket is just as good as another, and nothing of significance is lost if one is replaced by another. We saw earlier that people can be valued for their usefulness, but when only that happens, they are replaceable without loss of value by someone else with similar extrinsic qualifications. Valued only for usefulness, one capable quarterback is just as good as, and can be readily replaced by, another one; one qualified machine tool operator is just as valuable as, and is readily replaceable by another machine tool operator. The same may be said when people are valued only systemically; one qualified philosopher as such is just as good as, but no better than, another equally well qualified philosopher. And so it is with every human role in which people are valued merely as means to ends, no matter whether extrinsic or systemic. They are readily replaceable without loss of value by any other equally efficient means—even by machines and computers.

In some human contexts, individual persons are irreplaceable—as we know full well when we deeply respect and value ourselves, when we deeply cherish and love our friends and loved ones, and when we grieve profoundly over friends and dear ones who have been lost to death or in some other way. If we think that the people closest to us in life are readily replaceable without loss of intrinsic worth by someone else, we have not yet grasped the true significance of uniqueness, that is, of unique persons.

All together, these seven arguments—and maybe you can think of more—add up to a strong case for the conclusion that unique persons, not desirable universal properties, have intrinsic worth and are valuable in, to, and for themselves.

D. Uniqueness and Individual Worth

Up to this point, the concept of "uniqueness" has been much used but not yet defined or examined. Now we must ask about its logical meaning and its precise axiological significance. According to Robert S. Hartman, "unique" is the value category that belongs to the realm of intrinsic value, the highest form of value; "extrinsic goodness" belongs to instrumental or useful values; and "perfection" belongs to systemic or conceptual values (Hartman, 1967, 195, 197, 199). But what did he mean by "uniqueness"? And what does that word mean to the rest of us?

According to Hartman, uniqueness is not a property of an entity. Like "good," it is a "secondary property," that is, a property of its set of properties. Specifically, again like "good," it is the *completeness* of its set of properties. Apparently, Hartman had a hard time deciding on what he meant by "unique." If we survey his writings and publications, we will find at least three different and perhaps incompatible definitions of this key axiological concept. 1. Unique means having all its properties, 2. Unique means having at least one property that nothing else has, and 3. Unique means having a non-denumerable infinity of properties.

1. "Unique" he wrote, means that an entity has "all the properties that it has" (Hartman, 1960, 15). Unfortunately, this definition is inadequate if "uniqueness" is supposed to distinguish intrinsically good things from those that are merely extrinsically or systemically good. *All concretely existing things have all the properties that they have, whether individual persons, individual machines, or individual concepts.*

2. "Unique" usually means "having properties, or configurations of properties, that nothing else has." Hartman captured this sense in writing of "properties which the individual has uniquely" (Hartman, 1967, 97, 98), and of "properties which characterize this and no other thing" (132). He defined individual goodness as implying that there is "no other individual x exactly like this x with all these attributes" (Hartman, 1991b, 15). His most explicit affirmation was, "All intrinsic values are selves, and each self is unique, *i.e.*, has at least one property that no other being has" (Hartman, 1995a, 60). However, even in this, sense human persons are not uniquely unique. All existing extrinsic bricks are unique, if only with respect to having their distinctive locations in space and time, and all systemic universal

thoughts are unique in having their own distinctive meanings and uses. Alfred North Whitehead recognized that each "eternal object" (each universal systemic concept or its referent, as Hartman might say) is unique. According to Whitehead, "each eternal object is an individual which, in its own peculiar fashion, is what it is" (Whitehead, 1953, 159) and "any eternal object is just itself" (171). Even Hartman recognized that universal concepts or words can be unique (Hartman, 1967, 309), *so "unique" does not apply only to intrinsically valuable entities like human beings.*

3. In one discussion, contradicting 2. above, Hartman explicit denied that "unique" means "having at least one property that nothing else has" (Hartman, 1995b, 97). In place of this, he then proposed that "A thing is unique only if it has a non-denumerable number of properties" (96). This leaves us wishing that Hartman would just make up his mind! In light of the definitive arguments against Hartman's "proof" of human infinity given in section "F. Infinities: The Second Formality" of this chapter, we should probably stick with some combination of definitions 1. and 2. above. If we accept this third definition, *no actual human being is unique, for no human being really has a non-denumerable infinity of properties.*

The connection between the value of concretely existing human beings and uniqueness seems much more tenuous than Hartman claimed. Being an unrepeatable and intrinsically valuable human self is intimately connected with having one's properties, but the exact nature and significance of this connection requires more careful examination.

Uniqueness is a property of intrinsically good individual entities, but, as just indicated, it can also be a property of systemic and extrinsic entities. Uniqueness, like goodness, applies only to the total set of a thing's good-making properties, but it is not itself a good-making property. It leaves unanswered the vital question, What are the good-making properties of those unique beings that are intrinsically good?"*All intrinsically good entities (e.g., individual persons) are unique, but not all unique entities (e.g., ideas, things) are intrinsically good.*

Only unique beings that *also* exemplify the *specific good-making properties* of consciousness, self-valuation, others-valuation, thinking, deciding, feeling, conscience, etc., are intrinsically good. As Hartman said, *"All intrinsic values are selves"* (Hartman, 1995a, 60), and this is the real reason why unique bricks and thoughts are not intrinsically good. *Intrinsically good beings are a synthesis of uniqueness with the additional intrinsic-good-making properties of selfhood or individuated consciousness.*

Individuated consciousness in all its richness, not uniqueness, is the distinctive good-making property of intrinsic goodness. Uniqueness itself, like goodness, is not a good-making property; it is a secondary property belonging to unique configurations of consciousness. The good-making properties of all persons and animals are synthesized concretely into unique configurations that nothing and no one else has; and each unique person or conscious being possess some properties not possessed by anything or anyone else.

What is a "property?" Properties, as we know by now, are qualities or relations, some actual, some only possible. Hartman distinguished between thoughts of or words for properties, reserving "intensions" and "predicates" for these, and the actual or potential realities to which words and thoughts refer, reserving "extensions" and "properties" for these (Hartman, 1967, 31, 103). "Meanings" can be intensional, extensional, or both. Ideas are meaningful, but so are their referents. Some if not all qualitative predicate/properties are inherently relational in nature, most obviously intentional concepts like "desire" and "love," both of which require objects to complete their intensional and extensional meanings. Anxieties are usually *about* something. Desires are usually *for* something; love is usually *for* someone or something. Intentional concepts usually have *objects*, but not always. Some are only "free floating," seeking objects, but not always finding them. Individual people exist in time and are composed of uniquely configured, unrepeatable, temporally ordered sets of concrete determinate properties, including consciousness, but not that alone.

Hartman came very close to formulating this next definition when he wrote of "x's self, i.e., the integral totality of all of x's attributes" (Hartman 1991, 15) The best available Hartmanian definition of *a unique human person* is probably this: *A unique person is the integrated totality of all of his or her properties (qualities and relations.* For short, we are "our total property inventory." All the conscious and unconscious events, experiences, thoughts, decisions, feelings, and activities of our past, present, and future belong to our total property inventory. So do all the physical structures and processes in our bodies, past, present and future, for our bodies are integral aspects of what we are. We know very little about ourselves. Most of our past has slipped from our memories (though not from God's). Our total property inventory is incredibly richer than our present conscious awareness. Most of our total property inventory lies below the surface; consciousness is just *the tip of the iceberg of our total reality, but no less valuable for being so.*

Much that Hartman wrote adds up to equating our full individuality with our total property inventory. He clearly regarded individual persons in their full determinateness, concreteness, and uniqueness as intrinsically good, as opposed to the extrinsic goodness of mere things in the public sensory world, and the systemic worth of mere ideas or concepts. A unique or "singular" fact (like an individual person), he wrote, "has the full concreteness of all its properties" (Hartman, 1967, 96) It is "in a class all by itself" (162). He says of "the totality of all the attributes which any actual x [or person] may possess" that this totality "is a unique configuration" (Hartman, 1991b, 16).

Taking Socrates as his example, Hartman wrote, "It is, I think, beyond doubt that the proper name 'Socrates' refers to all of Socrates and not to some section of his properties. It refers to the totality known and observed as Socrates" (Hartman, 1968, 26). Hartman recognized that "The individual exists in space and time. The concept of it is in the mind" (34), and he acknowledged that for many purposes we require concepts "where spatio-temporal existence itself is part of meaning" (36).

He gave organismic intellectual and artistic creativity as examples (36-43). In another article, agreeing explicitly with process theologians, he treated "God" as such a concept, writing that God, "by the necessity of his nature, is continuously surpassing himself—a necessary ever self-surpassing, self-concreting on-going" (Hartman, 1972, 275) and that

> Since God never exhausts his potentiality, the world is continually being created; and God and the world are continuously in the I/Thou relation of creativity. All past properties of the world were in God as predicates, that is, as thoughts to be realized; and all future properties of the world are in God as predicates to be realized (278).

Human beings, Hartman acknowledged, are constantly creative, thus constantly temporal, some much more creative than others, for "the vast majority of men stop at narrow ranges of creativity" (278). The temporality of the human self is more implicit in some of Hartman's writings than explicit, though usually explicit enough. His whole axiological psychology is about human self-development through time in multiple value dimensions. It pinpoints human shortcomings when self-development in three dimensions takes place asymmetrically or does not take place at all or as it should. He regularly emphasized the relationality of human selfhood, often quoting with admiration Kierkegaard's definition of the self as "a relation which relates itself to its own self" (Hartman, 1962b, 418). Perhaps Hartman was not always as crystal clear about the temporality of human selfhood as he should have been (Edwards, 1995, 41-50), but he was usually clear enough.

A Hartmanian understanding of unique personhood as "the integrated totality of all of our properties, both qualitative and relational," must be qualified by temporality. "Having all of our properties" is not a done deal. At any given moment, we have a vast plethora of properties, both actual and possible, but our total set of actual properties is unfinished until death do us depart. Aristotle suggested that no one could be *completely* happy until he (or she) is dead, because something bad might happen in the future to spoil everything. Without getting bogged down in that one, we can acknowledge that none of us have all of our actual properties *completely* until we are dead—and not even then if there is survival after death where things actually happen. We are temporally ordered unique selves, and "our total property inventory" is always unfinished and increasing as long as we live or survive. Hartman wrote, "The outstanding feature of a dead person is that nothing happens with him anymore, that he is no source any more of properties or features" (Hartman, 1968, 43). What our future selves will be like depends significantly on the decisions that we make here and now.

What kinds of properties constitute unique human selves and their well-being? Hartman would answer in terms properties that correspond to three basic kinds of value—systemic, extrinsic, and intrinsic. All three are integral parts of our uniquely configured total property inventories and our unique personal worth. As Hartman said, "Our inner or moral Self, our outer or social self, and our systemic or thinking self, comprise our total value pattern, our Personality" (Hartman, 1994, 61).

Systemic properties are thought properties—language, ideas, concepts, words, beliefs, rules, laws, ritual forms, mathematics, logic, and the likes of such. Philosophical, theological, and scientific belief systems are composed of systemic properties or entities. To the extent that they are within us, they partly constitute who we are, our total property inventory. Systemic properties are systemic value-objects, so we are partly composed of systemic values. As we think and learn conceptually, our systemic properties are enriched; the pursuit, capture, and contemplation of knowledge enrich the systemic parts of selfhood, of ourselves.

Extrinsic properties are spatiotemporal properties existing in our common perceptual environment, our shared everyday world of space-time as given to us in ordinary sense experience. Philosophers traditionally defined "extrinsic values" in terms of actual or potential usefulness, and Hartman himself affirmed that extrinsically valuable things are good with respect to their function (Hartman, 1991b, 14). However, Hartman most emphasized their actual or potential existence as things, processes, and activities in our common public perceptual space-time world—hereafter, "things," for short. He wrote, "The subjects of extrinsic valuation are everyday things and persons ... in space and time" (26).

Colors, odors, sounds, tastes, shapes, sizes, motions, etc., and all their actual and possible combinations, no matter how intricate, are extrinsic properties. Extrinsic properties are indefinitely but not infinitely numerous. We value things in space-time as extrinsic values to the degree that they fulfill our expectations of them, that is, fulfill the standards we apply to them, including their overall actual or possible usefulness.

Our own bodies and behaviors consist of extrinsic properties that are integral parts of our total personal property inventories. Thus, they are integral parts of who we really are. As we nurture, care for, and act through our bodies, we are enriched with additional good-making extrinsic properties. As embodied, we are, in part, physical beings, and we live in a spatiotemporal universe, a physical environment of things, processes, and actions that can enrich our experiences and our lives. As we take the properties of objectively existing spatiotemporal things into ourselves in conscious sensory perception and in affective appreciation, they become parts of our own personal property inventories, parts of ourselves, our extrinsic selves, or the extrinsic parts of ourselves. To the extent that things, processes, and behaviors fulfill our expectations and the standards we apply to them, they are extrinsically good.

Intrinsic properties include *all* our properties, our total inventory, including our systemic and extrinsic properties. However, some human properties are *distinctively intrinsic*; that is, they do not belong to our systemic and extrinsic property inventories, for example, our consciousness and self-awareness plus all conscious contents, experiences, capacities, and activities. This includes our creativity plus our abilities to identify intimately with entities valued, to love, to empathize, to be compassionate, to act deliberately and conscientiously. Distinctively intrinsic properties also include our moral and spiritual virtues, such as, fulfilling our self-expectations, being true to ourselves, exercising self-control, being courageous, fair or just, faithful, hopeful, honest, sincere, trustworthy, and the like.

As we intensify and develop our distinctively intrinsic value-enhancing properties and capacities, our personal property inventory is enriched with the very best or richest personal good-making properties of all. Intrinsic properties have the highest value. Like our extrinsic and systemic properties, our distinctively intrinsic properties are integral parts of who we are; but they are also the core of our personal realities. Our total enduring selves with all our properties, including the constitutive qualities, relations, and configurations that make us unique, are intrinsic goods; and we are ends to, in, and for ourselves. This claim about our intrinsic worth pertains to our total temporally-ordered unique selves, not just to the transient self of the present moment, and definitely not to some self beyond all time and space (like Kant's "noumenal ego"). Our distinctively intrinsic properties, including those at the cores of our personalities, change, develop, increase, and further enrich out total property inventories through time, throughout the years of our lives. Thank God for the fullness of time!

We share many universal properties with others, but in each of us, all the aforementioned shared (universal) properties are concretely configured in unique and distinctive ways. Each of us also has additional individuating properties that belong exclusively to us as unique persons and to no one else. Of each of us it may be said that "After God created us, he threw away the pattern." The details of our integrated total property inventory are still being created by both us, others, nature, and God. Our total reality is inherently temporal, social, conscious, affective, mental, moral, spiritual, and active or creative.

E. Self-concepts and Individual Intrinsic Worth

So, good is concept fulfillment. Does this apply unproblematically to individual persons? Maybe so maybe not. Go back and re-read section 2 C above on "Intrinsically Good Things" to refresh your memory on how being an intrinsically good person involves fulfilling, realizing, or actualizing our own concepts of ourselves. It consists in being an authentic person, being true to ourselves, being faithful to our own self-expectations and self-ideals, even though these change with time. Robert S. Hartman defined "intrinsic value" as "the fulfillment of the singular intension" (Hartman, 1967, 254). But is that the whole story?

At least three significant philosophical questions must be asked about measuring intrinsic worth by anyone's *self-concept*. In dealing with these, we will revert again to "universal" first person language that applies to each of us. First, what if I have *a really screwed-up concept of myself?* Second, and closely related, why must the relevant concept of myself, the "singular intension," measuring my intrinsic worth, be *my own*; why couldn't it be *someone else's*? Third, if all people have *equal* intrinsic worth, how could there be *degrees* of intrinsic worth based on degrees of self-realization, that is, on degrees of self-concept fulfillment? In other words, is axiology's affirmation of equal intrinsic personal worth compatible with its recognition that we do not all fulfill our concepts of ourselves equally well, that we do so only by degrees, that we are not always true to ourselves?

First, what if I have *a really screwed-up concept of myself?* "Self-concept" here is normative as well as descriptive. Using "universal" first person language that applies to all of us, it includes both who I know I am and who I aspire to be. It includes the normative ideals by which I regulate my living and acting, as well as my knowledge of my purely factual or descriptive past and present reality. How could I (or anyone) have a really screwed-up concept of myself? Consider two obvious ways. I could have a *morally* screwed-up self-image, or I could have a *psychologically* screwed-up self-image.

Morally, I could have predominantly non-moral or even immoral self-ideals. If I did, would my intrinsic worth consist in fulfilling my non-moral or my immoral self-concept? Look again at the project of fulfilling self-ideals by the "I" in section 2 C. of this chapter. The person described there was quite a decent person. As long as the "I" is that of a morally decent person, it is quite plausible that my intrinsic worth consists in fulfilling my self-concept. The claim becomes much less plausible, however, when applied to someone like Hitler, Stalin, serial killers, serial rapists, or child molesters. If we could ask *them* if they are fulfilling their own self-ideals, they would in all likelihood answer with an emphatic "YES." So, how should Hartmanian axiology deal with people who have morally screwed-up self images?

Hartman's own strategy was to deny that anyone is really and deeply immoral. According to Hartman, "The person will be the more moral the more he fulfills his concept of his Self;" (Hartman, 1967, 306) and "Thus, in the degree that I am I, I am a morally good person. Moral goodness is the depth of man's own being himself" (Hartman, 1962a, 20). The upshot of this is, don't believe what they say if and when grossly immoral people claim that they are being true to themselves and fulfilling their self-ideals. Such people are profoundly conflicted or confused within. They have a moral conscience deep within them, and their superficial immoral self is in violent conflict with their deep moral self, which is their real and true self, but they are confused about who they really are. They may be out of touch with this true self, but it is there, nevertheless, telling them the difference between moral right and wrong.

Many immoral people probably are thus conflicted and confused, but does this explanation really hold for everyone? Is every immoral person really a profoundly moral person deep inside? The main problem with this assumption is that in some cases it seems to be question-begging. It postulates a universal moral self lying deeply within grossly immoral people, some of whom seem to believe quite sincerely that they have no such deep moral self. Even if they have a conscience, they might say, *their* conscience does not tell them that mass murder, serial killing, rape, and pedophilia are wrong. Pedophiles have been studied axiologically (by Wayne Carpenter), and they don't believe they are doing anything wrong! They and many other evil persons would probably think that Hartman does not really believe that intrinsic goodness is fulfilling *their own* concept of themselves; rather it consists in fulfilling *Hartman's* concept of themselves!

We can at least hope that Hartman is right about people with screwed-up moral self-images. We can hope that at a deep level, all human beings, even the worst ones, share a common human nature and a common moral conscience. We can hope that moral goodness is an integral and inescapable ideal requirement of who we all are, even though each of us has to actualize it in his or her own distinctive way and circumstances. But are we really sure about this?

Contemporary psychology says that some people really do seem not to have much of a moral conscience, if any at all, or else their conscience does not give them the same moral directives that the rest of us get from ours. Today, such people are classified as "psychopaths" or "sociopaths" who, by definition, do not have a moral compass within to guide them. They know that other people disapprove morally of what they do; they know that others may try to penalized them in various ways if they do not conform to common "external" moral standards. But, to them, living and acting morally would be conforming to other people's ideals and concepts of them, not to their own concepts and expectations of themselves.

When we get to ethics in Chapter Four, we will consider more carefully whether there are any universally valid moral ideals. Even then, we may have to exempt sociopaths. For now, let's concede that *intrinsic goodness as fulfilling my concept of myself applies only when my self-concept is not morally screwed-up, or psychologically screwed-up,* as discussed next. Also, shouldn't the relevant self-ideals be those of mature adults, not those of children or otherwise immature persons? Surely, not every "my self-concept" counts equally.

Second, why must the relevant concept of myself, the "singular intension" measuring my intrinsic worth, be *my own*; why couldn't it be *someone else's*? After all, we do have concepts of and ideal expectations for other unique people as well as ourselves. Just ask any parent, counselor, psychologist, moral teacher, or spiritual guide! Hartman never posed this question. He always assumed that the relevant singular intension to be fulfilled had to be *my own, not someone else's*. Hartman expressed this while explaining his understanding of "conscience."

> This self-reflective and self-directive part of a person is usually called the person's conscience. In the case of a person our definition may thus be formulated: "x is a good person if x is as x's conscience demands" or "x is good if x follows his conscience," or in some similar fashion (Hartman, 1991b, 15).

In other contexts, Hartman clearly recognized that individual persons can be axiologically deficient in many ways, including their self-concepts. He clearly acknowledged that axiological deficiency can and does spill over into psychological deficiency. He wrote, "... In the social field we are very adept. But we fall far short of living in the full depth of ourselves ... We live rather shallow lives. We are not fulfilling ourselves. We are only living a small fragment of ourselves. We are not, really. We don't live what we could be" (Hartman, 1962a). He also affirmed quite explicitly that counseling or therapy is in order and proper if and when deficiencies in self-concepts are sufficiently great. This comes out in many of his writings, but perhaps most emphatically in the *Manual of Interpretation* (Hartman, 2006) that he wrote to go with The Hartman Value Profile.

The Hartman Value Profile, of which he was the principal author, assumes that *our values are the real keys to our personalities.* Today, the HVP is extensively used in consulting and counseling. In clinical psychology, it can help diagnose many psychological disorders, prescribe, where indicated, axiology-based regimens of treatment, and measure progress during the course of treatment. Parents, psychologists, moral guides, and spiritual counselors are constantly trying to change people's self-concepts and self-ideals, thus rejecting Hartman's assumption that everyone's self-concept is OK as is. These "experts" may have better ones to offer! Very often they do, especially when people have serious mental disorders, or if they have what Hartman called an "axiological astigmatism," the inability to bring the value dimensions into clear focus. Someone has an axiological astigmatism "if one of the dimensions is seen more clearly and the others less clearly, or one less clearly and the other two more clearly" (Hartman, 2006, 233).

So what would a "better self-concept" for me be, even if not my own? Why couldn't my best self-concept be Hartman's concept of me rather than my concept of myself? Recall that "better" means "richer in good-making properties or predicates." Clearly, some self-ideals are clearer, richer, and more harmonious in good-making predicates than others. At times, other people can definitely offer us, or direct us toward, better self-concepts, richer-in-goodness self-concepts.

Assuming that *you* have some very good ideas about how *I* could live a much richer, more satisfying, and more abundant life, why should not *my* intrinsic self-actualization consist in fulfilling *your* concept of myself, rather than my own? Moral problems arise, no doubt, when coercion rather than persuasion is used to force someone else's "better self-image" upon me; but if acting upon my own self-ideal is self-destructive or significantly harmful to others, the use of force seems appropriate and necessary. We involuntarily institutionalize mentally ill people who are "harmful to self and others," even if their self-concepts tell them to do it. We criminalize and imprison mentally sane people who have actually harmed self or others, even if their self-ideals allow them to do it. That is why we do and should have police, prisons, punishments, involuntary psychiatric commitments, and defensive (but not preemptive) armed forces. Not everyone's self-concept is good enough. Sometimes, others know better.

Third, if all people have *equal* intrinsic worth (e.g., if *everyone's* cardinal number is $\aleph_1$), how could there be *degrees* of intrinsic worth corresponding to degrees of self-realization or of self-concept fulfillment? Is axiology's affirmation of equal intrinsic personal worth compatible with recognizing that we do not all fulfill our best concepts of ourselves equally well, and that we do so only by degrees? Hartman clearly conceded that self-concepts can be and usually are fulfilled only by degrees, thus that there are degrees or gradations of intrinsic value to the extent that this consists in self-ideal fulfillment. He wrote,

> Dorothy may be singular and yet single; by no means seen as possessing the fullness of her possible concretion. There are, in other words, gradations of intrinsic value. Intrinsic value, as the other forms of value, may be *more or less fulfilled.* The singular concept may be more or less differentiated (Hartman, 1961, 418).

If human equality is to be affirmed, it must be in the intrinsic value domain. Clearly, we are not all equal systemically and extrinsically. Some of us are obviously much smarter and more learned than others, systemically. Extrinsically, some people are obviously much more practical and/or socially useful than others. Differences in extrinsic social worth are expressed in hierarchical social institutions, though not always with exactitude. Within business organizations, and in society as a whole, differences in social utility are recognized and expressed in differences in titles, prestige, salary, pay, bonuses, and fringe benefits. Presumably this is why football players make much more money than college professors! But maybe the correlations between social worth and compensation are not all that exact!

The point is, in every social order, some people are definitely judged to be much more intelligent (systemically valuable) and/or socially useful (extrinsically valuable) than others. If we are to affirm equal human worth, this must be in the dimension of intrinsic values, not in the extrinsic and systemic domains. This is where Hartmanian formal axiology locates it, but how is intrinsic equality to be reconciled with Hartman's admission that there are "gradations of intrinsic value"?

In Hartman's transfinite Axiological Calculus, human equality is expressed in and affirmed by his symbol for intrinsic value-objects. His symbol for intrinsically good beings, individual persons, is "$\aleph_1$." This symbol is applied equally to everyone, and there are *no degrees of $\aleph_1$*. One basic formality of Hartman's formal axiology, the Axiological Calculus, says that there are no degrees of intrinsic worth. The other basic formality, the Form of the Good, allows that people do not equally fulfill their own self-concepts, so there are degrees of intrinsic worth. Applying one formality, we get equality; applying the other formality, we get inequality. So does axiology just boil down to nonsense? Maybe so, maybe not.

Some self-concepts are definitely too screwed-up to be fulfilled. Yet, some people, perhaps quite rare, are perfectly true to themselves, and their self-image is both morally and psychologically sound. Most of us fall somewhere between these extremes. Most of us aren't all that true to ourselves, or we are so only by degrees, and we need to improve our self-expectations as well as our conformity to them. Thus, formal axiology seems to be trapped in a contradiction: "No degrees? Yes.

Degrees? Yes." Are the two primary formalities of formal axiology, the Form of the Good, and the Axiological Calculus (when based on transfinite math) logically incompatible? Is there any way out? Perhaps.

We might refuse to affirm that people have a non-denumerable infinity of good-making properties, as assumed when the equalizing "$\aleph_1$" is applied to everyone. Perhaps we do not all have an exactly equal number of good-making properties, particularly a non-denumerable infinity of them. Without getting bogged down in infinity just yet, what else might we do to escape this apparent impasse?

Without infinity, we could nevertheless affirm on other philosophical grounds that all of us have equal intrinsic human worth. After all, we are all both equally human and equally unique. That "We are all equal in the sight of God," and "God loves us all equally" are commonplaces among religious people, and some of us (perhaps too few) take this very seriously. Democratic societies affirm that "We are all equal in the sight of the law," and democracies strive to protect "equal rights for all." Even if we were not all exactly equal in intrinsic worth and entitled to equal rights, we could not afford practically to act and live otherwise, for any other practical assumption would be subject to too much abuse too easily. Viewed axiologically, human rights function to protect the hard core of intrinsic individuality in each of us from unwarranted intrusion by or harm from others. Axiology must recognize that we live in a very tough world in which the intrinsic worth of everyone needs equal protection, thus equal rights, just to avoid the disastrous consequences of assuming otherwise, if for no other reason. Social orders that do not recognize equal human rights are miserable places to live, as history and contemporary political structures show over and over again.

Can a serious commitment to equal intrinsic human worth be reconciled with the obvious fact that people do not equally fulfill their best self-concepts? Consider the following proposal. *First*, we could at least affirm a *minimal* equal intrinsic worth for everyone that entitles all to equal respect, equality under the law, and equal moral rights. This equality would be absolute, but only minimal; it is the ground floor of human worth that should not be compromised, no matter what. No person's intrinsic worth falls below that minimum, (even though there may be disagreements about what counts as a "person," e.g., in abortion or other "marginal cases." These are all metaphysical or theological problems, not ethical problems).

Second, once minimal equal intrinsic worth is recognized, fully respected, and not compromised, there is ample *room on top of that* for individuals to build lives that are more or less abundant in good-making properties—in all three dimensions. Most of us desire to live as abundantly and meaningfully as possible. This is a large part of nearly everyone's self-concept, even if not absolutely universal or always clearly and consciously understood.

Axiologically, all of us have, or should have, the self-ideal of living a life that is as rich as possible in systemic, extrinsic, and intrinsic values. Some of us are truer to this ideal than others, so this axiological ideal is usually fulfilled only by degrees. Still, *minimal equal intrinsic worth holds for unique persons, no matter what.* This is where our strong social obligations to respect and not harm one another come into play. Once equal basic worth and security for all are guaranteed, increasing degrees of self-realization and abundant living are then up to each individual. Without logical conflict, the Form of the Good comes into play with individuals once equal minimal rights and intrinsic worth have been secured for all. The former is our duty to ourselves; the latter is our duty to others. We should make these duties to self and others conscious parts of our own self-concepts or self-ideals. Intensive moral and axiological education and training at public expense should help to make it so.

To be consistent, formal axiology must recognize (1) a minimal or foundational level of goodness at which all unique persons have equal, (even if not infinite), rights and intrinsic worth. No one ever falls below that level of equal rights and intrinsic worth. But on top of this minimal and egalitarian foundation, there is (2) a superstructure of degrees of self-realization, according to which some people (e.g., Abraham Maslow's "self-actualizing persons") are far more self-actualizing, that is, more developed intrinsically and otherwise, than others.

These two assumptions may be difficult if not impossible to express mathematically, but the philosophy behind them is clear enough. All of us are equal in basics, but some people are truer to themselves than others, some actualize their own ideas or ideals of themselves better than others, some are more introspective, thoughtful, disciplined, conscientious, loving, empathetic, and compassionate than others, some are more practical and useful than others, some are more thoughtful, learned, and intelligent than others, and so on. Given foundational equality and superstructures of degrees of self-realization, what kind of people come out on top? Obviously, those whose lives are richest in good-making properties, whether they be systemic, extrinsic, intrinsic, especially all of the above. Such people are not only most fully human, they are also most fully themselves, most faithful to their experiences of and their best concepts of themselves. They are the most-self-full-filled. Their lives are as rich in good-making properties as human lives can be. They live as abundantly as human beings can live. What more could we want?

F. Infinities: The Second Formality

What more could we want? Well, we might want infinite value, not just intrinsic value, for ourselves. That is clearly what Robert S. Hartman wanted, but perhaps he was not able to have it or defend it. The book you are now reading was not written for "True Believers." True Believers accept everything that is offered to them and have no critical perspective on their beliefs. This book presents the basic elements of Hartmanian Formal Axiology along with critical perspectives and significant additions and improvements. This critical approach to introducing and defending formal axiology reaches its climax in this section of this chapter.

Several logically independent features of Hartmanian Formal Axiology have now been identified and explained—the Form of the Good, the Three Dimensions of Value, and the Hierarchy of Value. All three are logically independent of one another. They cannot be deduced or inferred from one another, so each requires a separate philosophical rationale or justification. Once they become available, they can be applied and related to one another, but they are logically independent of one another and require justification separately. The same sort of thing must now be said of the next feature of Hartmanian Formal Axiology—transfinite mathematics, or the mathematics of set theory. It is logically independent of all else that we have seen thus far, and everything presented thus far is logically independent of it. It depends on nothing else that has been explained thus far, and nothing else explained thus far depends on it. Thus, we may accept everything presented thus far without accepting this next feature, and there are very good reasons for not accepting it.

Hartmanian Formal Axiology incorporates *two formalities, the Form of the Good, and Transfinite Mathematics* as applied to or associated with the three value dimensions. The first works remarkably well, as we have seen. The second does not work very well, as next explained.

Hartman wanted to do one more thing with systemic, extrinsic, and intrinsic values. He wanted to number them, and he regarded this as very important. He thought that there could be no real science without mathematical formulas. Initially, this objective seems quite commendable, given his project of creating a "science of value" that could bring logical order into value theory. It would do so by combining values with formal systems, just as the physical sciences combine "facts" with mathematical formulas. But what kind of math is relevant? Even if some branches of math are relevant, Hartman may have selected the wrong one, and we may need to search further for a viable mathematical framework for an axiological calculus.

i. Numbering the Value Dimensions

Here is how Hartman numbered the value dimensions. With each of the three dimensions or types of value, Hartman associated a number taken from set theory and transfinite math, as follows.

Systemic values were associated with "n" for finite. This means that systemic value-objects have only a finite and definite number of good-making properties, and their relative worth is to be measured axiologically with correspondingly finite concepts.

Extrinsic values were associated with "$\aleph_0$" for denumerably infinity. This means that extrinsic value-objects have a denumerably infinite number of good-making properties, and their relative worth may be measured axiologically by correspondingly rich concepts. In transfinite math, infinities come in higher and lower orders, some being larger than others. Denumerable infinity is equivalent to the complete set of all whole numbers—from zero to infinity. A denumerably rich value-entity would have a set of distinct good making properties that correspond one to one with all the whole numbers of arithmetic, which are endless. This set has no last member.

Intrinsic values were associated with "$\aleph_1$" for non-denumerably infinity. This means that intrinsic value-entities would have so many good-making properties that they exceed all the whole numbers of arithmetic and require correspondingly rich concepts to be measured axiologically. For now, let's just say that non-denumerable infinity is a kind of "infinity of infinities," something that exceeds or is "larger than" all the whole numbers of ordinary arithmetic.

Why did Hartman associate the three basic value dimensions with the finite/transfinite numbers of set theory? The most accurate answer seems to be that he correlated the three forms or dimensions of goodness with three varieties of language (Hartman, 1967, 19, 31-43, 79-92, 255-259), then took off from there. We cannot be sure about how he arrived at the correlation. Originally, he may have reasoned that there are three basic kinds of value *because* there are three basic kinds of concepts, or he might have reasoned that there are three basic kinds of concepts *because* there are three basic kinds of value. *In neither case would the three forms of value be derived or deduced from the axiom of axiology, the Form of the Good.* This Form can be applied to them, but they cannot be inferred or derived from it, despite his claim to the contrary.

Hartman eventually concluded and affirmed that the three kinds of value are determined by the existence of three kinds of concepts (305). In any case, he contended, each value dimension involves concepts, since good is concept fulfillment, and each correlates with distinctive linguistic forms or kinds of concept.

•*Systemic values or value-objects* correlate with and fulfill "synthetic" concepts—formal constructs like those of logic, mathematics, computer programs, definitions, the Form of the Good, etc.

•*Extrinsic values or value-objects* correlate with and fulfill "analytic" concepts—empirical class concepts abstracted from experience.

•*Intrinsic values or value-objects* correlate with and fulfill "singular" concepts—proper names, personal pronouns, metaphors.

•*Systemic value-objects* are supposed to correlate with and fulfill concepts that we *construct with our minds.* Hartman originally conceived of systemic value-objects only as what we earlier called "pure conceptual constructs," but he gradually expanded the scope of "systemic concepts" to include all concepts. Eventually, it came to include all ideas, thoughts, or words whatsoever—definitions, beliefs, doctrines, laws, scientific systems, philosophical systems, theological systems, legal systems, ritual systems, and all formalities, you name it. Many of these, like definitions of words in ordinary language, include empirical elements and are not merely formal constructs which, by definition, refer only to themselves.

According to Hartman, pure conceptual constructs have very important and interesting properties, and some of these were very significant for his original association of systemic values with the number "n."

1) Conceptual constructs are terms that have no meaning all by themselves; they take their entire meaning from the systems of which they are a part. The numbers 1, 2, 3, 4, and 5, for instance, mean nothing by themselves; they have only relational meanings within the inclusive system of arithmetic. 2) Conceptual constructs refer only to themselves or their systems, not to anything outside or beyond themselves. They have no empirical content, no meaning drawn or abstracted from any kind of experience, whether it be sensory or introspective. This is supposedly how pure conceptual constructs differ from analytic or empirical concepts. 3) They are constructed completely by our minds, not derived from anything else or in any other way, so they mean only and exactly and definitely what we intend for them to mean. 4) Even though they do not *refer* to anything other than themselves, numbers, logic, and other conceptual constructs can be *applied* to other things. 5) Since they refer only to themselves, their extensional and intensional meanings are identical. 6) They have completely clear, definite, precise, and finite meanings—like the concept of a "circle" discussed earlier. 7) They function in "all or nothing," "black or white" ways; so if any part of their meaning is distorted or omitted, the results are meaningless. 8) Since their intensional and extensional meanings are identical, there are no degrees of conceptual construct fulfillment; their fulfillment is always either perfect, or nothing at all.

Although pure conceptual constructs are supposed to have these properties, most of our ideas and beliefs (i.e. most of our systemic values) are not like this at all, as explained in Chapter One, so these properties do not automatically carry over to *all* systemic values or ideas, as Hartman assumed. Hartman wanted especially to carry *definiteness, precision, finitude,* and *perfection* over to over to all systemic values (Hartman, 1967, 80-81, 112). The only value-words appropriate to the systemic value domain are, *"Perfect, or nothing,"* he claimed (112, 194-195). Also, because all systemic values contain only a finite number of good-making properties and have very definite meanings, *they have only finite value.* Thus "n" is the appropriate number for them.

Hartman hoped to develop an axiological calculus that would enable us to calculate mathematically the real value of all value combinations. The appropriate mathematics for this, he thought, is transfinite mathematics or set theory, but we may not want to follow Hartman in applying transfinite mathematics to the three dimensions of value. Even without transfinite logic, systemic, extrinsic, and intrinsic values, as well as the Hierarchy of Value, are very real.

ii. Why Transfinite Math Will Not Work

At its annual meeting in October, 2008, held in Cuernavaca, Mexico, the Board of Directors of the Hartman Institute adopted five important goals or strategies for the future. The fifth of these was, "To develop a formal Calculus of Value that really works." This presupposes the inadequacy of Hartman's own calculus of value, based as it was on applied transfinite mathematics and set theory. It is not inadequate in every respect; axiologists can do remarkable things with it; but it is inadequate in many significant ways. Occasionally its results are strongly counterintuitive, and its philosophical foundations are indefensible. What follows will explain in some detail why this is so.

Three caveats are important at the very beginning. First, this critique does not in any way challenge transfinite math as such or calculations made with it. It challenges only their application to the three value dimensions recognized by Hartmanian axiology. Second, this critique does not in any way challenge or threaten the Hartman Value Profile and the math used in scoring it. Transfinite math is not used at all in scoring or validating the HVP; only ordinary arithmetic and statistics are used. Third, this critique does not in any way call into question the vast majority of Hartman's significant achievements in value theory, such as his definition of "good" as "concept fulfillment," his distinction between three kinds of value and valuation—Intrinsic, Extrinsic, and Systemic, or his applied Hierarchy of Value—people are more valuable than things, and things are more valuable than mere ideas. *This critique only challenges the way Hartman chose to number such things.* Now for the problems.

●*Systemic value-objects.* The first troublesome thing about set theory applied to the three value dimensions is with the number "n" for "finite sets." Difficulties with infinite sets and transfinite numbers will come later. Hartman maintained that all systemic values have "n" worth, but this claim is dubious from the very outset. Within Hartman's framework, something as simple as the thoughts of "green" or "x" both have "n" value; likewise, something as complicated as all the ideas contained in all the works of Plato and Aristotle have only the very same "n" value. No matter how many "n"s we add up, they amount to only "n". "N"s always equal "n", no matter how many or how few. If Hartman is right, the ideas of "green" and "x" have just as much worth, n worth, as all the thoughts in all the books that have even been written; and all the thoughts in all the books that have even been written have no more worth than "green" or "x." Something of great significance gets lost when the "n" of set theory is applied equally and additively to all systemic values, to all ideas and compilations of ideas. Frank G. Forrest, the principle developer and defender of applying set theory and transfinite math to the three value dimensions, ends his book with the admission that such a valuemetrics is a "blunt tool"(Forrest, 1994, 170). Blunt indeed!

One might also wonder why at least some concepts like "infinity" do not have infinite rather than finite worth. Here is why. The numbers n for finite, $\aleph_0$ for denumerably infinity, and $\aleph_1$ for non-denumerably infinity are words or thoughts that exist within our minds; thus, by his own reckoning, as systemic value-objects, they should have only finite value. Hartman correlated them with the three kinds of value, systemic, extrinsic, and intrinsic; but this book rejects this, as indicated.

The distinction between intensions and extensions is relevant here. Intensions are just words, thoughts, or ideas that exist within our minds. Extensions are the realities to which these thoughts refer. "Animal," for example is a word or thought that refers to real animals. "Animal" is the intension; the real animals to which this word refers are the extensions. The three numbers of set theory are intensions. If there are any corresponding realities, they would be the corresponding extensions, but the intensions and extensions of conceptual constructs are supposedly identical, and there are no relevant realties beyond themselves. Yet, these three numbers, as used in Hartmanian axiology, are supposed to quantify precisely the number of good-making properties possessed by certain realities to which they refer or to which they are applied—namely, systemic, extrinsic, and intrinsic objects of value.

To concentrate on infinity, confusing the thought of infinity (the intension) with some reality that actually possesses an infinite number of good-making properties (the extension) might lead someone to jump to the conclusion that real numbers have intrinsic or infinite value. But this would indeed be a serious confusion. Traditionally, God alone was thought to be the only reality who has an infinite number of good-making properties.

Our intensional thought of "infinity" is not itself an extensional reality that has or consists of an infinite number of good-making properties. Our thought of infinity is not infinite, and it is not God. Indeed, our thought of "God" is not God—just as our thought of a "tree" is not a tree. Thoughts do not themselves have the properties of the realities to which they refer. Philosophers point out that our thought of "blue" is not itself a blue thought. Bertrand Russell pointed out somewhere that our thought of "three" is not three thoughts. It is only one thought, just as our thought of "one" is only one thought. To extend Russell's argument to "infinity," our thought of "infinity" is not an infinite number of thoughts; it is only one thought! Thus, it does not consist of an infinite number of good-making systemic or thought properties. It is only one thought property. *One* good-making thought property, e.g., "infinity," has finite value, not infinite value, and this explains why our thought of "infinity" does not itself have infinite worth; it does not consist of an infinite number of good-making properties. Simply put, the word "infinite" is just one word; it is not an infinite number of words.

Hartman gradually expanded the realm of systemic value-objects beyond his starting point of pure conceptual constructs, but he tried (unsuccessfully) to carry many of the alleged properties of pure conceptual constructs over to *all* ideas or systemic values. This becomes very problematic, however, once all definitions, including those containing empirical concepts, are classified or recognized as systemic value-objects. It becomes even more problematic after Hartman included concepts like "sovereignty," "citizen," "the state," "corporation," "the general will," and all belief systems, pseudo-systems, and ideologies (Hartman, 1991a, 199-204). Most dictionary definitions and ordinary thoughts, all of which axiology eventually treats as systemic value-objects, contain words that have empirical content, that have been abstracted from experience, that refer to things other than themselves, that contain words that themselves must be defined by indefinitely many other words, and that are adequate by degrees rather than all or nothing. Thus, most systemically valuable entities are not like conceptual constructs with respect to *definiteness, precision, finitude,* and *perfection.*

Even conceptual concepts or constructs may not always have the precise or definite, finite, and totally non-empirical meanings that Hartman attributed to them; the lines separating systemic, extrinsic, and intrinsic concepts may not be as sharp as Hartman assumed. Like the affective aspects of valuation, the conceptual aspects seem to merge gradually into one another. The real differences may be only with respect to *degrees* of definiteness, precision, and finitude, not in absolute kind. Hartman repeatedly used "circle" as his prime example of a precise systemic concept. Its precision "consists in the complete determination of its meaning a minimum of terms" (Hartman, 1967, 81). However, the defining words of "circle" like "curve," "closed," "points," "equidistant," and "center" have to be defined by other words, and then by other words, and then by other words—perhaps indefinitely; and some of them have minimal empirical content. We may arrive at them not purely *a priori* but by a process of extensive abstraction from empirical concepts. For example, from empirical lines, we may abstract only distances between beginnings and endings, and by ignoring or omit thickness we get purely geometrical lines having only length but no breadth.

Nevertheless, ideas, whether pure constructs or not, constitute a very significant and distinctive domain of value. Hartman's originality in recognizing this must be acknowledged, and his insight about this must be affirmed. Still, we need a more adequate mathematics than the one Hartman selected, as further explained later.

• *Extrinsic value-objects* are measured by extrinsic or analytic value concepts that have supposedly been *abstracted* from our sensory experience of the world, Hartman maintained (Hartman, 1967, 113). But what of psychological concepts that are abstracted from introspective experience? We do indeed find the things of the world useful to us, either actually or potentially, either now or later. They belong to general classes like tables, cars, fingers, and figs. These classes have definitions, definitional predicates. As Plato recognized, wherever two or more things are called by a common name, they share at least one common property. Since there must always be two of them having something in common, extrinsic values are not considered with respect to their uniqueness, Hartman argued.

Instances of general classes must exemplify their definitional properties, or else we don't know how to classify or evaluate them. "Chair" for example is defined as "a seat with four legs and a back." Is a broken chair with one severed leg, or having no legs or back at all, still a chair? We can still think of a broken chair that has lost some of its definitional properties under the concept of "chair" when we want to have it fixed or when we recall its former function. The goodness, badness, or in-between worth of members of extrinsic classes are not supposed to depend on their definitional properties, however; they depend instead entirely on their expositional properties, but what are expositional properties, and how many expositional properties are there? In theory sensory objects possess a denumerable infinity of properties, Hartman maintained; in practice, he reluctantly conceded, we always deal with only a finite number of them.

In principle, extrinsic value-objects and the analytic concepts by which we measure them are indefinitely, indeed infinitely, large in good-making properties/ predicates, Hartman thought, though we need not and should not follow him quite this far. In this respect, they are radically different, supposedly, from systemic concepts that always have only finite and precise meanings. Analytic or empirical concepts consist of words that are defined by other words, that are defined by still other words, and "so on to infinity"—a denumerable infinity. An infinite number of good-making properties are there, correspondingly, in all extrinsically good things, Hartman contended. Thus, in principle, extrinsically good things are infinitely valuable because they have an endless number of good-making properties. As Hartman put it,

> According to a theorem of transfinite mathematics, any collection of material objects is at most denumerably infinite, that is to say, can be put, at most, into one-to-one correspondence with the series of rational numbers. The cardinality of, or appropriate number for, this series is $\aleph_0$ (Hartman, 1967, 117).

In practice, however, Hartman admitted, our extrinsic value concepts or standards are always composed of only a finite number of good-making predicates, to which only a finite number of their actual good-making properties could ever correspond. (Hartman, 1967, 113, 194, 195, 221). In other words, even if extrinsic value-objects have an infinite number of good-making properties, in practice this makes no difference whatsoever. In extending Hartman's poorly developed axiological calculus, Frank G. Forrest proposed that we use the letter "k" for what he called "elastic sets" of indefinitely large but still finite sets of properties/ predicates; and he used "k" instead of Hartman's $\aleph_0$ (Forrest, 1994, 9-10) in numbering extrinsic value-objects.

Why did Hartman assume that physical objects, processes, and actions do in fact have a denumerably infinite number of good-making properties? This assumption can certainly be questioned. The only reason for this that Hartman ever gave is that this is "a theorem of transfinite mathematics."

Following Hartman himself, some of Hartman's interpreters seem to get an argument of sorts for the non-denumerable infinity of human experience from a play on the dual concepts of "continuous" and "continuum." The play consists in identifying the two, but there are some very good reasons for not doing so. First, they are two quite distinct concepts. "Continuous" is an empirical concept that means "being linked without interruption," as when two or more things are spatially, temporally, or causally linked. "Continuum" is not an empirical concept at all; it is a formal mathematical construct that means "a set with the same transfinite number as the set of real numbers," which is the same thing as "denumerably infinite." (Sometimes "continuum" is identified with "non-denumerably infinite," but this makes no difference to the present argument.) Identifying these two meanings is sheer confusion, resulting from a mere play on similar sounding words. The argument begins empirically with the continuity of human experience, then leaps from there to a mathematical construct, a continuum. If a moment of human experience is a unified gestalt in which many things are at once linked with one another, so many that we cannot practically count them, this does not mean that it can be divided up into an infinite number of real good-making parts or properties. Simply identifying "continuous" with "continuum" is question-begging, for the question is whether any experience can be divided up into an infinite number of real parts that are also good-making, and we cannot simply make this true by definition.

Infinitely divisible lines in space may be used as examples of such alleged infinities, but for many reasons it is very hard if not impossible to get infinite extrinsic worth, much less infinite intrinsic worth, from such examples. First, if a line is divisible into an infinite number of points, does this really make it infinitely valuable? Does this make it intrinsically valuable? Might not some properties, like points on a line, be of such trivial significance that they are not good-making at all, that they alone, no matter how many, could never add up to actual infinite or intrinsic worth? Are infinitesimally small points good-making properties, or are they just too trivial or irrelevant to matter? If infinitesimally small points are only systemic conceptual *constructs* (they have an absolute position but no size or shape), could they even count at all as actual *empirical* good-making extrinsic properties? Might not some physical objects, properties, and actions have no extrinsic value at all, no usefulness, either actual or potential, to say nothing of having no intrinsic significance? Doesn't quantum theory tell us that nothing in nature has an absolutely precise position, and that real lines (or any other physical entities) are *not* infinitely divisible into real parts, even if mathematically imaginary ones are? According to quantum theory, *below certain measurable finite quanta, nothing real exists at all.* Infinitesimals are conceptual fictions, not real objects in experienced space and time. Perhaps we can imagine no point at which we would have to stop dividing imaginary lines, but quantum theory says that we can and do find natural units at which we must stop dividing real lines. Do systemic imaginary properties count as actual extrinsic good-making properties? Is potential worth equivalent to actual worth? Might not the good-making properties of empirical objects, processes, and actions just be indefinitely large without being infinitely large, especially if their alleged infinity makes no practical difference whatsoever?

Frank G. Forrest admitted that the axiology of transfinite math is a "blunt tool." This is very obvious, as previously explained, when it treats all ideas and combinations of ideas as having equal worth, no matter how trivial or profound, no matter how sparse or numerous. One word or thought in Plato's *Dialogues* has n value; but all the words or thoughts in all of Plato's *Dialogues* have only n value when we apply cardinal number arithmetic (transfinite math) to them. The same sort of problem arises if we assign "$\aleph_0$" (denumerably infinite) value to everything in the physical universe. This means that the penny in my pocket is worth $\aleph_0$, but all the gold in Fort Knox is also worth only $\aleph_0$. Thus, my penny is worth all the gold in Fort Knox, and all the gold in Fort Knox is worth no more than my penny! Something is seriously wrong with this axiological logic!

All useful things are equally useful if all have the same axiological value (Hartman's "$\aleph_0$" or Forrest's "k"), but this is blatantly false. Obviously, something very important gets lost when axiology applies transfinite math to the ordinary world of empirical "stuff." Given a choice between a bookkeeper who uses axiological math, and one who just uses plain old arithmetic, most of us would much prefer the latter! Using transfinite math in business bookkeeping would mean that there would never be any profits, gains, or losses! It seems very obvious that with the things of the world, other formal or mathematical systems seem to work much better! Transfinite math is definitely not isomorphous with the domain of extrinsic goods or of systemic monetary values.

Hartman's association of extrinsic values with a denumerable infinity of properties is very questionable, but extrinsic value-objects are no less significant, even without Hartman's excursion into the transfinite. We just need a different mathematics to understand their significance.

●*Intrinsic value-objects* supposedly correlate with and are measured by what Hartman called "singular" concepts or "unicepts." These are proper names like "Joe," "Ike," "Mary," and "Dorothy." They also include personal pronouns that stand for proper names, words like "I," "me," "my," "you," "your," and "they." They also include metaphors, Hartman thought, though we will have deal with them later. They are concepts that apply or refer only to unique conscious individuals. They do not apply or refer to classes of things, as do extrinsic analytic concepts, and they do not apply to mere words or ideas, as do pure conceptual constructs.

The appropriate transfinite number for every unique conscious human being, Hartman claimed, is "$\aleph_1$," a non-denumerable infinity. Every intrinsically valuable human being supposedly contains within himself or herself a non-denumerable infinity of good-making properties, specifically—thought properties, Hartman argued, and for that reason, "$\aleph_1$" is the correct cardinal number for every person. However, if this claim is false, then "$\aleph_1$" is *not* the appropriate number for us, and a transfinite calculus built upon it does not apply to us and is without foundations or justification. Instead of abandoning hope for developing an axiological calculus, we should just abandon transfinite math and search for something less misleading.

iii. Hartman's Faulty "Proofs" of "The Infinite Value of Man"

That all people contain within themselves a non-denumerable infinity of good-making properties is a very large and surprising claim! Why should we believe it?

Hartman gave the most detailed account of his reasons in an article titled "Four Axiological Proofs for the Infinite Value of Man," (Hartman, 1964). Later, in less detail and using less "sexist" language, he presented his single "Proof for the Infinite Value of the Human Person" in *The Structure of Value* (Hartman, 1967, 116-119). In his original "Four Proofs ... ," Hartman gave four arguments for the conclusion that we unique human beings have an infinite number of good-making properties. This conclusion, he claimed, follows from each of the following four premises.

1. We can think a non-denumerable infinity of thoughts.

2. We have our own definitions of ourselves within ourselves, and each such definition is infinitely rich in meanings or thoughts.

3. We are the "mirror of all things," that is, we can think an infinite number of thoughts about an infinite number of things in the world.

4. We are self-actualizing beings, and our self-ideals are infinitely rich in thoughts or meanings.

Since "Proofs" 2, 3, and 4, all depend on thinking an infinity of thoughts, they reduce to the first proof. This may explain why Hartman presented and defended only the first "Proof" in *The Structure of Value* (116-119). His essential argument boils down to this:

1. We can think a denumerable infinity of thoughts corresponding to all possible extrinsic properties.

2. We can think that we are thinking, that we are thinking, that we are thinking, ... each of these thoughts an infinite number of times, and this gives us non-denumerable infinities of the first infinity of good-making properties.

So, we have within ourselves a non-denumerable infinity of good-making properties, namely, thought properties, and this means that we have non-denumerably infinite worth.

Hartman's "Proof" has been discussed and critiqued in many publications. (See, for example, Edwards, 1973; Edwards, 1991, 83-87; Dicken and Edwards, 2001,139, 146-149). In a nutshell, here is why it will not work and why our value as unique human beings cannot be represented appropriately by "$\aleph_1$."

1) The most telling objection to Hartman's "Proof" is that his two premises are blatantly false. We simply can't do it. We cannot think even a denumerable infinite number of thoughts, and we can not think that we are thinking each of those thoughts an infinite number of times.

According to Hartman's "Proofs ...," we *actually have* a non-denumerable infinity of good-making properties, thought properties, and for this reason we have non-denumerably infinite worth, precisely and only because we can actually think a non-denumerable infinity of thoughts. The trouble is, we can't, and that is all there is to it. As a contemporary mathematician says of the project of correlating two infinite sets, "Putting two infinite sets into one-to-one correspondence is an infinite task, and we don't pretend that we can do it (that is, finish it) in finite time" (Suber,

1998). In a finite lifetime, we can't actually think a denumerable infinity of thoughts, much less a non-denumerable infinity of them. In an early version of his "proof," Hartman himself explicitly admitted as much, writing that "Obviously, no individual can actually think all these thoughts. The demonstration of man's infinity refers to ideal man" (Hartman, 1961, 410). In later versions of the "proof" this fatal admission was simply dropped without explanation.

Well, Hartman's "ideal man" is a mere conceptual construct, so his "proof" does not apply to real people. With respect to extrinsic things in space-time, Hartman says that he is only talking about an "upper limit" of an *actual* infinity of properties (118, 222), but he still adds that "that every individual person is as infinite as the whole space-time universe" (118). He further claims to "have shown that the human being has literally infinite value" (Hartman, 1991a, 194). The trouble is, he has not shown this at all! We can't literally do what he claims we can do!

That we cannot actually think a denumerable infinity of properties, much less a non-denumerable infinity of them, should be obvious enough. If we could think a mere denumerable infinity of thoughts, we would (or could) know everything there is to know about everything that can be counted, but we don't. Infinite means "having no limits," whether they be denumerable or non-denumerable. Yet, all of us have only limited knowledge and only a very finite, though indefinitely large, ability to think an inventory of thoughts. Our finitude, in every conceivable way, not our infinity, is an integral in escapable feature of our individual human reality. This ontological truth cannot be dismissed lightly. The mathematics of denumerable and non-denumerable infinity has no legitimate application to our human actuality.

To the objection, "I could just count through the numbers – that would be an infinity of thoughts, but it wouldn't imply that I know all there is to know" (Steinhart, 2008) there is a plausible response.

Aside from just not living long enough to count through all the numbers, there is a serious problem here about our *capacities*. "Being able to do something" is a capacity concept that does not refer merely to a single exercise of that capacity. Being able to think an infinite number of thoughts, whether denumerable or non-denumerable, is a capacity—like being able to walk, or being able to speak a language. A single use of a capacity does not add up to having that capacity, just as a single step, a child's first step, does not add up to the habit of walking. When we have capacities, we use them more than once. This particular objection assumes that if we had the capacity to think an infinite number of thoughts (which we do not), we would use it only once. However, the single use of a capacity is not equivalent to having that capacity; when we have capacities, we do use them more than once. If we are *capable* of thinking an infinite number of thoughts, we could not use that capacity just once to count through "all the numbers" (even though there is no "all" in the sense of a last number). Instead, we could use it an indefinite number of times—so much so that we could know all that there is to know, not just about our universe, but about all possible universes in which things can be counted. At least, we would be capable of knowing all there is to know, even if we were too lazy or lacking in curiosity to do the work; *and not using it more than once would be a manifestation of finitude.* Yet, none of us are omniscient—another obvious truth!

Here are some additional telling objections to Hartman's "proofs" of the infinite value of "man."

2) The proofs are totally systemic in that they depend entirely on our ability to think. They make no appeal whatsoever to our capacities to love or to identify intensely or totally with others. Thus, they have nothing whatsoever to do with the most appealing features of intrinsic valuation, as explained in the following chapter.

3) The proofs have nothing whatsoever to do with "uniqueness." They depend entirely on properties that all human beings have in common—our ability to think. The "proofs" appeal only to allegedly universal human properties, not to human uniqueness, not to properties that each of us alone possesses, not to the total set of our properties, only to our thinking and then thinking about thinking. Thus, the "proofs" fail to show the very thing they are alleged to show—that *unique* persons have infinite intrinsic worth.

4) When developed into a value calculus using transfinite rules of calculation, "$\aleph_1$" applied to persons has drastically counterintuitive implications. For example:

● The applied calculus leads to the conclusion that loving a hundred people has no more value than loving one person since $\aleph_1$ added to $\aleph_1$ a hundred times just yields $\aleph_1$, nothing more. In transfinite math, no matter how many times you add or subtract, you end up right where you started. Applying transfinite math to people says that the existence of a hundred people is no better than the existence of one person, and that the death of a hundred people is no worse than the death of only one person. This really gets embarrassing when applied to killing people. It implies that the mass murder of a hundred people is no worse than killing just one person, which seems utter ridiculous! The math for killing people is slightly more complicated, (See Dicken and Edwards, 2001, 148-149); but that's the way it comes out.

● The applied calculus leads to the conclusion that it is just as valuable for a person to love the number "1" ($n^{\aleph_1}$), or a grain of sand ($\aleph_0^{\aleph_1}$) as it is to love a person ($\aleph_1^{\aleph_1}$) because all three of these formulas are equivalent to exactly the same thing—$\aleph_2$ (Forrest, 1994, 50). This, also, seems utterly counterintuitive. Surely loving a person has more value than loving an idea or a grain of sand. A transfinite axiological calculus may lead us far astray.

● No matter how often they occur, the presence or absence of the "intrinsic value enrichers" discussed earlier—truth, beauty, goodness, knowledge, enjoyment, pleasure, happiness, the moral law, love, freedom, creativity, desire fulfillment, interest fulfillment, etc. as normally experienced in everyday life—makes no difference whatsoever to $\aleph_1$ intrinsic worth. Only when evaluated intrinsically, only when we totally identify with them, do they make a difference that shows up in the math (Forrest, 1995, 154-155).

● When the transfinite calculus is applied to the eighteen value combinations that make up the Hartman Value Profile, many important distinctions simply get lost. The eighteen are reduced to only eight, and many vital distinctions are "hopelessly lost," as Mark A. Moore put it (Moore, 1991, 184-188).

Other objections can be raised (Richards, 2008), but this much shows that Hartman's application of transfinite math to the systemic, extrinsic, and intrinsic value distinction is in serious trouble. No one within the Hartman Institute has ever attempted to reply to the preceding definitive objections.

iv. Refuting Hartman's Own Reply

The only available reply was written by Hartman himself shortly before his death (Hartman, 1995c, 111-117). It may be summarized as follows.

1) The "infinite value of man" is still a valid theoretical truth, even if not an empirical truth.

2) It is also an empirical truth since a few people, the mystics, really do think an infinite number of thoughts, even though most people don't and can't.

3) "Thinking" is a far richer concept than some people think because it includes "dreaming, imagining, memory, anticipation, etc."

4) Future people will be able to think to infinity, even if presently existing people can't.

5) We are made "in God's image," which is infinite, so we are infinite too, but at a lesser order of infinity.

A few minor details are omitted in this summary, but this is the essence of Hartman's reply.

Hartman's response is completely unconvincing (Dicken and Edwards, 2001, 158-159) because:

1) If only theoretical people can think an infinite number of thoughts, this still leaves all of us real people wallowing in finitude. Theoretical people are only systemic constructs, not real people like us.

2) That mystics think or experience to infinity is an interpretation that comes after the fact of mystical experience itself, and mystical experience can be, and probably should be, interpreted in other ways. Most importantly, if only mystics can do it, this still leaves most people, all of us non-mystics, as finite clods; and it implies radically unequal value between infinite mystics and finite non-mystics.

3) Human dreaming, imagining, remembering, and anticipating are also finite. And Hartman's argument omits love, compassion, mercy, identification, etc.

4) Hartman gives no account of how, or evidence that, the transition will be made some day between us finite dullards and our supposed infinitely-cognitive super-person posterity. This gap between man and superman is an infinite gap. It still leaves presently existing people with only a finite number of good-making properties, thus with only finite value.

5) The "image of God" argument seems to involve resemblances between human and Divine capacities to know, think, love, and so on; but traditional theologi-

ans (whether Christian, Jewish, Moslem or whatever) correctly and consistently reject "infinity" as a point of resemblance implied by the *imago deo*. Almost universally, theologians emphatically contrast God's infinity with our finitude. Traditionally, ascribing an inherent infinity of good-making properties to any of God's creatures would be heresy and a blasphemous self-deification of our finite selves. The concept of the "infinite value of man" was first created by 18th and 19th century German romanticists—definitely not by traditional theologians reflecting on the "image of God" in us (Edwards, 2000, 236-239), and definitely not anywhere in the Bible.

Traditional Christian theology was much more inclined to call us human beings infinitely bad than to call us infinitely good, something that Hartman never realized or considered. God is not neutral toward us as sinners, we were told. God hates us infinitely in our sinful state, some say, despite the Bible's claim that God loves us while we are yet sinners. Jonathan Edwards, for one, explicitly claimed in his sermon on "The Justice of God in the Damnation of Sinners" that justice is the very last thing that sinners could want from God because disobedience to an Infinite Being is an infinite offense, and an infinite offense deserves infinite punishment. Since *all sinners are infinitely odious* to God, justice requires that they be infinitely punished in Hell. Sinners in the hands of his angry God are in infinitely deep trouble! What sinners need is mercy, not justice, and God can give that to whomever he pleases (J. Edwards, 1830, 501 ff). Such themes are commonplace in the writings of Jonathan Edwards and many other theologians. Of course, Edwards never explained why an infinitely loving God does not please to be merciful to all. "Inscrutable sovereignty" just doesn't cut it!

Other theologians see any attempt to claim infinite worth for ourselves as a profound manifestation of vanity, pride, and sinfulness. The Twentieth Century theologian, Reinhold Niebuhr, for example, wrote that "Men are tempted to protest against their finiteness by seeking to make themselves infinite. Thus evil in its most developed form is always a good which imagines itself, or pretends to be, better than it is. The devil is always angel who pretends to be God" (Niebuhr, 1956, 83). Would Niebuhr see Hartman as just such a devil in disguise, a finite being pretending to be infinite?

Traditional Christianity clearly did not affirm that we have infinite value because of properties that we inherently possess. In that respect, we definitely do not exist in the image of God. The possibility remains, of course, that we are infinitely valuable, not in ourselves, but relationally; we are infinitely valuable because we are loved infinitely (not hated infinitely) by God, even while we are yet sinners. The infinities here are not Biblical, but an axiological theology might want to make such a claim anyhow. The trouble is, this *relational infinite worth* is very different from our being able to think an infinity of thoughts, or our *possessing within ourselves* an infinite number of any kind of good-making properties.

The claim that "the infinities here are not Biblical" may need explaning. Most obviously, "the infinite value of man" is not a biblical expression. "Infinite" is never applied to human beings anywhere in the Bible. Hartman wrote that "Jesus is that person who for the first time in human history articulated the nature of man's infinity in God" (Hartman, 1994, 131). The trouble is, Jesus never once used the word "infinity." Hartman clearly puts words into his mouth that were never there.

In conclusion, Hartman's "proofs" for the infinite worth of human persons fail catastrophically. The Form of the Good works great; the Transfinite Axiological Calculus does not work, even though remarkable things can be done with it.

G. Axiology as a Future Science

Robert S. Hartman hoped to turn axiology or value theory into a real science and to move it beyond mere philosophical speculation. Most current members of the Robert S. Hartman Institute share that aspiration. How well did he succeed?

Before defining "real science," we should note first that no science is any better than the philosophical assumptions upon which it is grounded, and all sciences are grounded in philosophical assumptions like the uniformity of nature, the ontological status of space and time, the reality of causation, and the existence of other minds. Science is a social enterprise that requires repetition or replication of results by other competent scientists, other minds. Without other minds (philosophically presupposed), there is no science. The hope of completely divorcing science from philosophy is utterly naive. Clearly, the *application* of all formal and empirical systems depends upon philosophical assumptions. If a true science of formal axiology is ever developed, it will never empower us to dispense with philosophy, even though some of Hartman's remarks pointed in this direction (Hartman, 1967, 14-15, 30). Here are some serious arguments supporting the claim that Hartman's "axiological science" did not and could not dispense with philosophy.

1) The three value dimensions are *philosophical* through and through; they are philosophically derived and cannot be deduced from his axiom, "Good is concept fulfillment."

2) Hartman's use of transfinite math in applying axiology to human beings was grounded in his failed *philosophical* "Proofs for the Infinite Value of Man."

3) *Purely formal* axiology has no subject matter. Only *applied* axiology has human beings, things, and ideas as its subject matter, and *philosophical* arguments are required to justify these three applications. Only applied axiology answers G. E. Moore's question, "What things are good?" Hartman's application of it to us human beings makes many controversial philosophical assumptions, such as that we are capable of thinking a non-denumerable infinity of thoughts, that systemic thoughts are intrinsic-good-making properties, etc. If we can't think a non-denumerable infinity of thoughts, Hartman's way of applying his transfinite formalities to us does not work, and his position cannot be defended philo-

sophically. Maybe there is some other way to do it, but that also will have to be explained and defended philosophically. Formal axiology will just have to find another math, one that does not require us to make absurd philosophical assumptions. We always bring our philosophical assumptions with us, both in selecting relevant formal systems and in applying them. This is especially true in value theory of any kind, formal or not. Axiological science will never be any better than the philosophy that grounds it, and it will never be able to divorce itself from philosophy, despite what Hartman occasionally suggested.

ii. What is Real Science?

Next, whether Hartman succeeded in creating a "real science of axiology" cannot be answered until "real science" is clearly defined. Hartman definitely did not equate real science with natural science. When most people with an American education hear the words "real science," they almost immediately identify this with "natural or empirical science." Hartman came from a much broader European tradition that takes "science" to be any organized body of knowledge. In this tradition, "science" is just "orderly thinking," as Hartman put it (Hartman, 1967, 4). Science in general is a *"thought pattern applied to a set of objects"* (Hartman, "The Science of Value: Five Lectures on Formal Axiology," unpublished, 11).

In this older European framework, theology was "the queen of the sciences," but a science nevertheless. Because Hartman came from this European background, he did not identify "science" with "natural science," and he regarded this identification as fallacious (Hartman, 1967, 130).

Hartman had a very specific understanding of what we are calling "real science." It involves mathematics, but it is something much more specific than mere "mathematical rigor." He thought that creating a real or proper science involves identifying a formal system (a formal axiom or numbering system of some kind) with an empirical subject matter (Hartman, 1967, 4-5, 9, 14, 41, 72-77). An axiom is "the *symbolic form of the core of a phenomenal field,*" and it is known by "a direct and immediate intuition" (41). Axiology identifies the Form of the Good with the core of what Hartman called "value phenomena" (97). A true science applies some formal system to a phenomenal field or subject matter. A value science would apply some formal system to value phenomena.

Hartman did equate real science with *scientific method,* but not as usually understood, not with the method of the physical or empirical sciences, the so-called "hypothetical method" involving sensory observation, repetition or replication of experiments, verification or falsification, and empirical prediction and control of natural objects and processes (Hartman, 1967, 45-46, 127-130). Rather, he identified it with the synthesis of a formal system with the core of some subject matter or "set of objects." He wrote, "I define a "science" as "the combination of a formal frame of reference with a set of objects" (Hartman, 2002, 8). As he explained his understanding of science and scientific method,

> Science in general is a method and has nothing to do with any specific content; if there is a formal frame of reference applicable to a set of objects, then there is a science, no matter whether the subject matter of the science is spatio-temporal—and hence empirically observable and predictable—or not. Thus, mathematics, music, and axiology are sciences, and they *do* include experimentation, observation, and prediction even though they are not "empirical." For these operations are nothing but attempts to apply a frame of reference to a set of objects; whether these objects are spatio-temporal or not is irrelevant. Prediction, in particular, is nothing but the statement that the object conforms to the frame of reference. Thus, in music one can "predict" which note Wilhelm Backhaus is going to play next when he is playing a certain concerto; and in mathematics one can "predict" what will be the result of a certain operation. The same occurs in axiology. Given a certain situation and applying the axiological frame of reference, one can "predict" the axiological result. It is a peculiarity of natural science that its formal prediction coincides with a temporal process of its object; and this material process is confused with the formal predictability of any science as such (Hartman, 1967, 127)

Just any old formal system won't do, however. In a "real science," the relevant formal system must have the same pattern as (that is, be "isomorphous with") the subject matter to which it is applied (Hartman, 1967, 4, 9, 14). Hartman explained that an isomorphous system accounts "with the minimum of concepts for the maximum of phenomena" (14). In scientific axiology, "there is *an axiological pattern isomorphous with and formally structuring, the whole value realm*" (9).

Thus, according to Hartman, real science must have 1) a subject matter, a "set of objects," 2) mathematical formalities, or a formal "frame of reference," and 3) isomorphous patterning between 1) and 2). Particular sciences make use of whatever branches or parts of mathematics they happen to need, or that happen to fit (Hartman, 1967, 106-107; Hartman, 1991b, 10). Sometimes, scientists have to create entirely new branches of mathematics in order to find something that will fit. Logic and mathematics, as well as their applications, have historical origins, just like everything else in human culture. Logic and math did not just fall from the sky all at once and for all time. Socrates and Plato had no logic at all, which is probably why there are so many wretched arguments in Plato's dialogues. Plato's student, Aristotle, created the first logic, and creative logicians have been at it ever since. The same is true of various branches of mathematics.

Before Galileo (Hartman, 1967, 27, 31, 34-35, 45, 70-71, 146-147, 300), no one knew how to apply any branches of mathematics to the empirical world, so real natural science did not exist in ancient and medieval times. Real physical sciences (e.g., physics, chemistry, biophysics, etc.) apply some kind of isomorphous math to their subject matter, and *real non-physical science* (e.g., axiology) can do it too.

The two formalities of Hartman's science of axiology are: *1) the Form of the Good,* as "concept fulfillment" and *2) Transfinite Math,* as applied to the three dimensions of value. *Only the first counts as the "axiom" of formal axiology.* Hartman never claimed that transfinite math is an axiom of formal axiology. These formalities, Hartman thought, could bring order to the phenomenal field of values, thus creating a science of axiology. Axiology's phenomenal field is that of experienced values and valuations—that is, of what and how people value.

Hartman's first formality, the Form of the Good, works remarkably well and is isomorphous with its subject matter. *This is the formality he most emphasized the only one he called the axiom of his new science of axiology.* The second formality, Transfinite Math, does not work very well. The philosophical foundations of its application to human beings are too weak, and it is not "isomorphous" with its subject matter, as just explained. However, remarkable things can be and have been done with it (Forrest, 1994).

We are only halfway there in creating a science of value. Only the math, the weak part, enables computation, exactness, and developing a calculus of value. Having a formal calculus of value that is isomorphous with its subject matter still awaits the insights of creative mathematicians. We are still far removed from the day anticipated by Leibnitz, and championed by Hartman, when "two philosophers who disagreed about a particular point [in moral philosophy] instead of arguing fruitlessly would take out their pencils and calculate" (Hartman, 337, n. 4).

Axiologists today (as evidenced by articles in the *Journal of Formal Axiology: Theory and Practice)* tend to treat Hartman's infinities (e.g., "the infinite value of man") as metaphors that both express and invoke intrinsic valuations—for those capable of responding to mathematical metaphors. For many valid purposes, this is an excellent move, but *no real science is based upon math applied metaphorically.* Certainly, no effective calculus of value could be based on metaphorical math.

ii. Where Do We Go From Here?

Where do we go from here? There are at least three possibilities: 1) to develop a different and better proof of the infinite value of human beings, or 2) to develop and apply a better (more relevant) branch of mathematics, or 3) to ramify the Form of the Good and the three value dimensions into empirical axiological behavioral sciences like psychology, sociology, or political science.

1) A very different axiological "proof" of the "infinite value of human beings" has been offered, but it is valid only in a theological context (Edwards, 2000, Ch. 6). An infinite being (God) loving a finite being (a human being) results in an infinite value combination. In the following quote, Frank Forrest's "k" will used for our indefinitely large human finitude, and $\aleph_1$ will be used for God's infinity.

If we represent God's love to us as $(k)^{\aleph}{}_1$ that formula is logically or mathematically equivalent to $\aleph_2$. In this manner, we can express the value-increase required by Process Theology but not allowed by Hartman's $\aleph_\omega$. Our love to God, expressed as $(\aleph_1)^k$, is equivalent only to $\aleph_1$ and thus has less value than God's love to us. Either way, whether we love God or God loves us, we have infinite worth; and this is the ultimate proof of the infinite value of human beings! We have infinite worth only in relation to God, not because of any properties that we possess inherently. God's love to us has $\aleph_2$ worth; our love to God has only $\aleph_1$ worth; that makes much better sense intuitively than regarding them as equal in worth. Both lover/loved combinations are infinities, but the first is higher in order than the second. God's love to us is more valuable than our love to God, though both value combinations are infinities (Edwards, 2000, 236).

Thus, we would have infinite value either because we are loved by God, or because we love God. Hartman did not follow through with it, but he was aware of Kierkegaard's "proof" that "only when the self as this definite individual is conscious of existing before God, only then is it the infinite self" (Hartman, 1962b, 427). The transfinite calculus might be of excellent use in theology, though not in a "secular" human axiology that would be available outside of theology. The theological application does not say that we have infinite worth because we contain within ourselves an infinite number of good-making properties (i.e., that we can think an infinity of thoughts, as Hartman contended). It says that we have infinite value only relationally—because God loves us, or because we love God, because we exist before God, but these theological considerations do not carry over into "secular" contexts. This "proof" would be convincing only to those who believe in an infinite and loving God. It is definitely not the universally appealing secular "proof" that Hartman wanted. The transfinite math in the theological "proof" advances the science of axiology if you believe in God, but not if you don't. To human beings considered only in themselves, it reasonably assigns only an indefinitely large but still finite intrinsic worth.

2) Perhaps some branch of mathematics, a better branch, a more relevant branch than transfinite math, could be found or created. When applied to the three dimensions of value, it would have to be truly isomorphous in form with its subject matter. In application, it could not depend upon implausible philosophical claims like "We can think an infinite number of thoughts," and it would not have embarrassing logical implications like "A hundred people have no more value than one person." Hartman did not choose the best possible formal system to apply to the three value dimensions. Transfinite logic is not isomorphous with its axiological subject matter. Mathematicians and logicians can create, have created, and are continuing to create, a vast number of alternative mathematical and logical systems. Set theory and transfinite math, with their hierarchy of finitude and multiple infinities, is only one such system. Someone can do better, (but not the present author, who is not a mathematician).

Mark A. Moore, (Moore, 1995) showed us how to apply the alternative finitistic mathematics of quantum wave theory to the three dimensions of value. His initial efforts may need additional work (Richards, 2008, 198-205), but he shows decisively that the three dimensions of value can be numbered distinctly without resorting to infinities, and they can be divorced mathematically from their faulty grounding in Hartman's "Proofs for the Infinite Value of Man." In the future, other mathematicians may find other ways to apply other or different finitistic branches of mathematics that do not have strongly counterintuitive implications to the three value dimensions and other ways to calculate relations between them. Completing a true science of axiology awaits these further future developments. Without formulas, there is no science of formal axiology. About that we can certainly agree with Hartman and Frank. G. Forrest; but this is future science, not science today.

3) Perhaps new subdivisions of formal axiology can be created—empirical behavioral axiological sciences, for example—that give empirical support to, validation of, and testable clinical or even wider behavioral applications of the three dimensions of value. This, too, has now been done quite successfully by Leon Pomeroy in his book titled *The New Science of Axiological Psychology* (Pomeroy, 2005). In this remarkable book, psychologist Pomeroy develops in considerable depth an axiological psychology that works intensely and successfully with the three dimensions of value (applications of the Form of the Good) and the Hierarchy of Value and validates the Hartman Value Profile. However, Pomeroy's work does not use or depend in any way upon transfinite mathematics. Pomeroy's isomorphic math is statistics. His book shows profitably, persuasively, and definitively that scientific axiology can be taken in new directions that are entirely independent of Hartman's "Infinite Value of Man."

We can and should go very far with Robert S. Hartman without going all the way. This, for some, (like the author of this book) may be a slow and difficult lesson to learn. Later chapters will explore many additional and more constructive concerns about what and how we value that are immensely illuminated by Hartman's ideas and ideals. Even without transfinite mathematics, understanding what and how we value is immensely illuminated by Hartman's thinking. As Martin Luther said, we shouldn't "throw out the baby with the bath water."

Chapter Three

HOW WE VALUE: SYSTEMIC, EXTRINSIC, AND INTRINSIC VALUATION

In previous chapters, exploring value issues in non-technical language came first, and a "Philosophical Exposition" came later. By now, readers should be familiar and comfortable enough with the philosophical terminology of axiology, so this strategy can and will be dropped. Now and hereafter, philosophy and easy-to-understand explanations will run side by side.

By now readers should have mastered the Form of the Good (Chapter One), the Three Dimensions of Value, and the Hierarchy of Value (Chapter Two). And they should now have some critical perspective on axiological issues. What next?

So far, the words "value" and "values," broadly understood, were used to cover the things, objects, or entities that are judged to be good, fair, average, poor, and bad; and "value" and "valuable" in a narrower sense were used as synonyms for "good." As we turn now to another important value topic, additional axiological words will be required. "Valuation" or "evaluation" will now cover the many *ways we value, or how we value* good things, bad things, and those in between. Many good things exist, and we relate valuationally to them in many ways. *How* we value is significant and well worth considering. Robert S. Hartman had many illuminating things to say about *how* we value, as well as about *what* we value.

Note that the evaluators who do the valuing discussed in this chapter are the same as the intrinsically valuable beings identified in the preceding chapter. Evaluators are unique conscious beings like us, or God, or animals. As social beings, others always influence and have input into our own personal evaluations, so how we value need not be done in lonely social isolation. It can be and often is a social or collective enterprise.

So, how do we relate valuationally to items in the three basic dimensions of value? Everything in all of our experience and awareness has value in one dimension or another, so *how do* we evaluate anything and everything? Ideally, *how should* we evaluate anything and everything? Let us account the ways.

1. Conceptual or Rational Valuation

We definitely relate *conceptually or rationally* to the things that we value. Earlier "emotivists" who thought this impossible were certainly mistaken about that. Previous discussions of the Form of the Good and how it applies within each of the three value dimensions explained how we relate conceptually to the things we value. We evaluate things in each value dimension by applying the Form of the Good to them with our minds. Being rational about values consists largely in understanding and using or applying the Form of the Good. Some philosophers, for example the emotivists, said that having values and making evaluations are nothing more than just having and expressing feelings, but clearly this is not the whole truth. Evaluation definitely has a rational or conceptual component—understanding and applying the Form of the Good, the Axiom of Axiology—"Good is concept or standard fulfillment." First and foremost, evaluation involves applying the Form of the Good. First and foremost, evaluation is a rational or conceptual affair. Since the Form of the Good can be applied within each value dimension, there are Systemic, Extrinsic, and Intrinsic variations on the theme of conceptual or rational valuation. For details about the conceptual aspects of how we value, go back to Chapters One and Two.

Hartman strongly emphasized the rational features of valuation, sometimes describing valuation in purely cognitive terms. He wrote, "Valuation is a matter of thinking" (Hartman, 1991b, 18), of subsuming facts "under the logic of value" (17). He defined "valuation" as the "combinatorial arrangement of the thing's properties" (Hartman, 1967, 215, 217). By this he meant that "The valuer dissolves *sets of* secondary properties, that is intensions; and he recombines their elements into new configurations, which *are values*" (217). This process gives us many axiological distinctions like those between fact and value, and between good, fair, average, poor, and bad. Whenever we *think* about values, we are relating rationally to them. We do not always do this optimally, but we do it regularly, and we can learn to do it better.

2. Active or Dynamic Valuation

We also relate *actively or dynamically* to the things we value. We *do stuff* with the things we value. We actively combine good (or bad) things with other things that we value (or disvalue), as discussed previously. Value combinations can occur naturally or by human design, choice, and effort. When a beautiful natural scene is bathed in sunlight, twilight, or moonglow, extrinsically good things are naturally combined with one another in value-enhancing ways. Value combinations also occur through human choices and actions; actively combining values is an integral part of how we value. One thing valuates another (affects its value) when the two are combined, and we can be the ones doing the combining. So can natural causes or processes. Dynamic value combination is an important feature of valuation itself.

We can evaluate either positively or negatively by actively combining values. Robert S. Hartman illustrated both negative and positive human dynamic value combinations when he wrote,

> But the combination of things can be bad: and bad is indeed nothing but the in-compatibility of things, or things in transposition....A good Buick and a good Ford transpose each other when they collide....The result is both a bad Buick and a bad Ford, or rather, a Buick disvalued in terms of a Ford and vice versa....The wreck, however, is a good wreck, fulfilling the definition of "wreck," which in turn means a combination of two bad cars. On the other hand, a good Buick and a good Ford in a showroom form a composition of values, ... and this complex is a whole whose concept contains the expositions of both automobiles (Hartman, 1967, 268).

Good things may be actively combined to get good results, as when Buicks or Fords are combined with attractive auto showrooms. Advertisers like to combine cars and other products with attractive men and women or with beautiful natural scenery. Much advertising works (irrationally) by associating some product with some other good thing that has no logical or causal connection with it. (When you get the car, you don't get the beautiful girl or handsome guy in the ad.)

Good things may also be combined to get bad results, as when a good Buick and a good Ford are combined in a crash to produce a good wreck but bad cars. Such a good wreck is bad for the Buick and the Ford as family sedans.

Bad things can also be combined to get good results, as when offenders are corrected, institutionalized, and/or required to make reparations through their own efforts or expense. Disvalues as well as positive values in each value dimension can be actively and intentionally created through active value combinations. Advertisers and propagandists work irrationally to create appealing or unappealing value combinations. Immoral people act deliberately to create morally undesirable value combinations. Moral people act deliberately to avoid or prevent morally undesirable value combinations and to bring about morally desirable value combinations. Much more will be said about active or dynamic value combinations when moral actions are discussed in Chapter Four on ethics.

Combining positive values into more valuable wholes can occur within and between all three dimensions of value.

Systemically, we can actively combine one thought others to produce more creative or inclusive thoughts or belief systems. We can also think constructively about things, as when we design a house, and about people, as when we judge that someone is a morally good person or needs our help, or when we use words to *think*, "I love you" or to *tell* others that we love them.

Extrinsically, we can actively combine things with things, as when we knowingly buy, build, repair, or paint a house or any other artifact. We can also combine things with thoughts, as when we "put our money (or our actions) where our mouth is," that is, when we act practically to support the causes, ideals, policies, or projects that we favor. And we can combine things with people, as when we build a house for a specific person, or give a gift to a friend.

Intrinsically, we can actively combine people with people, as when we propose or consummate marriage, or shake hands, or hug affectionately. We can actively combine people with things, as when people live in houses and make them into homes. And we can actively combine people with ideas, as when scholars devote their lives to the pursuit of knowledge and truth.

Everything that we do involves combining values. Try to imagine additional examples.

3. Affective Valuation in Three Dimensions

Although Robert S. Hartman most emphasized the rational or cognitive features of valuation (how we value), he never denied and often said quite explicitly that feelings are also involved in valuation. He emphasized that valuational feelings cannot and should not be separated from rationality, and that we should not confuse valuation or how we value with nothing more than feelings, as some philosophers are inclined to do. He wrote, "Valuation is no more nor less a matter of feeling than is music. It is a matter of feeling structured by laws—feeling following definite laws. The feeling of value is nothing arbitrary" (Hartman, 1967, 129). Our affective approval or disapproval of goodness or badness has a logical structure (246-248).

So, we relate to the things we value not only cognitively but also through *feelings, emotions, attitudes, preferences, likings, and desires*. Though not the whole story, this also is definitely a big part of the story of how we value, and to these evaluative affections we now turn. So, which feelings are relevant to valuation? The answer is: "All of them!" This answer is so inclusive that it borders on chaos; but by thinking more about our valuational feelings, we can find much order in this chaos.

We can begin to order the initial chaos of our value feelings by dividing them up into *positive* and *negative*. Hartman explicitly recognized that our intrinsic involvement with what we value "may either be positive or negative, that is to say, either intrinsic valuation or intrinsic disvaluation" (Hartman, 1967, 298-299). In all value dimensions, we have positive or affirming feelings, emotions, desires, prefer-

ences, and attitudes; we also have negative or aversive feelings, emotions, preferences, desires, and attitudes.

Positive feelings manifest attraction toward; negative feelings push against or
away. Except for ill-defined "free floating" feelings, all of our feelings, emotions
and desires have objects, value-objects. Positive feelings pull us toward their
objects; negative feelings repel and push us away. Positive feelings include approval, attraction, pleasures, and desires for continuation and repetition. Negative
feelings include pains, disapproval, aversion, revulsion, and desires to avoid or
eliminate. Feelings can be roughly divided into "pro-attitudes" and "con-attitudes."
We normally have pro-attitudes toward the things that we value positively, to good
things. We normally have anti- or negative attitudes toward what we disvalue,
toward bad things.

The Hartman Value Profile consists of nine positive value combinations and
nine negative value combinations. Ranking them properly involves having pro-
attitudes or con-attitudes toward them by degrees. We do not always get the overall
ranking right, and this can be very revealing for self-knowledge purposes and for
understanding others.

Through feelings, we relate either positively or negatively toward the particular
things or value-objects that we value or disvalue. Feelings are also relevant in
selecting the "good making properties" that compose our value standards or concepts-to-be-fulfilled. More about this later.

We can further order the initial chaos of our feelings or attitudes by dividing
them according to *strength or intensity*. By degrees, variations in the strength or
intensity of our pro- and anti- attitudes correlate closely with the whole gamut of
our value words—good, fair, average, poor, and bad. Intensity variations also
correlate closely with the three basic kinds of value—systemic, extrinsic, and
intrinsic. Value-objects come in three basic kinds: systemic, extrinsic, and intrinsic.
So do the emotional and other affective components of how we value.

Systemic, extrinsic, and intrinsic valuational feelings exist on a continuum of
richness or intensity, and these gradually merge into one another. Affectively, no
sharp lines separate them, but we can recognize clear-cut cases when we encounter
them. Oddly, even though I, E, S valuations exist on a continuum, I, E, S values do
not, at least when transfinite math is applied to them, for Hartman's three transfinite
number are absolutely discrete and can never be merged or combined into a continuum. We may need to rethink this.

With respect to valuational feelings, according to Hartman,

> These dimensions indicate, precisely, the distance of the valuer from the valued
> object. This distance gives us the feeling tone accompanying the valuation. That
> we are most involved in intrinsic and least involved in systemic value means, pre-
> cisely, that in intrinsic valuation the distance of the valuer from the valued object
> is closest, up to identification, while in systemic valuation it is farthest (Hartman,
> 2006, 237).

The affective continuum aspect of valuation was well expressed in Hartman's analysis of a situation described by Ortega y Gasset. In this situation, a great man is dying, and his wife, his doctor, a reporter, and a painter react to the scene with different "attitudes" (Hartman, 1967, 259-260).

The least affectively involved person is the painter, who just happens to be there. His reaction is systemic. He "looks on impassively"(259). "All he sees are lines, shapes, colors, systemic aspects of an event whose intrinsic meaning escapes him and indeed does not interest him. 'In the painter we find a maximum of distance and a minimum of feeling intervention'"(260).

The next least affectively involved person is the reporter, who is just there working at his newspaper job because a famous man is dying. His reaction is mainly extrinsic, or "extrinsic-systemic." He is "present for professional reasons" (259). He "observes it with a view to telling his readers" (260).

The doctor is more affectively involved than the reporter. His reaction is intrinsic-systemic. He "is involved in it, not with his heart but with the professional portion of his self" (260).

The most profoundly involved person present is the wife. Her intense affective reaction is one of intrinsic valuation. She is "all grief;" she is "an intrinsic part of" the scene. Her dying husband "becomes one with her person;" she "values a whole life" (259).

With approval, Hartman notes, "Ortega *measures* these aspects of the situation by a common denominator: *'the emotional distance between each person and the event they all witness.'* This measure coincides with our value hierarchy" (260).

A continuous line of degrees emotional involvement runs through systemic, extrinsic, and intrinsic valuation; but, as Hartman makes clear, with respect to value-objects themselves, there is no necessary logical, temporal, or psychological progression from one type to another. This may also be true of how we affectively or experientially value such objects.

> The hierarchy of values is not static but dynamic. The value dimensions do not follow each other in experience in any order....Experience continuously oscillates between these dimensions; and each experience is a pattern in which these dimensions are arranged in different ways....The hierarchy of values is a theoretical order that must be recognized in its dynamic variations in experience (265).

With fluctuating degrees of feeling and emotional intensity, we react to the things we value or disvalue. The feeling aspects of *how* we value deserve special attention. The following concentrates mainly on positive affective valuations or pro-attitudes. Our feelings naturally or typically vary in intensity by degrees as we relate to systemic, extrinsic, and intrinsic value-objects, perhaps with sudden shifts, even though logically our valuational affections exist in a continuous sequence. Natural or typical variations in feeling intensity will be called "Affective Systemic Valuation," "Affective Extrinsic Valuation," and "Affective Intrinsic Valuation." (Hartman himself did not use this terminology.) Affective systemic valuation is the natural correlate of systemic values; affective extrinsic valuation is the natural correlate of extrinsic values; and affective intrinsic valuation is the natural correlate of intrinsic values. Such natural variations and correlations are not inevitable, but they are commonplace, and at their edges they merge into one another.

A. Affective Systemic Valuation

Affective systemic valuation is our least involved type of emotional involvement with what we value. How do we typically value and relate affectively to thoughts, ideas, statements, rules, laws, beliefs, etc? Though not inevitable, we tend to value them with emotional detachment, at least in our truth-seeking moments. Especially in the academic, scientific, philosophical, and legal realms, systemic detachment is the ideal; and being "disinterested" or "objective" is the corresponding intellectual virtue. Judges, jurors, teachers, scientists, historians, psychologists, philosophers, and even academic theologians are expected to relate to their subject matter with minimal emotional passion and affective involvement. They are supposed to have "cool heads" and "shed light, not heat." They are expected to evaluate their subject matter "disinterestedly," "objectively," or "fairly." Hartman called this "rational detachment" (Hartman, 1967, 5, 14).

It happens, but we should never confuse "disinterestedness" with "uninterestedness." Being uninterested in X means not being involved with X, not applying any concept-fulfillment standards to X, not being interested in X, not having any feelings toward X whether positive or negative. It means not valuing or disvaluing X at all. However, truth-seekers, intellectuals, judges, jurors, teachers, scientists, psychologists, philosophers, and theologians are all very much involved with and interested in their subject matter. They have definite feelings about seeking and having knowledge. They regularly apply concept-fulfillment criteria to and within their disciplines. They positively value their subject matter. They are detached but not totally unattached. "Uninterested" does not describe how they evaluate affectively. They value their subject matter disinterestedly, not uninterestedly. They approach their subject matter with a fair and open mind, not with indifference.

Relating disinterestedly to systemic values like ideas, systems, rules, laws, and beliefs means being fair and open minded about them. Certain feelings, but not all feelings, are known to interfere with being fair and open minded, and only those particular kinds of emotional reactions have to be curbed in order to achieve intellectual honesty and rational objectivity. Systemic disinterestedness or objectivity excludes only those emotional reactions that would interfere with achieving the "Good-making predicates for rational belief systems" that were outlined in Chapter Two [most of which were explicitly affirmed by Hartman himself (Hartman, 1967, 298)]. Recall that good belief systems:

1. are logically consistent
2. are confirmed by experience
3. are not refuted by experience
4. cover everything intended
5. do not cover too much
6. have the simplest possible number of explanatory principles or entities
7. have explanatory power
8. are elegant or beautiful
9. are fruitful for future research and discovery
10. can be applied in daily living
11. bring about intersubjective agreement.

Some but not all affective responses interfere significantly with objective searches for truth. Some feelings predispose us to cling to inconsistencies; others blind us to what is there to be seen; others make us see stuff that is just not there; others dilute or spread our thinking too broadly; others make us too narrow minded; others dispose us to make things too complicated; others incline us toward explanations that do not explain very much, if anything at all; others obstruct or ignore our appreciation for conceptual or systemic beauty and elegance; others block further paths of inquiry and discovery; others tie us to views by which we cannot practically live; others predispose us against people who do not agree with us, and against their beliefs and criticisms. Only emotions like these, feelings that interfere with fair and open mindedness, are excluded from systemic disinterestedness; we commonly call them "prejudices."

Not all emotions are excluded, however. Systemic objectivity is minimal interestedness, not complete uninterestedness. It is minimal emotional involvement, minimal affective valuation, but not total emotional uninvolvement. *On the continuum of emotional involvement, one thing lies beyond systemic disinterestedness, namely, indifference or uninterestedness.* Hartman says that the indifferent person just "refuses to value" (Hartman, 1967, 299). Indifference is off the axiological chart! Moving toward zero on the continuum of human feelings, indifference falls way beyond disinterestedness or rational detachment. Yet, it has great *moral* significance. Indifference is a moral vice, not the intellectual virtue of rational detachment.

Hartman identified another feature of systemic valuation that has both conceptual and affective components. He said that systemic valuation is "black or white," "all or nothing," "perfect or non existent." This feature of systemic valuation is logically independent of both fair-mindedness and applying the Form of the Good to ideas. Thus, it does not necessarily apply to either of them or to every systemic judgment. The tendency to judge conceptually and emotionally in all or nothing, black or white terms is a more or less accidental feature of systemic valuation. *Some* systemic valuations are like this, but *others*, perhaps most, are not. We can make rational judgments without prejudice or oversimplification. Still, we will need to keep track of "black or white thinking" when considering how we value.

B. Affective Extrinsic Valuation

Positive Affective Extrinsic Valuation involves attitudes, enjoyments, feelings, emotions, preferences, and appetites that are more intense than those of systemic valuation, but less intense than those of intrinsic valuation. Extrinsic value-objects are the familiar things, natural processes, human bodies, and human actions of everyday life. They belong to the realm of practicality. We want to be as practical as we can, but some of us are better at this than others, more practical than others. According to Hartman, "Extrinsic valuation is that of everyday and works well as such"; in most people it is the most developed and articulated kind of valuation (Hartman, 1967, 253). Practical-minded people are adept at using, coping with, controlling, and manipulating the everyday things, objects, processes, and activities that are given to us in normal sense experience. Predominately practical people live in, with, and for the things of the world. They are skilled in using, producing, owning, and controlling both material things and people regarded as material things. They aspire to be materially and socially prosperous and successful. They want not only the basic physical resources or necessities of life but also wealth, security, luxury, high social status, and honored or exalted social roles.

Typically, people have stronger positive attitudes toward, interests in, desires for, and emotional responses to ordinary physical things, objects, processes, and actions than they do to mere ideas. The level of affective involvement naturally or typically correlated with everyday things can be called "everyday interestedness." Everyday practical extrinsic interestedness tends to be more intense than systemic intellectual disinterestedness, yet less intense than total personal intrinsic involvement and identification. Extrinsic evaluation is liking but not loving. A continuum of feelings runs throughout the three dimensions, so no sharp affective lines separate them. Our affections affect us by degrees.

Practical-minded people are adept in dealing with extrinsic value-objects, but practical skills vary considerably from one person to the next. Practicality is extrinsic valuation. Practicality can be taught, improved, better understood.

Being practical means, first, being proficient in learning about, coping with, controlling, manipulating, producing, acquiring, and possessing extrinsically valuable things—sensory objects, processes, and actions in public space-time.

Second, it means knowing how to apply the Form of the Good to the things of everyday life at home, at work, at play, or wherever. Extrinsic valuation manifests good common sense. "Being practical" requires a clear understanding of the good-making properties of familiar things, objects, processes, and actions, as well as skill in applying this understanding to particular instances. When making things, doing their jobs, shopping, selling, negotiating, planning ahead, or whatever, practical people know what to look for, recognize the good stuff when they see it, remember it, or imagine it, and act effectively on this knowledge.

Third, being practical means being skilled in making comparisons—at applying the Form of the Good to more than one similar thing at approximately the same time. Intrinsic value-objects, e.g., people, are "one of a kind," but extrinsic value-objects belong to classes having at least two members, usually more. These members share not only definitional but also expositional properties in terms of which they may be compared or measured with respect to degrees of goodness, degrees of value-concept fulfillment. Some things measure up better than others. Practical people make informed choices between two or more options on the basis of the extent to which they fulfill the Form of the Good.

Fourth, being practical also means having typical or normal "everyday interestedness" levels of feeling for and about the things, objects, processes, and social encounters of everyday life and experience. It involves liking things but not passionately loving them or "going overboard."

As indicated earlier, ideal norms or expectations are built into the very way we conceive of or understand certain *social roles* like father, mother, son, daughter, grandparent, employer, employee, athlete, coach, teacher, preacher, or whatever. In learning these role-words, we learn their integral behavioral expectations; we learn how to compare and distinguish between comparatively good ones and less than good ones. We have typical or normal human affective responses to the people who play these roles well, so-so, or poorly.

Ideal norms, expectations, and typical affective responses are also built into the very way that we conceive of, understand, and classify the *non-human things, objects, and processes* of everyday life. Aesthetic qualities and value standards are built into every "brute fact." Philosophers sometimes say (mistakenly) that what "is," and what "ought" to be, are so radically different that they cannot be brought together, and one cannot be derived from the other. The real truth seems to be that every "is" contains an "ought," and every "ought" contains an "is." Strictly speaking, nothing in human awareness is affectively, conceptually, or valuationally neutral, though for practical purposes some things approach or approximate neutrality.

We have ideal expectations of and feelings about fathers, mothers, sons, and daughters, but this is equally true of hammers, nails, cars, trucks, trees, weeds, rocks, rills, hills, dales, computers, scooters, desks, desktops, tables, chairs, apples, and oranges. When children (as we all once were) learn the meaning of so called "descriptive" words, they learn more than their mere minimal definitions. They also learn what to expect of such things, how to compare them, and how to feel about them. Definitional properties, expositional properties, and appropriate affective responses or attitudes are learned all together. This is why, even with "brute facts," we can tell the difference between comparatively good ones, bad ones, and those in between.

"Facts" are just typical minimal sets of positively or negatively valued definitional and properties; "norms" are more inclusive but partly overlapping sets of good-making expositional properties. All belong to the total set of anything's property inventory. Any time we notice something, we value it in some way. Those who name and define things for us have a tremendous influence over our values and evaluations. Both definitional and expositional properties have been noticed, thus valued, by someone. We never learn the one (definitions) without the other (expositions). They are two sides of the same coin. In learning about coins, we always learn about both sides. We also learn how to feel about their descriptive properties and the descriptive properties of everything else. All classification is purposive or teleological. Every "is" contains its "ought;" every "ought" contains its "is;" so, as Hartman indicated, the distinction is somewhat obsolete (Hartman, 1967, 225). Every definition has an additional exposition. Descriptive properties are good-making properties; norms contain descriptions as criteria of goodness. "Goodness" and "natural properties" are one within the other without being identical.

We also have natural, typical, or "everyday interestedness" level attitudes about, feelings toward, and emotional responses to all extrinsic or descriptive definitional and expositional properties—toward everything that we experience in our common sensory space-time world. All experiences have feeling tones, including sensory experiences. All sensations and facts are value-laden.

Though not invariant, the good-making properties of things, wisdom about how to compare them, and appropriate human affective responses to them, are ensconced in social traditions handed down through generations. Recognized authorities and experts are the custodians and teachers of such traditions. *Authorities or experts* on extrinsic values are a dime a dozen. They are conspicuously present, for example, as judges in social events like car shows, animal shows, flower shows, state fairs, music or dance competitions, amateur hours, beauty pageants, "reality" TV shows, and organized contests of every description. They are also conspicuously represented as authorities in consumer magazines and their counterparts on the Internet. They exist wherever any practical *grading* must be done. *Practical grading is just applying the Form of the Good to some subject matter.* Experts exist to represent and implement widely agreed-upon good-making standards. Experts apply them by making comparative judgments about particulars, and they model and communicate appropriate affective responses to others who trust and accept their expertise. Professional psychologists, for example, can tell us if our "affects" (feelings) are appropriate or inappropriate.

In everyday life, we rely heavily upon professional experts of every description. Sometimes though we just don't agree with them, and we treasure our freedom to disagree. At times, even experts break with tradition and become innovators and trend-setters. Still, no social chaos of practical values and valuations exists because, when all is said and done, we human beings are so much alike, especially so within cultures and sub-culture groups. We can usually tell when people overvalue or undervalue the things of the world, that is, when people "go overboard," or when they are just being "impractical," "incompetent," or "uninterested" in practical affairs.

How are widely-agreed-upon good-making standards established in the first place? This is where philosophers who say, "Values are *nothing but expressions of feeling*," have their strongest inning. People typically have pro- or anti- attitudes and feelings not only toward composite objects like cars, but also toward their good-making component parts like motors, brakes, seats, lights, safety features, comfort qualities, accessories, and so on. Good-making properties are those toward which people have pro-attitudes or positive feelings, emotions, and appetites, either typically or individually. (Bad-making properties would be just the reverse.) Conventional standards (widely-shared sets of good-making predicates/properties) correspond with widely shared pro-attitudes, positive feelings, emotions, and desires. *Good-making properties **proper** are those properties or features toward which people have pro-attitudes after careful consideration, that is, under conditions of knowledge or enlightenment, impartiality or freedom from bias, and in the absence of internal or external coercions or constraints.*

Individuals do not always conform to conventions about good-making properties or appropriate feeling-responses because they sometimes have atypical feelings about them. At times we disagree with authorities, experts, moguls, innovators, and trend setters either because we feel differently about, or disagree with, their good-making criteria, or else because we think they have misapplied them. Some alleged good-making properties may not fulfill the above definition of "good-making properties proper," and we may have honest disagreements about what counts as a good-making property. This is why the Form of the Good is objective in theory but only subjective in application. We can understand sets of good-making criteria perfectly well but still not accept them *because* feelings as well as understandings are involved in valuation, and we do not share the feelings, or we do not have feelings refined by enlightenment, information, and impartiality or disinterestedness; or perhaps our feelings are somehow coerced or externally constrained rather than being free, uncoerced, or unconstrained. Hartman wrote,

> It is not the case that axiological judgment would differ from man to man only because one man did not know the expositional properties of the thing in question, but rather because one man does, and another does not, approve of these properties as exhibited by a phenomenon (Hartman, 1995e, 87).

A *direct* positive emotional, affective, or attitudinal involvement with or approval of the alleged good-making properties of a thing is essential for *fully* embracing the judgment, "X is good because it fulfills the norms applied to it." To agree completely, we must make that cognitive judgment *and* feel affectively that the norms themselves are appropriate. Ideally, we would meet these conditions only after careful consideration. Nature has equipped us to approve of successful means to ends and of many practical, theoretical, moral, and spiritual ends or goals in life.

To judge that common things in our everyday world are good, must we actually have the feelings about them that people naturally or typically have? The answer is emphatically *"NO!"* This is where philosophers (like Hartman) who say, "Values are *something rational, something more than mere expressions of feeling,"* have their strongest inning. Formal axiology to the rescue! Evaluation definitely has both rational or cognitive and feeling components. The Form of the Good is the rational component. *Establishing or accepting relevant good-making criteria* in the first place is the affective component. *Feelings* (desires, interests, enjoyments, emotions, pro-attitudes) *set the standards* (select the good making properties); *reason applies them* (judges that some X does or does not fulfill these standards).

Philosophers ask if *professional graders* must have the same feelings about what they grade that other people (e.g., consumers) typically have. For instance, must an apple-grader in a fruit processing plant feel as keenly about the apples being graded as the people who buy the apples? (Hartman, 2002, 248-249, 253). The answer is, "No." Grading apples on an assembly line quickly becomes routine if not downright boring. Still, apple graders know how to do their job correctly. How so? They know how to apply the Form of the Good on a rational or cognitive level, even if and when the typical or normal affective components of valuation are missing. They know rationally that good apples are expected to be of a certain size, shape, color, pleasant tasting, nutritious, pesticide-free, etc. They conceptually understand conventional good-making criteria for apples, or whatever they are grading, and they know how to apply them. When they inspect apples or whatever, they can rationally distinguish "Grade A" specimens (the ones that satisfy all the good-making criteria) from those that fall short by degrees, that is, from those that are only "Grade B," "Grade C," and so on. *Someone* has to approve or feel positively about the criteria, the good-making predicates/properties of "good apple," but *not necessarily those who apply the criteria.* So, to apply the Form of the Good, graders or judgers need not have normal feelings about that to which they are applied. Normally, however, people do.

John W. Davis nicely summarized the multiple conceptual/affective components of extrinsic valuation when he wrote,

> Conceptually, extrinsic valuation is a matter of measuring a thing's properties by means of a concept, as is also the case with both systemic and intrinsic valuations. But some valuations have an affective or emotional aspect....What then of the extrinsic? On the one hand, the process of measuring the extrinsic value of a thing can be characterized, like the systemic, as objective, impartial, and dispassionate, for a set of predicates is compared with a set of properties. The evaluator need not take a "pro-attitude" toward the thing being measured. On the other hand, the determination of the set of predicates used as a measure may involve emotion. "Extrinsic valuation is the model of everyday pragmatic thinking," writes Hartman. But such thinking involves human desires and interests. We order and classify the things that we interact with in space and time for all sorts of purposes. Our ab-

stract concepts help us get what we want. However, this is not to say that there is no logic involved in the formulation of such concepts (Davis, 1991, 72).

Evaluation has both rational and affective components. Philosophers who try to separate them completely always fall at least halfway short of the mark.

C. Affective Intrinsic Valuation

On a purely rational or cognitive level, intrinsic valuation is measuring an individual person by expectations for that person in his or her uniqueness and concreteness. As long as people are mature, decent, and sane, the relevant expectations or aspirations should be their own. Typically, this is so. People are somehow special, so very special, says the Hierarchy of Value, that they have more overall worth than systemic values or extrinsic values. Good reasons for thinking so were provided in Chapter Two. Respecting their worth involves respecting their choices, self-concepts, and self-expectations.

Intrinsic valuation involves applying the conceptual Form of the Good to individual persons, beginning with oneself, but it too has affective components. It also involves feelings, pleasures, pains, interests, desires, emotions, preferences, and attitudes. Hartman heavily emphasized the emotional or affective components of intrinsic valuation, along with the cognitive and dynamic or action components. Consider these quotes from *The Structure of Value*.

> Intrinsic valuation is the valuation of poets and artists, lovers and mystics, magicians and advertisers, chefs de cuisine and politicians, creative theologians and scientists. It is empathic—and empathetic—valuation (113-114).

> The relationship between systemic, extrinsic, and intrinsic value corresponds to a process of continuous enrichment with definite leaps from one value dimension to the next. Thus, if I buy a package of cigarettes from a saleslady I am in a legal, a systemic relationship with her. If I take her out for dinner I am in an extrinsic relationship, and if I take her to church and marry her I am in an intrinsic relationship with her: my total being is joined with her in a common intrinsic Gestalt (223-224).

> Systemic measurement is the abstract, formal kind of measurement used by the scientist, objective and detached. It is the way axiology itself measures value, or rather "value"—it measures the value measure. Extrinsic measurement is by the value terms "good," "fair," etc.—and it is more "subjective" in application although as objective in theory as is systemic measure. This kind of measurement is acted out, thought through, judged, in short, is lived in everyday life. Intrinsic measurement is exalted experience, enjoyment, involvement in the thing valued, indeed, the stages of involvement are this measure—yet, theoretically, it is as objective as are the other kinds of measurement (251).

This form ["We ought to choose or prefer what is good."] is equivalent to [A. C.] Ewing's definition of good as the object of a pro-attitude ([Ewing's] *The Definition of Good*, pp. 48-49).... If for "choose" we put the more general term "to have a pro-attitude toward: then "x ought to choose what is good" is equivalent to "x ought to have a pro-attitude toward what is good."....A logic of preference may be based on formal axiology (345-346, n. 20).

Music is the articulation of feeling, and so especially in the intrinsic dimension is formal axiology (357, n. 25).

The sense of values is a talent similar to the musical which sees in a given harmonic structure its possible variations; only that the sense of values seems to be the *general* talent of which the musical—and other artistic talents—are species (258).

Intrinsic measurement is exalted experience, enjoyment, involvement in the thing valued, indeed, *the stages of involvement* are *this measurement*—yet, theoretically, it is as objective as are the other kinds of measurement (251).

Rationally, intrinsic self-evaluation involves applying the Form of the Good to oneself, Hartman claimed, so we might expect the primary affective components to be primarily self-directed or self-focused. What words or concepts express this? "Self-respect" is a good place to begin. According to Robert S. Hartman, "The sensitivity to value arises out of sensitivity for the value of the self, of self-respect. Only where there is self-respect there is respect for the essentials both in men, things, situations, and problems" (Hartman, 1991b, 28).

What is self-respect? Reverting once more to the universal "I" that applies to everyone, if I respect myself, I *think* positively about myself, but I also *feel* positively about myself. The affective as well as the cognitive component of intrinsic valuation are very significant. If I know myself, I feel good about myself, I accept myself, I am satisfied with myself, I am content with who I am, I forgive myself if I have fallen short, I am at peace with myself, I have a keen *sense* that I deserve to exist, I take care of myself, I am grateful for being who I am, and I rejoice and delight in my very existence. In short, I both know and love myself and am emotionally centered within myself, but without being egoistic or self-centered. Assigning immense intrinsic worth to myself is not egoistic or selfish. Selfishness is not a matter of overvaluing myself; it is a matter of under-valuing others.

Affective intrinsic self-valuation is loving myself as a unique individual, not as a mere instance or representative of a system or set of beliefs, not just because others approve of me, not just for what I can do, and not merely for my social worth or usefulness to others. It is feeling positively and intensely about my total integrated property inventory, my very being in its completeness, *all* my combined systemic, extrinsic, and distinctively intrinsic properties. This includes my work, my good works, and all my social roles, activities, and responsibilities, but far more. It includes my beliefs applied to myself, but far more. Affective intrinsic self-evaluation involves a deep appreciation for who I am in my total being, not just for what I do, and not just for what I think or believe, though these are included. It is loving my unique reality comprehensively, everything about myself—all the ways I am similar to others, all the ways I differ from others, my conscience or inner compass, my self-acceptance and self-forgiveness, all my special talents, interests, and projects, my power to make my own decisions, everything about myself. It involves loving the integrated totality of *all* of my properties—my enduring self—what Hartman used to call "Self with a capital S."

Affective intrinsic valuation, properly understood, *typically differs significantly by degrees* from affective systemic and affective extrinsic valuation. Logically, all valuations are on a continuum of feelings; the lines between them are never drawn with exactitude; but we can recognize hard-core cases of each. We don't know exactly where to draw the lines cognitively between the ancient world, the middle ages, and the modern world, but these are still useful concepts, and we can recognize hard core instances of each. We don't know exactly where to draw the lines cognitively between youth, middle age, and old age, but we know paradigm cases of them when we see them. So it is with the affective components of each type of valuation. Systemic valuation involves high cognition but only minimal feelings; extrinsic valuation involves ordinary cognition and feelings; intrinsic valuation involves rich cognition combined with extraordinary or profound feelings. Intrinsic valuation proper involves comprehensive awareness as well as keen, intense, complete love, empathy, compassion, and identification-union—as good as it gets. We can and should value ourselves and others in all three ways.

Intrinsic valuation readily *spreads beyond oneself*. It spills over onto others. Cognitively, we apply an exceptionally rich Form of the Good to ourselves as unique individuals; we also apply it to *other people* as unique individuals, despite Hartman's heavy emphasis on *self*-concept fulfillment. Intrinsic valuation may involve not just my concept of and expectations for myself, but also my concepts of and expectations for other people, and their expectations for me—as the unique and richly complex conscious individuals that we are. Other people can and do have ideal expectations for me, and I for them, as unique persons, not just for their usefulness or class memberships, and not just as instances of ideals and ideologies. Axiologists must take seriously the fact that we can and do apply the Form of the Good to others as well as to ourselves intrinsically, not just extrinsically or systemically.

Of course, other people may have axiologically inadequate ideal concepts of me, just as I may have axiologically inadequate ideal concepts of them. The correction to both inadequacies is *the first principle of ethics*, as more fully explained in the next chapter—*We ought always to identify-with, prefer, choose, and do what is best, that is, what is likely to be richest in good-making properties*.

In most people, systemic and extrinsic valuations are mainly left-brain activities or functions, though not exclusively so; intrinsic evaluation is primarily right-brained, though not exclusively so. Learning to value self and others intrinsically, lovingly, empathetically, and compassionately, to be completely one with all, is largely a matter of getting in touch with and actually using the right side of our brains. Comprehensive valuation in all three value dimensions is a whole-brained activity. It is not half-brained systemic/extrinsic valuation alone, or the-other-half-brained intrinsic valuation alone. Our educational system is oriented primary toward developing left-brained people, who grow up to be half-brained adults. When budget cuts are made, right-brained activities are the first to go!

What would it be like to live for a prolonged period of time almost exclusively in right-brained consciousness? For a unique first-hand account, read *My Stroke of Insight: A Brain Scientist's Personal Journey*, New York: Viking, 2006. This was written by Jill Bolte Taylor, Ph.D., who was a distinguished young neuro-anatomist at Harvard when she suffered a severe left brain stroke that shut it down almost entirely for quite some time. As she describes it, her left-brain consciousness was almost pure intrinsic valuation consciousness, as axiology represents it, though she does not use this terminology herself. For a prolonged period of time after her stroke, she had few if any systemic and extrinsic capacities and no sense of self-identity or unique-individuality-value. These gradually returned to her only as she slowly regained her left-brain capacities. Being 1) a *loving and compassionate* person with 2) *a unique self-identity* requires whole-brain consciousness.

The affective components of intrinsic valuation readily spill over onto other people, but they do not necessarily stop there. We can intrinsically value animals, God, and more. This means, we can learn to love them. Affective intrinsic evaluation involves *loving others* as well as *loving ourselves*. Ideally, perhaps, it involves loving and being just as compassionate toward others *as* we love and are compassionate toward ourselves. More discussion of intrinsically valuing self and others will follow in the next chapter on "Ethics and Other Applications."

D. Complete Intrinsic Valuation

Valuation is the process or activity of conscious cognitive, active, and affective involvement with valuable objects. It is how we attach value to such objects cognitively, actively, and affectively. Valuation is conscious personal involvement—by degrees. We are complex persons, and we value in complex ways. Consciousness is intentional, that is, it is normally involved with objects of awareness; thus, consciousness is valuation, but only by degrees. Uninvolved conscious awareness is indifference, which is never absolute as long as consciousness remains. Minimally involved conscious involvement is systemic valuation, more involved is extrinsic valuation, and most involved is intrinsic valuation. As Hartman wrote, "Intrinsic valuation means dedication of the whole person and all its capacities" (Hartman, 1991b, 29).

The highest or most complete manifestation of intrinsic valuation with any X is *complete personal identification* with X. If we are highly conflicted selves, we do not fully identify with ourselves, but we can get beyond this. If we are morally and spiritually undeveloped selves, we do not fully identify with others or with Ultimate Reality, but we can get beyond this. *Paradigm intrinsic valuation is complete self-identification-with-something.* At its moral/spiritual maximum, it is *complete self-identification with everything and everyone (except evil).* As complete, it involves all our thinking, all our feeling, all our acting, all that we have and are—focused or concentrated on that with which we identify ourselves. In intense love of, compassion for, empathy toward, and concentration upon others, we fully identify ourselves with them. In the intense concentration of extrinsic creativity, we fully identify ourselves with works of art or with practical discoveries and inventions. In the intense concentration of profound and creative thinking, writing, and reading, we intrinsically identify ourselves with thoughts, ideas, ideals, beliefs, truths, and knowledge. Anything can be evaluated in any or every dimension.

Hartman was convinced that all dimensions of value and evaluation are included within intrinsic value and valuation, but some aspects of this are *distinctively intrinsic*, and focusing upon and developing our distinctively intrinsic values and valuations would improve our dealings with all the other dimensions. As he explained,

> This is the important thing; you cannot fully be systemic or extrinsic unless you are fully intrinsic. In other words, the moral man will also be a better accountant, pilot, or surgeon. The value dimensions are within each other. The human contains the social, and the social the systematic. The lower value is within the higher. The systemic is within the extrinsic, and the extrinsic within the intrinsic. The more fully you are yourself, the better you will be at your job, and in your social role, and in your thinking. Out of your intrinsic being you summon the resources to be anything you want to be. Thus, the intrinsic, the development of your inner self, is not a luxury. It is a necessity for your own being yourself in all three dimensions (Hartman, 1962a, 31).

Emphasizing the *cognitive* aspects of intrinsic valuation or self-identification-with-X, Hartman wrote,

> In intrinsic valuation the subject and object of knowledge form an inseparable unit, and the subject, in the process of knowing, completely interpenetrates the nature of the object. Knower and known form an organic unit, a community; the object known is part of the knowing subject, and the knowing subject is one with the object known. Knowing and being fuse into one (Hartman, 1991b, 29).

Similarly, when we identify ourselves totally with another person, we become one with that other person axiologically, psychologically, and practically. Emphasizing *complete* intrinsic identification with other realities, including persons, Hartman explained,

> The apprehension of the singular thing is apprehension of the thing in the fullness of its concretion, in its total *Gestalt*. Such apprehension presupposes a greater cognitive effort than either abstraction or construction—it presupposes the agent's appropriation of the thing, ultimately with his own being, his making it "his own." The singular thing is ultimately apprehended by *identification*, by *interpenetration* (Hartman, 1961, 408).

> In the intrinsic dimension all intrinsic selves are one. Identification with the other is the very core of this reality....People in contact with this realm are self-actualizing, in Maslow's sense, and have the capacity, as Viktor Frankl and others have shown, to survive the most horrible experiences. They summon their inner resources. Within themselves, they are one with their beloved ones, and through identification with others and with the world, they become united with themselves (Hartman, 2006,137).

In the union of the intrinsic evaluation of other people (or conscious individuals), the ontological or existential differences between us and them do not disappear or dissolve, but they no longer matter, and they are little noticed, if at all. We become what they are; and, if reciprocated, they become what we are; we "interpenetrate" as Hartman put it. What happens to them happens to us; the evils that befall them hurt us; the good that befalls them becomes our good; in love and empathy, their goodness becomes our goodness; in compassion, their evils and sufferings become our evils and sufferings. Great comfort and consolation are experienced in having fellow-sufferers who feel our pain and understand our suffering, (and especially so if the fellow-sufferer is God).

Our intrinsic actions are both other-benefiting and self-benefiting at the same time, for the distinction between "I" and "Thou" just disappears psychologically and axiologically, but not existentially. In mutual intrinsic evaluation, each becomes the other without ceasing to be themselves. What we do is both for ourselves and for those we love, without distinction; their tragedies become our tragedies; their sins become our sins; their strengths become our strengths; their good-making properties become our good-making properties. Yet the existential or ontological differences between us remain. Throughout intrinsic valuation identification, we continue to be distinct, individuated, embodied, separated centers of conscious experiences, free and responsible choices, self-directed activities, and values and valuations. We become one with others morally, spiritually, psychologically, axiologically because our differences, though intact, no longer matter and may not even be noticed consciously. I become one with another "without giving up myself," as Hartman says below. "That art Thou," "We are They" in complete intrinsic-identification valuation.

In one of his last-written descriptions of the experience of intrinsic valuation, Hartman explained,

> Subject and object form one close continuum; ... the Other, no matter whether a person, a thing, or a thought, becomes a Self identified with The valuing Self, a Thou to the I....I identify myself with the other without giving up myself but, on the contrary, deepening myself in the degree that I penetrate in the other. In this sense, the universe of intrinsic value could be called, were it not for the unfortunate yet significant ambiguity of the expression, the universe of intercourse.... Sexual intercourse is indeed an example of such a self-enclosed world out of this world; but any intrinsic value experience has the same structure (Hartman, 1974, 98).

Self-identification with others is the ultimate way to find ourselves by losing ourselves. Our old, narrow, self-centered selves get lost, pass away; but new, deeper, more expansive, everyone-centered selves get born anew. Finding a richer-in-goodness-self through identification with others is not selfishness. Just the opposite, but it is unintentionally self-beneficial, nevertheless, not to our old, narrow, self-centered selves, but to our new, radically transformed, and immensely expanded intrinsic selves. We are personally enriched by taking *any* good-making properties into ourselves, especially those previously called "intrinsic value enhancers." When we take all of the good-making properties and intrinsic value enhancers *of another person* into ourselves, we are doubly enriched! We live twice as abundantly. This is good for us, and the more people we identify ourselves with, the more abundantly we live. People who do not love abundantly do not live abundantly. Abundant living is not achieved by aiming selfishly and exclusively at one's own abundant living. That is the paradox of the axiologically abundant life!

Narrow selfishness or self-centeredness is oblivious to all of this, which is why it is so pathetic. I (we) lose out on living abundantly if I concentrate exclusively on my isolated self, try to gain everything only for myself, and value myself alone. I miss all of the unintended, unexpected, indirect, serendipity benefits of loving, empathetic, and compassionate self-identification with others. I miss my chance to take the good-making properties of others into myself and make them my own by rejoicing in them as they exist in others.

4. Combining Values and Valuations

Combining *valuable objects* with other valuable objects in *other dimensions* was discussed previously. Recall that ideas can be combined with things and people; things can be combined with ideas and people; and people can be combined with ideas and things. When done positively to enhance value, such combinations are technically called "compositions." When done negatively to diminish value, such combinations are technically called "transpositions."

Now we must consider combining our own *valuations* with value-objects in all dimensions. We can evaluate every value-object that belongs to each and every value dimension, and we can do this in ways that belong naturally or typically to each distinctive dimension. As Hartman put it, "Anything whatever, from the lowest to the highest, can be valued in all three processes, systemically, extrinsically, intrinsically" (Hartman, 1991b, 31; compare Hartman, 1967, 251, 294). Hartman used *evaluating formal axiology itself* to illustrate how anything can be valued in all three dimensions.

> Such a theory [formal axiology] is a mental construct. Hence, in our terms it is a systemic value. Since, however, anything can be considered in all three value dimensions, a value theory can also be regarded as an extrinsic and as an intrinsic value. In the former case, it is seen as a tool functioning in the space-time world among similar such tools, or a member of the expositional class of value theories. In the latter case, it is regarded as unique and incomparable, and some person as fully involved with it (Hartman, 1967, 294).

Evaluating any value-object in any dimension needs further clarification. We can evaluate anything whatsoever in at least three basic ways, each of which has three sub-divisions. We can evaluate any X:

1. by applying concepts to it,
   - a. systemic concepts,
   - b. extrinsic concepts,
   - c. intrinsic concepts,

2. by acting toward, for, with, or upon it,
   - a. as if it were a mere concept,
   - b. as if it were a "thing" in public space-time
   - c. as if it were a "person,"

3. and by responding toward it with feelings (desires, emotions, attitudes, etc.).
   - a. disinterestedly or dispassionately
   - b. with ordinary everyday practical desires, emotions, attitudes, etc.
   - c. through passionate identification with it—as in profound love, empathy, compassion, and concentration.

Every such way of evaluating things can be applied to anything or any value-object in any dimension of value. The above outline should also help us to understand and appreciate how every dimension of value can be within every other dimension. This will now be explained in terms of systemic, extrinsic, and intrinsic patterns of evaluation.

Every way of evaluating can also be applied positively or negatively to both individual values and to value combinations. Everything and every value combination in any value dimension can be valued either positively or negatively in any dimension. In technical terminology, evaluations in any dimension can be either compositions that sustain or increase value, or transpositions that diminish value. Evaluation always creates and is itself a value composition or transposition.

In Hartman's writings, two levels of symbolism are used. We are now somewhat familiar with Hartman's unworkable symbolism of n, $\aleph_0$, and $\aleph_1$. However, we can still be faithful to Hartman by using a different formalistic symbolism that he also used, one that does not necessarily presuppose implausible infinities.

We can just let "S" represent systemic values and valuations, "E" represent extrinsic values and valuations, and "I" represent intrinsic values and valuations. *Positive* value combinations (compositions) can have the form (X^X), and *negative* value combinations can take the form (X_X). For example, the positive systemic valuation of an intrinsic value like "counting people" would be (I^S), and the systemic disvaluation of an intrinsic value like "People don't count" would be (I_S). As Hartman explained, "All formulae must be read backward ... *e.g.* (I^S) means "the systemic valuation of an intrinsic value" (Hartman, 1967, 289).

A. Systemically Evaluating Everything in all Dimensions

Systemically evaluating anything whatsoever involves:

  i. Applying systemic concepts to it,
  ii. Acting upon it as if it were a mere concept,
  iii. Responding disinterestedly or dispassionately toward it.

Typically, we evaluate systemically valuable entities in these three ways. Systemic value-objects are the natural home turf of systemic valuation, but we can also evaluate extrinsic and intrinsic value-objects systemically. Consider now the conceptual and attitudinal or affective aspects of positive systemic valuation; acting on systemic concepts and feelings will be assumed and illustrated throughout.

i. Applying Systemic Concepts in Three Dimensions

Recall that Hartman originally conceived of systemic concepts as finite meaning sets or intensions with definite or precise meanings. However, as previously explained, many of our ideas, definitions, beliefs, rules, laws, rituals, and scientific, philosophical, and theological ideologies are immensely and indefinitely complex and are far from being definite or exact. Nevertheless, "applying systemic concepts to extrinsic and intrinsic value-objects" could be taken to mean "relating to them *as if* they were finite and precise in meaning." People actually do that often enough, sometimes but not always with disastrous results. Hartman focused on "all or nothing" thinking and valuing in situations in where systemic thinking turns into devaluation, when it is employed to reduce, diminish, or ignore anything's or anyone's good-making properties. Systemic thinking is objectionable when:

- It inordinately finitizes or oversimplifies.
- It sees things as black or white, all or nothing, perfect or imperfect, and recognizes no shades or grey; thereby, it treats things or people as worthless if they have even the slightest imperfections.
- Some concept combinations are inherently unintelligible.

But not all systemic thinking is like this. A great deal of systemic thinking and valuing is trouble free and does not abuse language or its proper objects.

Consider first the troublesome varieties.

- Applied to ideas (S^S), things (E^S), and people (I^S), some systemic thinking *inordinately finitizes or oversimplifies* and thereby diminishes value. According to Hartman, in systemic thinking,

> All the elements are on the lowest common denominator, namely, as elements of the system, and all their intrinsic or extrinsic differences are erased; they are, as individuals, unavailable. There is nothing but a mass of interchangeable, formless elements: Chaos numbered and indexed. The culmination of such systemic organization was Nazi Germany (Hartman, 1991b, 20).

> The subjects of *logical or systemic* valuation are things in a minimum relationship: as elements of a system or as schemata. A schema is less real than any empirical thing. When human beings are valued systemically they are less real than, say, a piece of paper. If a bureaucratic procedure a person does not exist unless he has a birth certificate. At a border he does not exist unless he has a passport....In Europe and Asia, where systems are stronger and less flexible than in this country, people without papers have for weeks and months oscillated between borders, living on ships, unable to get off at any port. On the other hand, the more impressive the paper, the more important the person (Hartman, 1991b, 25).

> What counts in a system is the system and its procedures and nothing else. This goes not only for the system's victims but also for its agents. They act as elements of the system and as nothing else. The system, as a body of legal rules, lends their actions both justification and sanctification. Therefore, the love of the uniform in Europe, Asia, and South America which cancels individuality and gives anonymity and prestige in uniformity. Therefore also the self-righteousness of the professional bureaucrat. The world of systemic value is the haven of those who lack Self, that is fully differentiated intrinsic value, and it is hell for those who are alive consciously in their own inner Self (Hartman, 1991b, 25).

Explaining as much as possible with as little as possible, that is, with as few assumptions, principles, or entities as possible, is an important ideal of all objective, scientific, and rational thinking. So-called "Ockham's razor" captures and expresses this ideal. The trouble with seeking simplicity, however, is that it can be pushed too far. It can oversimplify at the expense of another important rational ideal, comprehensiveness, which requires that everything relevant be included or considered. Adequate belief systems should be both as simple and as comprehensive as possible.

Many systemic evaluations (disvaluations) fail to consider or include everything that is relevant. "*Reductionism*" (sometimes "reductivism"), as it is called, tends to oversimplify, to finitize belief-complexities inordinately, whether in natural science, philosophy, theology, or whatever. Alfred North Whitehead recognized this; he advised us to "Seek simplicity and distrust it." In giving this advice, Whitehead warned that "We are apt to fall into the error of thinking that the facts are simple because simplicity is the goal of our quest" (Whitehead, 1971, 163). Needless to say, we can inordinately finitize not just ideas but also things and people by forcing them into restrictive molds that just do not fit. All stereotyping is oversimplification, as is all prejudice, dogmatism, and authoritarianism. Consider these examples of oversimplifying systemic thinking.

– Our thoughts, aspirations, emotions, and loves are nothing but "matter in motion" in our brains.
– A man is dying, but, as a painter, I see nothing there but colors, lines, and shapes.
– The only value of this music is its market price, its cash value.
– This house is nothing more than four walls and a mattress.
– This car is just a set of wheels.
– You are only as good as your word.
– This person has a mental disorder, so he is utterly irrational and can't give informed consent to anything.
– Human beings are just rational animals, nothing more.
– Human beings are just tool-using featherless bipeds, nothing more.
– The chemicals in our bodies are worth less than a dollar, so that's all we are worth.

● Applied to ideas (S_S), things (E_S), and people (I_S), some systemic thinking (devaluation) *sees only black or white, all or nothing, perfect or imperfect, and nothing in between.* It is blind to all complexities, nuances, and shades of gray. It treats people, things, and ideas as worthless if they have the slightest imperfections. Falling into the "all or nothing" trap when relating to ideas, things, and people is commonplace. In explaining "black or white thinking," Hartman wrote:

Constructions of the human mind thus have only two values, which we shall call *systemic values*: either perfection or nonvalue. This is the model of the black and white valuation of things, the simplest kind of valuation there is. Since it belongs to constructions of the mind it is obvious that when applied to actual things it "prejudges" them—it is the model of prejudice. This kind of thinking is based on the logical category of limitation: the variety of the world is limited to only two distinctions: A and non-A (*e.g.* white and non-white; Communist and non-Communist). Such persons are limited, *bornées*, value blind, in the same sense in which a person is unmusical who only knows two tunes, the one that is the Star-Spangled banner and the other that is not. Systemic valuation is the model of schematic and dogmatic thinking (Hartman, 1967, 112).

The reason is that systemic valuation denies all degrees of value and sees things in either black or white; the thing either is or is not a member of its class, it either is *perfect* or *no good*. In a systemic organization you either belong or you don't belong. Shades and differences of opinion and character are not tolerated. The one value is conformity and the one disvalue non-conformity—which leads to expulsion or "liquidation." All members of a system must be the same or else be no members (Hartman, 1991b, 20).

Consider these examples of objectionable black or white systemic thinking:

– There is an error in this belief system, so nothing in it is believable.
– If we admit that even one statement in this book (e.g., the Bible) is false, we will have to throw out the whole thing.
– We can't throw out the whole thing, so there must be no error whatsoever in this book.
– If the stock market goes down 10 percent, that would be a total collapse.
– We must get rid of all federal regulations on businesses, no matter how many people get hurt.
– The plumbing in one unit of this apartment complex is bad, so I am not going to pay the builder for anything.
– My new car just got its first dent, so now it's totally ruined.
– You are either for us or against us.
– Better Dead than Red.
– Questioning any of my beliefs is a direct attack on my personal integrity and intrinsic worth.
– This person is confused about a few things, so he must be utterly crazy.
– As an "A" student, I will commit suicide if I ever make a "B."
– If you don't belong to my social (or religious) group, you are just trash or riffraff.
– If you are a "liberal" you have no right to exist.
– "Tolerance" is just another name for "Treason."

Needless to say, oversimplifying and black or white systemic thinking (disvaluation) can be both intellectually dishonest and morally troublesome. Radio and television talk show hosts are experts in black or white thinking. They do it for ratings, entertainment, power, and money, not for truth. Sadly, black or white thinking can and often does spill over into action. It can empower or authorize us to treat things and people as if they were mere ideas, nothing more. It can result in stupid behavior and immoral actions.

Please do not jump to the conclusion that all systemic thinking is intellectually dishonest or morally troublesome. All thinking whatsoever is systemic thinking. Systemic values just are thoughts, and all thoughts are systemic values. Every application of concepts of any kind (not just formal constructs) to anything whatsoever is systemic thinking. Not all thinking is like the examples above. We can think clearly, morally, and systemically with integrity. Thinking with formal constructs like logic and mathematics can be trouble free. Not all systemic thinking is objectionable. Not all is negative or disvaluational. Not all is black or white.

● Hartman recognized a third language-abusive (disvaluational) way of combining systemic value-objects (concepts) with one another. *Some concept combinations are just plain unintelligible.* Hartman recognized two types of unintelligible concepts, *nonsense* and *counter-sense.*

Nonsense statements make no sense at all and can be neither true nor false. Hartman himself gave these examples:

- The number 3 is masculine.
- The Mediterranean Sea is hypocritical.
- Robert is á – 13.
- The mathematics of the transfinite is black and red.
- Green is or (Hartman, 1967, 269).

Counter-sense statements are logical contradictions; they are analytically false because their subjects and predicates have logically incompatible meanings. Hartman gave these examples:

- A thing can be and not be at the same time.
- A pentagon has twelve sides.
- Physical being is immeasurable.
- Two bodies may occupy the same place at the same time.
- Houses cannot be lived in.
- Bachelors are married.
- War is peace (Hartman, 1967, 269-270).

False statements, though not unintelligible, are also systemic disvalues. They misuse language by not accurately describing the facts. "Falsity," Hartman wrote, "is not formal but material, which means that "the predicate contradicts facts" (270).

Lying communicates false or misleading information. What it affirms just isn't so. When caught, liars try to pass it off by saying that they "mis-spoke."

Not all thinking oversimplifies, fails to see shades of gray, is unintelligible, or mis-describes facts. Genuinely systemic formal and precise concepts like those of mathematics and logic do not have to be applied in ways that oversimplify, fail to make important distinctions, omit much that is relevant, or are morally or otherwise degrading. Very often, systemic thinking in all dimensions is a very good thing. Very often, it is just what we need. We can think and evaluate systemically without being either stupid, mistaken, or immoral. Using the Form of the Good correctly is systemic thinking. The proper corrective of systemic lying is systemic truthfulness; the proper remedy for systemic nonsense and self-contradiction is clear and precise systematic thinking; the proper remedy for systemic oversimplification and black and white thinking is thoughtful systemic thoroughness and comprehensiveness.

We can appropriately and positively evaluate ideas (S^S), things (E^S), and people (I^S) using only formal concepts with fairly definite meanings. Combing formal concepts with (thus valuing) systemic, extrinsic, and intrinsic values is often highly desirable, very good. Consider some relatively trouble free instances of numbering or applying logic or other formalities or ideas, and to things and people.

- Is this claim logically consistent?
- What will you pay me for what I know, or what I have discovered?
- How many dialogues did Plato write?
- How many bases does a baseball diamond have?
- How many yards must the punter kick in order to score a field goal?
- How many acres of land are in the lot or plot that I want to buy?
- What is the price of this book?
- What will you charge to fix my car?
- What can "time and motion studies" tell us about our workers?
- How many students are in this class?
- How much money per week do I earn?
- Are you being reasonable?
- Should I obey the laws of the land?
- Are our laws good laws?

Neither these questions nor the answers to them need be intellectually or morally troublesome. Yet, they all apply formal concepts to ideas, things, and people. They involve systemic thinking and evaluation.

Hartman himself quite explicitly acknowledged that not all systemic evaluation is bad. With maternity wards in mind, he indicated, "Where numerical order is important, as in tagging the right baby of the right mother, there is no badness in the systemic valuation" (Hartman, 1991b, 33-34).

...Not all systemic valuation is evil. It is evil only when it is a transposition—when applied to situations where it is inappropriate. Many things in our individual and social life *must* be valued systemically. Scientific constructs must be valued this way, and the rigorous discipline of systemic valuation in general is necessary for modern society and is precisely what ... American education [is] lacking, as against European education. There are even life situations where systemic valuation is necessary: all situations where no play is allowed and it is a matter of either being or not being. Thus, when meeting a deadline, when making a train, when stopping at a red light or before a railroad crossing—you either do or you don't—and when you don't you miss, and sometimes [lose] your life. The saying that a miss is as good as a mile expresses systemic valuation. Systemic valuation is necessary in all situations that demand discipline. In this sense Kierkegaard said that the heart of ethics is energy, and that he knew as a boy he had to hand in his school work, and if not the world would come to an end. It is necessary in all situations of emergency. Discipline may, in this sense, be defined as voluntary emergency. Until a child develops this kind of self-emergency education must provide it, and it can only do so by force—this is the very nature of emergency. It is here where progressive education is axiologically deficient (Hartman, 1991b, 33).

Hartman's unspoken rule for combining value dimensions was that *valuations in any dimension are OK as long as they are compositions that sustain or increase value; they are troublesome morally or otherwise only when they are deliberately used to diminish value.* Can you think of any way to improve this rule?

ii. Responding Disinterestedly or Dispassionately in Three Dimensions

Responding dispassionately toward what we value can be quite appropriate, but not always. We will now consider applying formal concepts like those of logic, mathematics, and law *dispassionately* to ideas, things, and people.

No matter what is being counted, logically analyzed, or legally assessed, we normally expect this to be done disinterestedly or with rational distance and impartiality across the board. No matter whether we are thinking abstractly, practically, or personally, we expect logical reasoning, accurate counting and fair-minded applications of laws, beliefs, mathematics, science, philosophy, and all formal systems. We expect census-takers to count and tally accurately and without bias. Since fair representation in legislative bodies and governmental appropriations depends on an accurate census, we definitely do not want census-takers to fudge the numbers to promote political, self-serving, or ideological agendas. We expect banks and financial institutions to keep accurate, disinterested, and objective track of our account numbers, deposits, withdrawals, and interest payments. We expect our Social Security numbers, years worked, ages, and monthly payments to be handled accurately and dispassionately. When buying or selling anything whatsoever, we expect accurate and unbiased accounting.

As noted, fair and open mindedness (disinterestedness) is a principle intellectual virtue. It is not a moral or a spiritual vice. We expect it from judges, jurors, faculty members, teachers, scientists, researchers, and administrators. Every court of law and every department of our universities and public schools should approach their clients or students, their subject matter, their staff, and their colleagues without prejudices and with fair and open minded systemic evaluation. We expect officials in all of these roles to evaluate ideas (S^S), things (E^S), and people (I^S) disinterestedly. We do not want these social roles to be diminished, distorted, or exploited by and for personal extrinsic gain or by and for narrow and biased ideological or political agendas. At times, we definitely need to examine ourselves and our family members or friends more objectively and less sentimentally and unrealistically. We do not always live up to the ideal of intellectual or legal disinterestedness or fairness, but when we do not get it from others, then we suddenly become very devoted to it!

Of course, we do not want or expect disinterestedness everywhere. Sometimes we rightfully expect extrinsic or intrinsic interestedness.

B. Extrinsically Evaluating Everything in All Dimensions

Extrinsically evaluating anything whatsoever involves:

i. Applying extrinsic concepts to it,
ii. Acting upon it as if it were a "thing" in public space-time,
iii. Responding toward it with ordinary everyday practical feelings, desires, emotions, attitudes, etc.

Typically, we evaluate extrinsically valuable entities in these three ways. According to Hartman, "Extrinsic valuation is the model of everyday pragmatic thinking" (Hartman, 1967, 113). Extrinsic value-objects are the natural home turf of extrinsic valuation, but systemic and intrinsic objects of value can also be evaluated extrinsically. In the next discussion, the emphasis will be on extrinsic or practical concepts and on ordinary attitudes or feelings. Extrinsic actions will be assumed or illustrated throughout.

i. Applying Extrinsic Concepts in Three Dimensions

Recall that for *practical* purposes Hartman originally conceived of extrinsic concepts as indefinitely large but finite meaning sets or intensions composed of sensory predicates that have been abstracted from sensory properties and objects experienced within our public world of space-time. If extrinsic concepts are infinite in theory, as Hartman contended, they are definitely finite in practice, as he admitted. Practically, finitude is as far as we can ever go.

Applying extrinsic concepts (symbolized next as "E") positively to extrinsic value-objects or things (E^E) is no mistake. This is where they naturally belong. Yet, just as our observations may be in error, so may our thoughts about our observations and perceptions. After briefly inspecting a used car, we may conclude (mistakenly) that it actually has all the good-making properties that it is supposed to have. After buying it, we may discover that it does not have all these good-making properties (e.g., the engine is too worn or weak), or it does have many bad-making properties that we did not originally spot (e.g., the brake linings are worn out). The extrinsic value domain is not error-free, but applying extrinsic concepts positively to extrinsic value-objects is not one of those errors.

Extrinsic values and valuations can be applied negatively as well as positively to extrinsic value-objects. "One business cooperating with another" (E^E) increases value for both, but "One business competing with another" (E_E) can diminish value. So, cooperation is better than competition! Buying property is positive; stealing property is negative. Constructing a useful building or structure is positive; bombing a useful structure or building is negative. As someone has said facetiously, "Mechanical engineers build weapons; civil engineers build targets."

Negatively *applying extrinsic concepts (symbolized as "E") to systemic values* (S_E) might involve confusing concepts with things that we can see, hear, taste, touch, or smell. Here, vision and hearing seem to be the most relevant senses. Applying extrinsic concepts to things might involve confusing mental ideas with visually printed words or numbers, or with the "spoken word." Behaviorist in psychology inevitably make this mistake. For them, every psychological or conscious concept, including thinking, is redefined "empirically" in sensory terms. Thoughts become words on paper, or overt speech, or very quiet vocal-chord vibrations. "Pain" is nothing more than externally observable "pain behavior," but nothing is going on inside consciousness, which does not even exist. Behaviorism's great mistake is to confuse or "reduce" both systemic and intrinsic value-objects to extrinsic value-objects.

Extrinsically *acting* negatively upon or with ideas or systemic value-objects (S_E) could be something like babbling, talking nonsense, lying (communicating false or misleading information), broadcasting propaganda, shouting "Fire" in a crowded building when there is no fire, or just "crying wolf." Thinking negative or degrading thoughts about someone else's beliefs is one thing; uttering them in public is something else.

Extrinsically *acting* positively upon or with ideas or systemic value-objects (S^E) could be something like filing documents, typing words, writing memos, printing books, giving speeches, preaching sermons, lecturing, giving news reports, or just communicating positive ideas in some public arena or through some public medium. Using ideas to make and do constructive things positively evaluates them in terms of their practical results. Publicly praising or commending ideas and beliefs is one way to combine them with extrinsic activities.

Applying extrinsic (or systemic) concepts to intrinsic values, that is, to people is not always a bad thing. Counting people (I^S) and applying "social worth" and "social role" criteria to people (I^E) are not always undesirable. In the practical everyday world, we do this all the time. Recall Hartman's rule for combining value dimensions: There is nothing wrong with applying extrinsic or systemic value concepts to people, or acting accordingly, as long as this does not result in a "value transposition," that is, as long as it does not deliberately harm them or attempt to diminish their intrinsic worth. We can both systemically and extrinsically evaluate people in ways that do not "dehumanize" them.

Trouble arises when we evaluate people extrinsically in ways that do not at the same time respect and acknowledge their intrinsic worth, or in ways that actually diminish their intrinsic worth. Not paying workers fair wages and benefits degrades or disvalues them. More obviously, owning people as property (slavery) diminishes their worth; and killing people, whether in peace or war, whether intentionally or unintentionally, diminishes or demolishes their intrinsic worth. Any actions or practices that dehumanize, degrade, de-individualize, diminish, or destroy unique conscious individuals are morally bad, even if sometimes necessary as the "lesser of evils." Numbers can be used to dehumanize people, as when the Nazis tattooed numbers on the arms of their prisoners destined for enslavement and eventual slaughter. Numbers can also be used to confer high honors on individuals, as when the jersey numbers of outstanding athletes are officially retired from service.

Immanuel Kant said a few good things. One was that we should always treat people as ends in themselves but never *merely* as means to our ends (Kant, 1949, 46). The "merely" here is very important. It allows for treating other people as means to our ends (I^E) as long as *using them* also respects and does not diminish them as ends in themselves. Currently, the United States is said to be moving more and more toward a service economy, as opposed to a manufacturing economy. This means that a substantial number of jobs in our economy are oriented toward providing people with services. People working in service jobs are obviously being used as means to ends, but, perhaps less obviously, so are those who manufacture the products that we want to own. When we take advantage of their services, skills, and labors, we are using them as means to ends. This does not necessarily mean that we are using them *merely* as means to ends, however. As long as workers, whether in service jobs, manufacturing, or whatever, are paid decent wages and benefits, not treated disrespectfully on the job, and can fulfill their own desires and interests by and through their work, they can be valued and treated both as ends (I^I) and means (I^E) without being *mere* means (I_E), that is, without degrading their intrinsic worth.

However, workers *are* being regarded and treated as mere means (I_E) when they are exploited by excessively low wages, few or no benefits, get no respect, and if their work suppresses their creativity and frustrates their most basic desires and interests. Slavery is one of the worst economic (and most immoral) expression of treating people as mere means, as mere property. We are already getting into ethics, the topic of the next chapter, but understanding how to evaluate everything in every dimension does lead inevitably into ethics. Take a look at some of Hartman's ideas about how to organize economics and work environments in ethical ways in Hartman, 1991a, 193-199.

ii. Responding with Practical Feelings in Three Dimensions

Ordinary feelings, desires, emotions, and attitudes fall within the zone of the "Goldilocks effect,"or the "golden mean"—not too much and not too little. Too little affection or feeling moves toward systemic disinterestedness and, beyond that, toward apathetic uninterestedness. Too much affection or feeling proceeds in the direction of intrinsic valuation and complete self-identification with what is being valued and ceases being extrinsic evaluation. The lines between the three are not absolutely sharp, but we can recognize paradigm cases.

Most of the time we live within the "level headed" zone of ordinary or normal practical desires, interests, feelings, and attitudes. Most human evaluation falls within the "even keel" of extrinsic valuation, as far as feelings go. In our rarer more cool-headed "academic," "rational," or "impartial" moments, we value with systemic disinterestedness. In our very rare but more intense loving, empathetic, and compassionate moments, we value with intrinsic passion.

● *Responding to systemic value-objects extrinsically.* Positively valuing concepts, ideas, laws, and belief systems extrinsically (S^E) involves being interested in and attracted to them because they are useful, that is, because they can somehow help us to fulfill our ordinary practical desires, interests, emotions, and attitudes. We often distinguish between "pure science" and "applied science," or between "pure philosophy" and "applied philosophy." Systemic evaluation sides with the purities, extrinsic evaluation with the applications. "Pure knowledge" is "for its own sake," (metaphorically speaking) even though it may eventually have unexpected practical applications. "Applied knowledge" is more directly and obviously useful and serves our more immediate practical interests.

Negatively valuing concepts, ideas, laws, and belief systems extrinsically (S_E) sees them as either useless or harmful. Some people think that the ideas and laws passed or espoused by Democrats or Republicans, Liberals or Conservatives are extrinsically bad for business, or bad for themselves, or bad for their social class, and they have very hostile feelings toward them. Others are so exclusively focused on ideas that are good for business or good for themselves that they are hostile or indifferent to ideas and policies that are good for other people, good for world peace, or good for the environment.

● *Responding to extrinsic value-objects extrinsically.* Positively valuing sensory things, processes, and activities for their usefulness in fulfilling our normal or natural desires, positive feelings, and emotions is the native home of extrinsic valuation (E^E). We normally want, feel good about, enjoy, and act to get, useful things or objects. We desire, encourage, and try to sustain useful processes and behaviors. Our ordinary desires and interests are practical desires and interests.

We also know perfectly well that some things, objects, processes, and deeds will not work, will not do the job, will not satisfy us emotionally, will not produce the results we want, will not fulfill our basic practical desires for food, drink, shelter, clothing, and the necessities of life, or will not efficiently luxuriate or entertain us. Inefficient or harmful causes, things, processes, and activities are disvalued extrinsically (E_E); they are extrinsic disvalue-objects. So are property-destructive and status-diminishing things, processes, and activities.

• *Responding to intrinsic value-objects extrinsically.* Positively valuing people extrinsically (I^E) is commonplace, even if limited in scope. We normally feel good about useful people who fulfill their social functions as expected, and we want them to keep on keeping on. We like, appreciate, and encourage good workers, good bosses, good wives, good husbands, good children, and so on.

Correspondingly, we dislike, disvalue, disapprove of, and discourage bad workers, bad bosses, bad wives, bad husbands, bad children—people who do not fulfil their positive extrinsic social roles (I_E).

There is nothing wrong or troublesome about any of thus—as long as we do not lose sight of the intrinsic worth of both useful and useless people. We can treat people as means to ends as long as we do not treat them *merely* as means to ends.

C. Intrinsically Evaluating Everything in Three Dimensions

Intrinsically evaluating anything whatsoever involves:

i. Applying intrinsic concepts to it,
ii. Acting upon it as if it were a person,
iii. Passionate identifying with it—as in profound love, empathy, compassion, and concentration.

Typically, we evaluate intrinsically valuable entities in these three ways. Intrinsic values are the natural home turf of intrinsic valuations, but systemic and extrinsic values can also be evaluated intrinsically, that is with intrinsic passion and self-identification-with them. Consider next the conceptual and then the affective or feeling aspects of intrinsic evaluation. Intrinsic actions or activities will be assumed or illustrated throughout.

i. Applying Intrinsic Concepts in Three Dimensions

Recall that intrinsic concepts as such are singular concepts that refer to unique conscious beings who are ends in themselves—mainly human beings, but also God and non-human animals. Proper names, personal pronouns, and metaphors are obvious examples of intrinsic concepts. All such words have intensional and extensional meanings that can be applied accordingly in valuational processes. Before turning to metaphors, consider first how singular concepts like proper names and personal pronouns might be applied systemically, extrinsically, and intrinsically. Giving proper names to theories and things, as well as to people, can help us identify-with and appreciate them more intensely in their uniqueness and completeness, not just as abstract members of some general class.

Theories, ideas, ideals, doctrines, laws, rules, and other systemic constructs are frequently given capitalized proper names, as if they were persons, and they are often but not always associated with persons (S^i). Consider, for example: Euclidean Geometry, the Copernican Heliocentric Theory, Newtonian Physics, Darwin's Theory of Evolution, Einstein's Theory of Relativity, the Heisenberg Uncertainty Principle, Stephen Hawking's Theory of Everything, Aristotle's Ethics, Kant's Categorical Imperative, the Bush Doctrine (of preemptive war), Dow Jones Averages, Uncle Sam (for the United States of America) etc. Conceptual constructs like corporations (e.g., Enron, Bank of America, General Motors) and nation-states (United States of America, the Confederate States, France, Germany, etc.) are also given proper names and treated as "fictional persons" or "legal persons." Psychologically and axiologically, we may personify such things and devote ourselves passionately to them, as if they were unique persons worthy of our unqualified devotion. Consider, "In Dow we trust," and "My country right or wrong." Hartman said that in intrinsic valuation, even a thing or a thought "becomes a Self identified with the valuing Self, a Thou to the I" (Hartman 1994, 98).

We also give capitalized proper names (symbolized as "I") to extrinsic physical things and processes, as if they were persons (E^i). Named *things* are often but not always associated with persons. Examples would be: Edwards Air Force Base, Jefferson's Monticello, the Lincoln Memorial, St. Patrick's Cathedral, the Lady Bird Johnson Wildflower Center. Contrast these with: the Empire State Building, the Brooklyn Bridge, the Golden Gate Bridge, etc. Those of us who speak English often give proper names (e.g., "old Betsy") to personal possessions like our shotguns, pistols, cars, and pickup trucks. We personify *things* with which we feel closely, even intrinsically, connected. Ships and airplanes are personalized and referred to as "she." French and other languages personify and sexualize all nouns and pronouns; all things are either male or female. Such languages tend to personalize all the *things* of the world; they are anthropomorphic about everything! In painting and sculpture, we literally in-corporate persons into things like paintings, such as "Whistler's Mother" and "Van Gogh's Self Portrait," or into sculptures, like "Michelangelo's David" or a "bust of Beethoven."

Personifying things, and aesthetically appreciating or valuing them in their uniqueness, not just as in their class membership, is not at all uncommon. Normally, this is not a bad thing, but it may lead to confusion and overvaluation. Persons, of course, are unique; but uniqueness does not imply personhood and intrinsic worth. Things that do not have intrinsic worth may be valued as if they have it, as if they were persons; but that does not turn them into persons or conscious individuals. Aesthetics is the intrinsic evaluation of extrinsic objects, Hartman contended. We intensely identify with the art objects that we create or profoundly adore. However, such extrinsic objects remain non-conscious extrinsic objects even when they are being intrinsically evaluated. Aesthetics involves the intrinsic evaluation of extrinsic value-objects; ethics involves the intrinsic valuation of intrinsic value-objects. Aesthetics is not ethics, and it should not degenerate into animism, the view that every material object has a soul of its own.

Most appropriately, we apply intrinsic singular concepts like proper names to unique human persons, and we also use personal pronouns to refer to them (I^i). This is the native home of intrinsic concepts (symbolized as "I"), intrinsically good persons, and intrinsic feelings, as further explained shortly. Many of our words (proper names, personal pronouns) refer to unique individual persons in their full concreteness and completeness.

• Hartman also indicated that *metaphors can be words of intrinsic valuation*, and this deserves special attention. Metaphors are not always positive intrinsic evaluation words; they can be used to turn us against things, as in calling a person a "pig" or a "dirty rat." Hartman most emphasized positive metaphors; but he gave at least one example of a negative metaphor, "Fred is an ass" (Hartman, 1961, 416). When used as positive intrinsic evaluation words or phrases, metaphorical concepts are closely associated with the positive affective aspects of intrinsic valuation. Negative metaphors are strongly associated with negative feelings.

"Metaphor" in educated discourse has at least two meanings, one narrow, one broad. In the narrow sense, metaphorical words are contrasted with similes, analogies, poetry, myths, allegories, and other non-literal verbal expressions. In this sense, a metaphor says that "X *is* Y," whereas a simile says that "X is *like* Y." Both build upon likenesses or similarities. In the broad sense, "metaphor" stands for all figurative or non-literal language, and this includes similes, analogies, poetry, parables, myths, allegories, and the like. Hartman had this broad sense of "metaphor" in mind when he linked metaphors with intrinsic valuations. Positive non-literal language can both express and help to evoke intrinsic identification and evaluation.

Metaphors, broadly understood, can both express and help to evoke intrinsic identification with something. They are used to express profound appreciation for and deep personal involvement with that to which they are applied. They can evoke such appreciation and involvement in others and help to arouse and sustain it in ourselves. Robert Burns's simile, "O MY Luve's like a red, red rose," links the feelings he had toward red roses with the woman he loved. "Metaphor" is rooted etymologically in the notion of a "bridge." Metaphors provide bridges for linking or transferring keen intrinsic appreciation of and involvement with one thing to something else. They build upon likenesses to express and transfer deep intrinsic feelings and affections from one thing to another. Religious literature is loaded with such metaphors. "All people are children of God the Father" links all of us as metaphorical children with a metaphorical Father-like God. Moral discourse like "All people are brothers and sisters," can help spread our profound affection for and identification with literal brothers and sisters to metaphorical brothers and sisters.

Hartman spoke of metaphors as "words which may mean any other word in the language." He explained, "A metaphor is a set of predicates used as a variable. Hence it can, in principle replace every other word of the language—and even itself as an ordinary word rather than that of a metaphor, as in "a peach of a peach" (Hartman, 1967, 113).

The metaphor, "a peach of a peach," (E^I) expresses the intrinsic valuation of an extrinsic value—a real peach, but the same metaphor could express the intrinsic valuation of a systemic value, "a peach of an idea" (S^I) or the intrinsic valuation of a person, "a peach of a girl" (I^I). As Hartman further indicated,

> *Intrinsic* language deals with objects not as members of classes but as unique beings. Hence concepts must be used in unique senses and not in the sense of referring to classes. Such a use of concepts, as uniquely characterizing rather than as extensively classifying, is the metaphor. When I say of my wife that she is a peach I do not mean to say that she belongs to the class of peaches. Rather, I mean that the word "peach" connotes something which uniquely reminds me of my wife—and not of a peach or of any other thing or person in the world. Metaphors, thus, have no class reference nor do they have—for that same reason—any definite connotation. When I call my wife a peach, I mean a different peach than when I call my uncle "a peach of a man" (Hartman, 1991b, 30).

When Hartman says that metaphors do not have any "definite connotation," this should not be interpreted to mean that they have no connotation or conceptual meaning at all. The emphasis should be on the word "definite." The conceptual meaning of metaphorical words constantly shifts from one context to another, as when evaluating peaches, uncles, or wives as peaches. Metaphors capitalize on, link to, and transform similarities or likenesses that may vary from one context to another; yet some trace of the original meaning of a metaphor remains throughout all of its transformations (Hartman, 1974, 92-93).

Metaphors treat similarities as bridges that facilitate affective intrinsic evaluation and self-identification-with. They transfer feelings or emotions from one thing to the next, or they sustain or enhance already-existing intrinsic self-identification. Peaches, wives, and uncles are all "sweet" in some metaphorical sense of that term. Metaphors can express, sustain, and facilitate intrinsic evaluation. Metaphors do communicate something fairly definite both conceptually and emotionally, but exactly what this is varies from one context to another. Thus, they function as variables, as Hartman suggested.

ii. Responding with Intrinsic Feelings in Three Dimensions

Positively identifying ourselves with valued objects happens in profound love, empathy, compassion, and concentration. If we love anything with all our heart, soul, mind, and strength, we evaluate it intrinsically, we are one with it, and it is one with us axiologically and psychologically. Since we can evaluate anything in any dimension, we can love any value-object in any dimension. Anything that becomes the center of our existence, our ultimate concern, if only for a short time, is being intrinsically evaluated. Like all other forms of valuation, intrinsic valuation is in a constant state of flux, but when it happens, it is what Abraham Maslow called a "peak experience." We move dynamically back and forth between the three modes of valuation, but sustained intrinsic valuation would be bliss.

Intense and completely negative dis-identification of ourselves with or dissociation from disvalued objects is also possible. Our feeling-laden words for positive intrinsic identification usually have opposites that can be equally intense and passionate. The opposites of love are, by degrees, hatred, revulsion, contempt, or indifference. Many "existential" emotions are highly and intensely negative, and in their extreme forms they manifest intrinsic disvaluation. They may also be quite tame, mild, ordinary, and less extreme, thus extrinsic. Such existential emotions are fear, terror, anxiety, despair, depression, revulsion, jealousy, grief, and feelings of abandonment, forlornness, uncertainty, self-doubt, loneliness, and boredom. Hartman explicitly mentioned torture and grief as intrinsic disvalues (Hartman, 1995c, 64), and, of course, this covers the adverse sufferings thereof. Some negative actions and emotions intrinsically disvalue oneself; some intrinsically disvalue other people, things, processes, actions, ideas, doctrines, or formalities.

● *Responding to systemic value-objects intrinsically.* Sometimes, people love and identify themselves fully with systemic ideas, concepts, beliefs, doctrines, dogmas, ideologies, systems of knowledge, and formalities of every description (S^I). Generally speaking, intrinsically evaluating systemic values is a very good thing, unless this interferes with objectivity, involves overvaluation, or else hinders the intrinsic evaluation of even better things.

All of us have probably evaluated systemic values intrinsically many times, though we don't always have a name or word for it. Intense *curiosity* or *wonder* about anything is a wonderful thing. Normally, intense *concentration* on ideas, problems, thoughts, or the books or media in which they are extrinsically embodied, is a very good thing. Have you ever been *"lost in thought"*? If so, what was your state of mind like? To venture an answer, you were so intensely involved with and absorbed in some problem, idea, belief, book, movie, or TV program that you "lost yourself in thought," meaning that at the time you had no conscious awareness of yourself or your thoughts as distinct realities. You and your thoughts were fused into one. The kind or importance of the subject matter of our thoughts makes no difference; we can be "lost in thought" about anything, even trivial things, but this just means that we can intrinsically identify ourselves with and thus intrinsically evaluate any systemic values, concepts, beliefs, ideologies, or systems whatsoever. Creative thinkers often find themselves lost in thought, thereby finding themselves by so losing themselves.

If positive intrinsic affective evaluations were evenly spread over concepts, things, and people, the intrinsic evaluation of systemic values would be highly desirable. We would regard such people as saints, for to them everything (except evil) would be sacred, including thoughts and beliefs.

However, positive intrinsic evaluation does not always spread evenly across the board to all dimensions of value. Some people intrinsically evaluate *only* or at least *primarily* knowledge, beliefs, doctrines, ideologies, "red tape," rituals, or formalities. They value such things "for their own sake" and before all else, but this readily degenerates into disvaluing persons (I_1) and/or property (E_1) intrinsically or otherwise, or at least into ignoring or being indifferent to them. Authoritarian or autocratic mentalities in government, politics, law, science, philosophy, and religion are especially prone to do this. We call such people "bureaucrats," "ideologists," "dogmatists," "fanatics," "rule-worshipers," "authoritarians," and "dictators."

Systemic extremists love systemic value-objects more than anything else; they are intensely devoted to them with all their hearts; they put them first before all else. They readily sacrifice persons, practices, practicality, and possessions to or for ideas or ideologies—which is what the "ivory tower" metaphor means. Systemic extremists have little or no empathy or compassion toward or practical involvement with people as unique individuals; they can be very "impractical," "incompetent," "socially challenged," "absent minded," or "ivory tower" in dealing with or relating to things, objects, processes, activities, and people in our common everyday world. In extreme cases, they can be so out of touch with people and/or things that their evaluations of them are simply off the axiological chart—as in almost-complete indifference. Indifference to people is not off the ethical or moral chart, however, for it manifests extreme carelessness toward, unconcern about, and harmful neglect of people and of people-benefiting-property. Indifference is a moral vice, just as impartiality is an intellectual virtue, and they are not the same. Returning to the axiological chart again, we find explicitly disvaluing attitudes and practices like hatred, vengeance, resentment, snobbery, spite, and worship wars.

Evaluating systemic value-objects positively and systemically (with rational objectivity or disinterestedness) is highly desirable, but *systemic extremists do not value systemic value-objects systemically or disinterestedly. Instead, they value them intrinsically, with all their hearts, and at the expense of all else. They tend to value people and/or things disinterestedly, or, more exactly, indifferently*, that is, with little or no interest or concern.

At negative extremes, systemic ideologists disvalue people intensely because they do not fit or conform to their ideological systems and prejudices. To them, ideas are indispensable, but people are very expendable. Consider Hartman's insightful comments on systemically disvaluing intrinsic values, beginning with "All great historical crimes have been—and are being prepared to be—committed in the name of some category: an idea, an ideal, a dogma, a faith, a "cause," a "system" (Hartman, 1961, 397n), and continuing with,

> Any bureaucratic procedure that sees not humans but instances of a rule, any authoritarian person that tries to impose his will by using the rules of a system, any procedure that imposes conformity is guilty of this evil of transposition of the logical and the axiological. It is the use of a system which gives evil the power to extend its range and, at the same time, to assume the resemblance of good. All great evil is systemic evil. [Hartman's Note: This is particularly true of war. They are between systems, not between people. It is people who die for those systems. See Jacques Maritain, *Men and the State*, London, 1954, p. 47: "*Ce sont toujours les meles qui se font tuer.*"("It is always the same ones who get killed.")]
>
> The reason is that systemic valuation denies all degrees of value and sees things in either black or white; the thing either is or is not a member of its class, it either is *perfect* or *no good*. In a systemic organization you either belong or you don't belong. Shades and differences of opinion and character are not tolerated. The one value is conformity and the one disvalue non-conformity—which leads to expulsion or "liquidation." All members of a system must be the same or else be no members.
>
> Where there are no differences and distinctions between things, there can be no order. Things that are all the same are indistinguishable of one another and interchangeable. Order, however, presupposes distinction and variety among things. Systemic things, therefore, cannot be in order. Rather, one such thing being like the next, the only "order" prevailing is the system itself. But this, as far as the elements of the system are concerned, constitutes disorder; all the elements are on the lowest common denominator, namely, as elements of the system, and all their intrinsic or extrinsic differences are erased; they are, as individuals, unavailable. There is nothing but a mass of interchangeable, formless elements: Chaos numbered and indexed. The culmination of such systemic organization was Nazi Germany.
>
> Every dictatorship is of this kind. It always arises in answer to a real or imaginary emergency. To overcome chaos by systemization is always the first impulse of humanity. Thus, the age-old prescription for tyrants is first to manufacture emergencies and then appear as savior. Actually, the system only replaces one chaos by another; it even intensifies chaos by card-indexing it. The culmination of this kind of chaos were the German concentration camps. But any secret police falls into this pattern, when it imposes uniformity. Its order is merely a formal one (Hartman, 1991b, 20).

● *Responding to extrinsic value-objects intrinsically.* Sometimes, people love and identify themselves fully with the things of the world (E^I). Generally speaking, this is also a very good thing, a self-enriching thing, as long as it is not done at the expense of all else. If positive intrinsic affective evaluation were evenly spread over concepts, things, and people, the intrinsic evaluation of extrinsic values would be highly desirable. We would regard such people as saints, for they would find God and holiness everywhere and in all empirical things, including bodies, property, prosperity, material objects, and physical processes.

However, positive intrinsic evaluation seldom spreads across the board to all dimensions of value. Some people intrinsically evaluate *only* or at least *primarily* the things of the world. We call such people "materialists," not because they subscribe to the metaphysical doctrine that only matter exists, though they might. Rather, they are axiological materialists because they feel and think and act as if only material things have value or genuine worth, or at least supreme worth.

Metaphysical materialists tend toward axiological materialism because for them nothing else exists; there is nothing else to value; but axiological materialists need not be metaphysicians. For axiological materialists, it is enough that *things and only things are supremely good.* They value physical things, possessions, and processes for their own sake and before all else. This readily degenerates into indifference toward, or into the extrinsic disvaluation of, persons (I_E) and/or knowledge, thinking, and believing (S_E). Axiological materialists are practical persons of the world first and foremost, but if they are also thinkers, they might also be metaphysical materialists. For them, "Greed is good." People matter only because they can be used and exploited for profit and gain; but people are expendable and may be discarded when unprofitable—thus, layoffs, downsizing, and shipping factories, services, and jobs to other parts of the world where people are cheap. To extrinsic extremists, ideas are valuable only when immediately practical or useful. Art is valuable only because it has cash value. No knowledge for knowledge's sake, no art for art's sake, no people for their own sakes, for these folks.

• *Responding to intrinsic value-objects intrinsically.* Sometimes, people love and identify themselves fully with people, God, and other unique conscious beings like animals (I^I). The great moral and religious thinkers and leaders of the world tell us to respond to people and other intrinsically good entities with love, empathy, compassion, concentration, and complete self-identification. I^I, when sustained, is the acme of moral and spiritual development, but in most people it exists only by degrees and intermittently, and it has a lot of competition from lesser values and valuations. The supreme ideal of intrinsically evaluating intrinsic value-objects is expressed in the following "commandments."

- Love God with all your heart, soul, mind and strength.
- Love your neighbor as yourself.
- Love yourself as your neighbor.
- Love strangers (e.g., "illegal aliens) as yourself.
- Love your enemies as yourself.
- Do unto others as you would have them do unto you.
- Do good to those who persecute you and despitefully use you.
- Identify with people as ends in themselves and never use them merely as means.

Only "the Devil" and "devilish people" like Hitler, Stalin, and "sinners" intrinsically disvalue intrinsically valuable people, God, and animals (I_I). Many theologians and cynics believe that this sort of devilishness is very widespread. What do you think? We can at least hope that they are wrong. Ignorance of and indifference to the intrinsic may be even more widespread manifestations of devilishness, but with much the same results. Lack of intrinsic self-development causes most of the moral and spiritual evils of human existence.

Oddly enough, positively evaluating intrinsic values intrinsically, (I^I), can itself be overblown, overdone, overemphasized, overvalued. If positive intrinsic evaluation were evenly spread over concepts, things, and people, the intrinsic valuation of intrinsic values would be highly desirable, but it doesn't always work out that way. Some saintly masters of intrinsic evaluation may find God and holiness in themselves and other people, but not everywhere and in all good things, or in all positive thoughts. Even saints can be neglectful. The *scope* of what some saints love or value intrinsically may be inordinately limited. Although saintly people are very highly developed intrinsically, they may not be very well developed extrinsically and intrinsically. They may be very impractical and/or uninformed "romanticists," or "love slobs," or "holy ignoramuses," or "enthusiasts," who love only love, who do not express their love in deeds, and/or who act foolishly or stupidly without knowing what they are doing. Some "nominal" saints may lack some of the ideal good-making properties of true saintliness at its best. Their "hearts are in the right place," but they do not know how to understand, explain, express, act from, actualize, or organize goodness. Forms of saintly self-development that are even richer in good-making properties are conceivable.

D. Living Abundantly

Finally, with respect to evaluating people, consider one dramatic and unexpected implication of expanding the scope of our intrinsic valuations of others.

Most people draw the line somewhere between "insiders" and "outsiders." Just where the line is drawn in practice varies from one person to another, from one context to another, from one social group to another. The way this distinction works, insiders are loved or positively valued, but outsiders are hated or at least don't count. Many people love their immediate family members, but they have no real interest in or concern for outsiders beyond their family, and they may be very hostile toward them. Insiders may include both their friends and family, but they are unconcerned with or perhaps even aggressive toward outsiders beyond those limits. Some people include friends and family, but also intimate social contacts—members of their tribe, clique, clan, or church; but their sympathy, empathy, and compassion stop there. Nationalists or "patriots" may spread their intrinsic loyalty and concern only to fellow countrymen and women; but beyond that "foreigners" don't count, i.e., they are not intrinsically valued, or they may even be detested, i.e., intrinsically disvalued, as are today's "illegal aliens."

Progressively including more and more people within the scope of "insiders" is axiologically important. Biology seems to have equipped us to love kin and kind, but not outsiders. Moral and spiritual growth consists largely in overcoming this constrictive "natural" or typical aspect of "human nature."

Recall that the best lives are those that are richest in good-making properties in all three value dimensions. Recall also that when we identify ourselves fully with others, no matter how few or how many, we become so united with them that we take their good-making properties into ourselves and make them axiologically and psychologically our own. The physical and existential differences between us remain intact, but they cease to matter because axiologically, psychologically, morally, and spiritually, we merge into one, we actualize a more perfect union. When we love others (animals, people, God, strangers, aliens, enemies) and fully identify with them, their goodness becomes our goodness and their lives enrich our lives with their good-making properties. Our lives become better and better as we love others as ourselves more and more, and the more others we so love, the more abundantly we live. Overcoming barriers between insiders and outsiders results in the most abundant-in-goodness lives we could ever hope to live. People who love most narrowly live most narrowly; people who love most abundantly live most abundantly! Axiology tells us so!

Chapter Four

ETHICS AND OTHER APPLICATIONS

Near the end of his life, Robert S. Hartman acknowledged that most applications of axiology to such disciplines as aesthetics, ethics, religion, and political science were yet to be written, but it is clear that he intended to write them. As he explained,

> As for aesthetics, an axiological theory of aesthetics has yet to be written, just as with a detailed ethics. I am doing so in a book which I am writing at present, *The Universe of Intrinsic Value*, where I start with aesthetics, then ethics, religion, and political science. *The Structure of Value* gives the *foundations* of formal axiology, not the total system. It gives a method and directives about how value sciences can be written (Hartman, 1995e, 85).

In another reference to the same projected book, he added the subtitle, *An Axiological Introduction to Ethics and Aesthetics* (Hartman, 1995b, 63), so the complete title would have been: *The Universe of Intrinsic Value: An Axiological Introduction to Ethics and Aesthetics*. Sadly, Hartman died before he wrote the definitive book(s) on ethics and aesthetics that he wanted to write. The folder on "The Universe of Intrinsic Value" in the Hartman Archives in the Special Collections Library at The University of Tennessee contains a very few research materials but no written text. Apparently, no writing was ever done on this project. Thus, we do not know in detail what an ethical theory derived from formal axiology, or as applied axiology, would look like from his perspective.

However, scattered throughout his writings, Hartman did give some very general clues about ethics, along with many examples of ethical thinking, so we can start with these and begin to extrapolate and create an axiology-based theory of ethics. Along the way, we will look at how some of his successors have further developed his hints, and at some of the complications.

Hartman also gave a few clues about how formal axiology might be applied to other value-laden disciplines like aesthetics, economics, political science, psychology, and religion. In the last section of this chapter, many of these will be identified but not extensively developed, and references for further study will be given. The book you are now reading is intended to do no more than give readers a background for going further, but it is not and does not pretend to be a substitute for the works that do go much further.

1. Hartman's Understanding of "Ethics"

Hartman never developed a complete ethical theory, but he did define "ethics," and he did spice up his writings on general axiology with many ethical comments and illustrations. Readers were exposed to much of this in Chapter Three. Since he did not live long enough to write his next projected book, any attempt to extend his reflections on ethics will be just that, an extension. As an extension beyond Hartman, an ethical theory based on the fundamentals of axiology as explained in the three previous chapters can only be an educated guess as to how Hartman might have done it. But, here it is—an educated guess about an axiological ethics.

The logical place to start is with Hartman's definition of "ethics," which he usually treated as being synonymous with "morality." His hard core definition of "ethics" was repeated with variations several times in his writings, so we will take it as fundamental. Here are his expressions of it.

> Sociology may be defined as the application of extrinsic value to groups of persons, economics as the application of extrinsic value to individual things; ethics as the application of intrinsic value to individual persons, and aesthetics as the application of intrinsic value to individual things (Hartman, 1967, 114).

> We have defined morality as the application of intrinsic value to persons (Hartman, 1991b, 194).

> Intrinsic value applied to individual persons shows the uniqueness of each person and its fulfilling or failing to fulfill its own self. This is the science of *Ethics* (Hartman, 1967, 308).

What did Hartman mean when he defined "ethics" as "the application of intrinsic value to individual persons"? The answer can only be an educated guess, for he did not explain. Since axiological applications are valuations, perhaps this means, "Ethics is or accounts for evaluating individual persons intrinsically." If so *ethics as a cognitive discipline* would give a rational account of what is involved in evaluating individual persons intrinsically, and *being ethical* would involve actually valuing individual persons intrinsically, as opposed to evaluating them merely extrinsically, merely systemically, merely indifferently, or with disdain and hostility. This is only an educated guess, but let's see where it goes.

If ethical theory gives a rational account of what is involved in evaluating persons intrinsically, what is this account? What exactly is involved in evaluating persons intrinsically? To answer, we must draw upon the explanation of "intrinsic valuation" given in the preceding chapter. As we saw there, an intrinsic evaluation of anything has three components, the first systemic, the second extrinsic, and the third distinctively intrinsic:

- Applying intrinsic concepts to it,
- Acting upon it as if it were a person,
- Responding toward it by passionate identifying with it—as in profound love, empathy, compassion, and concentration.

So, *ethics involves* at least this much:
- Applying intrinsic concepts to unique persons—the systemic or conceptual aspect,
- Acting upon persons as unique persons—the extrinsic or behavioral aspect,
- Passionately identifying with unique persons, as in profound love, empathy, and compassion—the intrinsic affective aspect.

Ethical theory explains what is involved in:
- applying intrinsic concepts to unique persons,
- acting upon persons as if they were unique persons, and
- identifying affectively with unique persons.

It also explains their opposites. *Being ethical lives* them. Ethical theory also gives an account of what is "unethical," of what fails to fulfill the concept of the ethical.

The unethical consists at least in:
- Applying only systemic and/or extrinsic concepts to unique persons—the systemic or conceptual aspect,
- Acting upon unique persons as if they were merely extrinsic or systemic objects—the extrinsic or behavioral aspect,
- Being emotionally indifferent toward unique persons, or responding with profoundly negative emotions toward them, as in hatred, condescension, or snobbery—the affective intrinsic aspect.

This chapter on ethical theory can only give *an account* of evaluating unique persons intrinsically, or the opposites thereof; it's up to you, the reader, to *be an ethical person.*

2. The Meaning of "Ought"

The word "ought" is an essential cognitive tool in ethics. To explain and understand evaluating unique persons intrinsically, we need the word "ought." Chapter One introduced but did not explain G. E. Moore's "Third Question of Ethics," which was, "What ought we to do?" Ethics proper, according to most philosophers, is mainly about *what we ought to do*. The three axiological aspects of applying intrinsic value or evaluation to persons can be recast as questions about what we ought to do. How ought we to apply intrinsic and other moral concepts to unique persons? How ought we to act upon unique persons? How ought we to respond affectively to unique persons?

What does "ought" mean axiologically? Hartman defined "ought" as "equivalent to the relation, 'it is better than,'" and he explicitly applied this to actions (Hartman, 1967, 165). He wrote, "John ought to read 'Ivanhoe'" means that it is better for John to read it than not to read it, or that it is better for him to read it than to read something else" (165). Thus, "You ought to do something" (e.g., read something), means, "It would be best for you to do it."

Perhaps we can improve slightly on Hartman's analysis of "ought." Taken no further, Hartman's analysis lacks one significant feature of the "ought" concept that many philosophers have much emphasized—its imperative function or forcefulness. "Ought" usually says more than that it would be better to do it. "Ought" usually lures, nudges, or urges us toward action. This imperative element should be added to Hartman's understanding of "ought." When this is done, "You ought to do X" would mean "It would be better for you to do X, so do it."

Also, "better than" is not always strong enough for "ought," especially in an ethical context. If action X is better than Y, and Y is better than Z, which one ought we to do? "Better than" does not tell us, for both X and Y are "better than." We need Hartman's definition of "best," as given in Chapter One, to capture the full moral meaning of "ought." Axiologically, "best" means "having more good-making properties than anything else in its class of comparison." So, if action X is better than Y, and Y is better than Z, we ought to do X because it is the *best* thing we can do in that context. Ethically, "You ought to do X" would mean that "X is the best thing you could do morally, so do it."

The Form of the Good is the *basic axiom* of formal axiology, so, in application, the basic or *first ethical principle* of formal axiology is: *We ought always to identify-with, prefer, choose, and do what is best, that is, what is likely to be richest in good-making properties*. Frank G. Forrest calls the basic principle of axiology "the value creation principle," which he expresses as, *"Select courses of action, ideas, or forms of behavior that result in value creation or that, secondarily, are value neutral. Avoid those that depreciate it"* (Forrest, 2001, 40). Perhaps "the most" needs to be added just after his "that result in". Thus, we should strive ethically for *the most value creation*.

Just what this means needs more explaining, but, in terms of traditional ethical theory, axiological ethics is teleological rather than deontological. That is, its most fundamental concept is "good" rather than "right" or "ought." The definition of "good," not the definition of "ought," is the axiom or first principle of formal axiology.

3. Applying Intrinsic Concepts to Unique Persons

An ethical theory based on axiology tells us that when thinking about persons (and animals or God) we ought to apply intrinsic concepts to all unique conscious individuals. That is the best way to think about people, so do it. Beginning with thought, we ought always to see conscious beings or conceive of them in their fullest possible concrete individuality. This does not exclude thinking systemically and extrinsically about unique persons; it requires only that we first think intrinsically about them, that we not lose sight conceptually of the intrinsic richness and complete worth of unique human persons or other intrinsically valuable beings while applying systemic and extrinsic concepts to them.

How exactly do we go about applying intrinsic concepts to unique persons? Conceptually, is ethics just a matter of using proper names, first person pronouns, and metaphors? No, ethics requires much more than this. *Conceptually*, it requires understanding as much as we can of the incredibly rich meaning of any unique person's proper name and its corresponding pronoun, "I." According to Hartman, ethics requires understanding and applying to oneself the fullest possible answer to, "Who am I?" We must add that in relating to others it also requires understanding and applying the fullest possible answer to, "Who are you?" Consider Hartman's words.

> Let us look at the moral realm. Since goodness is conceptual fulfillment, moral value will appear as the fulfillment by a person of his own concept of himself. This concept is a singular concept, "I", whose intension, axiometrically structured according to the logic of singularity, will appear as the axiological measure of a person's moral worth. The person will be the more moral the more he fulfills his concept of his Self. Hence, moral terms such as "honest," "sincere," "genuine" will receive an exact axiological meaning, as will their opposites, "dishonest," insincere," and "not-genuine" (Hartman, 1967, 306. Compare Hartman, 2002, 252).

> The most important singular thing that each one of us possesses is himself. Each of us is given to himself and our task in life consists in knowing ourselves more and more, in familiarizing ourselves with ourselves more deeply, in becoming increasingly more who we are. Psychologically, this means becoming more and more integrated; axiologically, it means becoming more and more differentiated. The completely differentiated person is the person who is completely himself or, more specifically, the person who completely fulfills his concept of himself, which is the concept of "I." According to our definition of value, such a person is

a good person, and *this* goodness is the one we define as *moral* goodness. The various expressions for moral goodness, such as "sincere," "genuine," "honest," "authentic," "true to himself," all mean *being completely who one is.* This moral goodness is the subject matter of *Ethics* which is defined as *intrinsic value applied to the individual person, or the "I. "*Here we see how Ethics grows naturally out of axiology. (Hartman, "The Science of Value: Five Lectures on Formal Axiology," unpublished, 43).

I have moral value in the degree that I fulfill my own definition of myself. This definition is: "I am I." Thus, in the degree that I am I, I am a morally good person. Moral goodness is the depth of man's own being himself. That is the greatest goodness in the world. If every one of us and everyone in the world would just be himself and follow his own inner self or as we say, the voice of his conscience, then everything would straighten itself out, all the problems would just fall by the wayside. We wouldn't listen to false prophets, to politicians, to those who want to use us for their own ambitions. We would just be, and be ourselves. We would know the true values (Hartman, 1962a, 20).

So, on a conceptual level, before we even get to others, ethics consists in applying our own most fully differentiated concept of ourselves to ourselves. It consists in applying our "total integrated property inventory" to ourselves, which includes our ideals for our own futures. It consists first in knowing ourselves, then in being true to ourselves, in being authentic persons, in fulfilling our self-ideals and self-expectations. A great deal was said about this already in Sections D and E of Chapter Two. There we noted several important things about our concepts of ourselves that complicate Hartman's notion of ethics as applying "I" to oneself. These are:

A. We exist in time, so ethics has to take this into account.
B. Our self-concepts may be really screwed-up psychologically or morally, so ethics has to take this into account.
C. We think ethically about other people as well as about ourselves, so ethics has to be expanded beyond where Hartman left it. Ethics must also include not just our concepts of *ourselves* but also 1) our concepts of *other people* in their fully differentiated individuality, and 2) their concepts of us in our fully differentiated individuality.

A. Self-concepts and Time

We exist in time, so ethics has to take this into account. How can we be true to ourselves when much of what we will do and become has not yet been conceived or understood, much less created? What does being true to ourselves mean in light of the facts that we exist in time, that we are unfinished selves, that much of what we will do and become is not somehow already "out there" or even already "in us"

to be true to? Our "total property inventory" is incomplete and constantly growing or expanding. The "I" of the future is yet to be created, so how can we be true to it when it does not yet exist? Consider the *temporal* significance of Hartman's words above, now italicized: "Each of us is given to himself and *our task in life* consists in *knowing ourselves more and more*, in *familiarizing* ourselves with ourselves *more deeply*, in *becoming increasingly* more who we are. Psychologically, this means *becoming* more and more integrated; axiologically, it means *becoming* more and more differentiated."

If we are to know ourselves more and more, this means that we do not know ourselves completely right now, partly because we are *in process* of "becoming increasingly more who we are." The trouble is, there is no "we *are*" for our *future* selves; our futures do not yet exist; they are not given or available to us in the present tense; we do not foreknow them; they are not predestined. Our real task, aside from knowing who we have been and now are, is *to create who we will become*, to choose more fully actualized and differentiated selves for ourselves. *Becoming* authentic persons cannot be a matter of being true to something that already exists, something that is just out there waiting to be discovered. It involves *choosing who we will become*, or better yet, *who we ought to become, which includes what we ought to do.* Can axiology help us with that task? Perhaps so, in the following ways.

Theoretically, it should be possible to evaluate our past, present, and future selves in all three value dimensions—intrinsically, extrinsically, and systemically. Perhaps only the immediate present has the concreteness and vividness to be evaluated intrinsically, and we don't always do that. In one interesting (but possibly exaggerated) passage, Hartman explained that we can evaluate both the past and the future only systemically because they have only a finite number of properties in our memories and anticipations (Hartman, 1995a, 58). Despite what Hartman thought, we are finite through and through, even in the present as well as in the past and future, so finitude is not the real issue. The past typically lacks experiential vividness and concreteness, and all futures, including our own, exist only as relatively vague and indefinite possibilities. Are these qualifications insuperable obstacle to evaluating our past, present, and future in all three ways? Probably not. Even in their indefiniteness, we can and usually do identify intensely with (intrinsically value) our own pasts, presents, and futures.

Hartman maintained that comparative "better than" judgments can be made *only* in the realm of extrinsic values because having *two members of a given class* that can be compared is always extrinsic. Comparative judgments cannot be made about individuals, he claimed, because they are "one of a kind." However, this is an oversimplification when applied to people. *Intrinsic comparisons* can take place for better or for worse. Each of us unique persons can conceptually or imaginatively envision many futures for ourselves. *There are many future unique selves that we could choose to bring about or create, many future acts that we could choose to perform, many future thoughts that we might think, and these definitely can be compared.* Axiologically, our possible future selves *can* be compared as better or worse, even though they are only our own, and in doing so we can and should use the fundamental moral principle of formal axiology, which is: *We ought always to identify-with, prefer, choose, and do what is best, that is, what is likely to be richest in good-making properties.*

Our presently unfinished selves can indeed envision many different futures for ourselves, many different things that we might later do or become. We can imagine a diversity of more differentiated future selves, even if they are all somewhat vague, and *about these, we can make intrinsic comparative judgments.* We can determine that some of these future selves would be *better*, i.e., richer in good-making properties, than others. We ought to actualize the *best* of these.

For example, we might choose to further develop our intellectual talents at the expense of our practical and intrinsic capacities, or to further develop our practical talents at the expense of our intellectual or intrinsic capacities, or to further develop our intrinsic capacities at the expense of our systemic and extrinsic capacities. For our own futures, we could (and we usually do) choose to live axiologically impoverished lives, to be axiological underachievers in one or more value dimensions. A comparatively more excellent future for us is possible and conceivable—one in which we are *as fully and richly developed in all dimensions of value as we can possibly become.* That is the *best* of the multiple futures that we can choose for ourselves. Thus, it is the one future self that we ought to choose to become. Note that all of these possible futures for ourselves can be conceived and compared. Being and becoming *a fully ethical self* consists in choosing to become the most value-fulfilled persons that we can possibly become. *Living lives that are as rich in goodness in all value dimensions as we can possibly make them is the real axiological meaning of "being true to ourselves."*

Our given selves, our past selves, our personal histories, and our existing dispositions and talents, lay constraints upon what we as unique individuals can think, choose, prefer, do, and become. We are finite beings; we have limitations. None of us will ever become *equally* well developed or *fully* well developed in all dimensions of value. Having our own distinctive "natural bent" is actually an integral and inescapable part of being the unique persons that we actually are. If our strongest value capacities are practical and extrinsic, we should go with our strengths, while trying our best also to further enrich our lives by becoming more thoughtful and informed, and more loving and caring. If our strongest value capacities are primarily intellectual, we should go with our strengths, while working as hard as we can to become more practical and personable. If our strongest value capacities are primarily intrinsic, we should strive also to increase our practical and social skills as well as our learning and thinking skills, so that we won't be just "effete" intellectuals, mindless doers, or love slobs. Just how far we can push our own personal axiological growth in any value dimension depends on the specifics of our own concrete uniqueness and definiteness, including our willfulness.

Aristotle championed the ideal of the "mean between the extremes," but he recognized that the mean varies from one person to another. Too little food and exercise for the athlete would be too much food and exercise for the average business person or scholar. No exact formula exists to tell us how much axiological self-development in any given direction is enough. Making our lives as rich as possible in every dimension of value is relative to our unique individuality, which includes our distinctive interests, talents, and limitations. There is always room for growth in every value dimension, even if we will always be somewhat unbalanced. Personal growth should not be significantly unbalanced, even though it can never be perfectly balanced.

B. Screwed-up Self Concepts

Our self-concepts may be really screwed-up, so ethics has to take this into account. We don't always know what is best for ourselves, so ethics can't be a simple matter of *fulfilling our concepts of ourselves*, despite what Hartman said. We can't simply be true to ourselves or our total reality, because our future selves just don't exist to be true to; and we can't simply be true to what we now think is best for ourselves because our present personalities and self-ideals may be really screwed-up in more ways than one.

Personal inadequacies actually show up when people take the Hartman Value Profile. Depending on our age and other factors, we may have a very immature concept of "I." No matter what our age, we may have a very unclear, poorly developed, conflicted, immoral, or wrong-headed self-understanding. We may have one or more of virtually innumerable axiological astigmatisms. We may be very confused about who we are. We may be poorly integrated bundles of psychological conflict and want very incompatible things for and from ourselves. We may just be very immoral persons deep down inside, though in his optimism Hartman doubted that anyone was like this. Realists may know better!

We may need professional counseling for many serious "problems in living" that are based on distorted self-images or self-ideals. We may just need to talk to a friend or family member about who we want to become, because we really don't know. We may need help in setting or re-setting our priorities when we demand conflicting things of ourselves. We may have inflated aspirations that far exceed our real talents and abilities. We may have rigidly perfectionistic self-ideals or concepts of ourselves. We may need moral or spiritual counseling and development that far exceed our present imagination, self-understanding, and self-concepts. We may have a serious mental illness manifesting currently unavoidable irrationality. In such cases, telling us to be "true to ourselves" would be a gross and irrelevant oversimplification.

In more ways than we can imagine, *we may have unreliable concepts of ourselves that we should not try to fulfill.* Fulfilling them would be bad for us, not good for us! Fulfilling them would be unethical, not ethical! Fulfilling them would be irrational, self-defeating, self-destructive. Fulfilling them would be impossible if we are riddled with conflicts. As long as we are mature and mentally competent, it would be morally wrong for anyone to try to force a new self-ideal upon us or coerce us to fulfill it; but this does not mean that we should always be faithful to our present self-image or self-concept. Deep down inside, there may or may not be an unconscious and well integrated "real moral self" to which we should be faithful. Hartman thought so, but this may or may not be true. Certainly this possibility requires more serious consideration.

One weighty problem with defining "ethics" as fulfilling our concepts of ourselves is this. Exactly which self-concept is relevant, our confused, conflicted, and poorly developed present conscious concept, our "deep down" well integrated unconscious or semi-conscious concept, the self-concept that wise counselors might help us to create, the self-concept that axiology says we ought to have, or what?

The best axiological/ethical answer to all problems of screwed-up self-concepts is this: *The self-concept that everyone ought to fulfill is the one that is richest in goodness, that is, richest in good-making properties in all dimensions of value.* Axiologically understood, this is the self-concept that everyone should seek, but *it is not the self concept that everyone actually has.* This is the self-concept that all parents, relatives, friends, associates, counselors, consultants, professional helpers, and therapists should help others (as well as themselves) to find or create. This is the ultimate aim of what Hartman called "Axiotherapy," about which he wrote, "The healthy person who does not require psychotherapy or psychoanalysis yet desires a new meaning of his life, can be helped by the test [The Hartman Value Profile] to revise and reorder his values. This process is called Axiotherapy" (Hartman, 2006, 43). Whenever "a new meaning of his [or her] life" is sought, this implies that the old meaning (the old self-concept) is inadequate, and this person should not be true to it.

From an axiological point of view, the *best* meaning (self-concept) that all persons should seek is the one that, for them in their uniqueness, is as rich in value in all dimensions as is practically, humanly, and personally achievable. To arrive at such self-understanding, we often need help from others. *Sometimes, the self-concept that we ought to fulfill is not our own but the one that someone else has of us, someone with greater insight into and wisdom about how we might live more or most abundantly in all three value dimensions.* If other people can help us arrive at a self-concept-to-be-fulfilled that is better than the one we now have, axiological ethics requires us to take *their* concepts of what we ought to be like into account, and to change rather than to be faithful to our less-than-adequate concepts of ourselves.

So, ethics is not merely a matter of applying *our unrefined* concepts of ourselves to ourselves, or of acting to fulfill such self-concepts. Rather, ethics in the first person is applying the *best possible* concepts of ourselves to ourselves, and of acting to fulfill the best possible and available self-concepts.

C. Thinking Ethically about Others

We think ethically about other people as well as about ourselves, so ethics cannot be merely a matter of fulfilling our best available self-concepts. Ethics has to be expanded to include both 1) our concepts of other people in their fully differentiated individuality, and 2) their concepts of us in our fully differentiated individuality.

How do or should we think about other people ethically? Our answer to this question is an integral aspect of our own self-concept. What kind of a person am I, or should I be, with respect to how I think about other people and other conscious beings? My self-concept-of-others-that-ought-to-be-fulfilled includes not only the way I *think* about others but also the way I *act* upon them, how I *feel* toward them, and the degree to which I *identify* with them. The way we think about other people strongly influences how we act toward them, how we feel about them, and whether we can identify with them. The immediate questions is, "Who am I in the way that I think about other people (or other conscious beings like God and the animals)?"

We can think about other people or unique conscious beings in one of three, two of three, or all three ways—systemically, extrinsically, and intrinsically.

Sometimes, we think of others *only systemically.* When applying prejudicial or stereotypical labels to conscious beings, we are thinking of them only systemically. Thinking up ways to conceive of other people only systemically, can be quite ingenious, and doing so is socially prevalent. This happens in the business world when people are categorized as *only* laborers, managers, customers, capitalists, etc., and everything else about them is ignored. In the everyday world it happens whenever we use only racial or any other "black or white" stereotypes to drastically reduce the real significance of, and ignore the inherent goodness of, other people. Purely systemic thinking about people ignores the richness of their good-making properties and either reduces their significance to almost nothing, or to something undesirable or bad. People become "nobodies," or even something worse.

Consider what we might call "war-speak." In war-speak, persons are reduced to numbers, as on dog-tags, or to statistics, as in body counts or as casualty tallies. Civilian casualties are disguised as "collateral damage," and military casualties are merely "bomb damage assessments" or so many "body bags."

There is something morally pernicious about the familiar distinction between "soldiers" and "innocent civilians." This is not because the distinction exalts civilians; it is that it degrades soldiers; both soldiers and civilians should be equally exalted! Most people probably do not realize this, but it is worth serious consideration. When we put uniforms on soldiers, that says in effect that they are no longer persons, so it is OK to kill or maim them, but if people are not wearing uniforms, they are real persons, so it is wrong to kill or maim them. As Hartman explained, "If one contends, as has been done on many occasions, that it is not people but soldiers that are killed in war, then one simply is saying that soldiers are not people, which happens to be the crux of the problem of war" (Hartman, 1991a, 201). In other social contexts, soldiers may be very proud of their uniforms, but on the battlefield, uniforms are a license to kill. In modern wars where our "enemies" do not wear uniforms, no one knows who to kill and who not to kill, who is a real human being and who is a mere soldier.

Much military training and indoctrination involves conditioning new recruits not to consider enemy soldiers as real people. Soldiers cannot afford to think about the full concrete individuality of the "enemies" they have to kill, that is, about the richness of their lives, their strong and equal will to live, their plans and hopes for the future, their friends, families, wives, children, and loved ones. Using only systemic words to classify people as close to worthless, or as completely devoid of good-making properties, rationalizes immoral indifference, callousness, malice, and downright destructiveness. Such is war. Psychologically, shooting, bombing, injuring, maiming, incinerating, or otherwise destroying something that is "worthless" is very easy. The nightmares and Post Traumatic Stresses come later.

Sometimes we think of people *only* extrinsically. We connive to *use people* as mere means to our ends without respecting and honoring their own ends, desires, interests, or well-being. Recall that using people is not a moral problem unless we are *merely* using them. Thinking about other people *merely* as means makes it easy psychologically to treat them that way. How we *think* about other people has great moral significance. Using language to depreciate people is downright immoral, even if commonplace, generally accepted, and widely practiced. Purely systemic or purely extrinsic thinking about people reduces their real significance and ignores all their good-making properties except their usefulness or their systemic conformity and compliance. Merely systemic and merely extrinsic thinking about other people do not take their full concrete individuality into account. Both fail to conceive of other people as ends in themselves. Both ignore or devalue their total inventory of good-making properties, their unique intrinsic worth.

We might and often do think about other people in both systemic and extrinsic terms all at once. For example, "color of skin" as the only entitlement to moral standing and significance is systemically reductive, using only extrinsic properties like "color" and "skin" as indicators of significance, personal worth, and full membership in the moral community, or lack thereof. All merely systemic and extrinsic thinking about other people reduces their moral significance, disregards their full individuality, and fails to treat them as intrinsically valuable ends in themselves. As indicated, on the conceptual level, being *unethical* may involve "*applying only systemic and/or extrinsic concepts to persons.*" As we think in our minds, so we do, and so we become and so we are in our minds, hearts, and deeds.

Ethically, the best way to think about people is the intrinsic way. As long as this comes first, systemic and extrinsic thinking about people are morally permitted.

Ethics does not require us to ignore or be dishonest about our differences. Hartman mentioned thinking of *ourselves* as "sincere," "genuine," "honest," "authentic," and "true to ourselves," but we can also think about *others* in such terms. Many additional ways of thinking about ourselves and of thinking about how we think about others also have great ethical significance. Does our self-concept-to-be fulfilled include being loving, empathetic, and compassionate persons? Do we have intrinsic as well as systemic and extrinsic aspirations?

The cognitive "scripts" that we allow to run through our minds make an enormous difference to the way we actually feel and act. If we think fearful thoughts, we are likely to become more fearful; but if we think more courageously, we are likely to become and be more courageous. If we think pessimistic thoughts we are likely to become emotionally and dispositionally pessimistic and depressed; but if we think optimistic thoughts, we are likely to become more optimistic and healthy minded. If we think hostile thoughts, we are likely to become more hostile; but if we consistently think friendly thoughts, we are well down the road toward friendliness. If we think hateful, manipulative, callous, condescending, snobby, spiteful, or other-diminishing thoughts, we are likely to become hateful, manipulative, callous, condescending, snobby, spiteful, or other-diminishing; but if we discipline ourselves to think more lovingly, empathetically, and compassionately about others, we are likely to become more loving, empathetic, and compassionate. If we allow ourselves to think in immoral ways about other people, we are likely to become more and more immoral; but if we can train and constrain ourselves to think more morally about other people, we are likely to become more and more ethical. How we think about others and about ourselves is largely under our voluntary control, though we do not always realize it. We really can choose to think more ethically. Do we conceive of ourselves as ethically virtuous persons? Is that a central part of our own self-concepts-to-be-fulfilled? As people think of themselves and about others in their hearts and minds, so they are, and so they act.

4. Acting Upon Self and Others as Unique Persons

Although Hartman defined ethics as fulfilling our *concepts* of ourselves, he did not ignore *moral action.* Fulfilling requires acting; acting can be fulfilling. Conceiving spills over into doing. Do we conceive of ourselves, not just as *thinking* ethically about others, but also as *acting* ethically toward others? *How we should act toward others is an integral part of our self-concepts-to-be-fulfilled.*

Most philosophers understand "ethics" to be primarily if not entirely about how we *act* toward others. Hartman most emphasized self-fulfillment, thus duties toward ourselves, but some philosophers have doubted that we have any ethical duties at all toward ourselves. Kant, for example, thought that we always naturally do what is best for ourselves (a totally unrealistic view, as every clinical psychologist knows!), so we have no ethical duties to ourselves at all.

Philosophers (like Hartman) who think that we do have moral duties to ourselves also emphasize our moral duties toward others. Hartman himself wrote, "Ethics has as its subject matter human conduct. Systematic ethics, thus, deals with the knowledge of human conduct and makes this knowledge more precise" (Hartman, 1967, 58). The purpose of ethics, he wrote, is to "teach people how to live 'good' lives" (Hartman, 1991b, 12). Thus, axiologically understood, ethics as fulfilling our concepts of ourselves includes *conceiving of ourselves as acting toward others in morally acceptable and appropriate ways*.

Ethical acting should be in accord with the basic or first moral principle of formal axiology, which is: *We ought always to identify-with, prefer, choose, and do what is best, that is, what is likely to be richest in good-making properties*. In more familiar words, we ought to just *"Do good."* But more must be said about this. Our actions have consequences for others as well as for ourselves. Axiological ethics requires that we act to bring about the best possible consequences for ourselves and for others, and that we avoid acting in ways that are harmful to ourselves and others.

Historically, ethical theories were divided into "teleological" and "deontological" types.

Deontological ethical theories take moral concepts like "ought," "right," "rules," "laws," and "duties" as ethically fundamental; teleological theories hold that "good" is the most fundamental ethical concept, with "better" and "best" not far behind. Deontological theories sometimes say that we ought to do our duty, to follow moral rules, even when doing so will most likely result in less good than not following them, or than making exceptions to them. Teleological theories say that we ought to do what is likely to have the best results, and that moral rules are generally reliable but not infallible guidelines to fulfilling that purpose. Deontological theories hold that doing our moral duty, that is, doing what moral rules require us to do, is an end in itself, valuable for its own sake, no matter what. Teleological theories hold that only unique conscious individuals are valuable as ends, valuable in, to, and for themselves, valuable for their own sake, and that our duty is to treat unique conscious beings in value-sustaining and value-enhancing ways, or at least to choose the "lesser of evils," if evils there must be. Deontological theories hold that we exist for and should act for the sake of moral rules; teleological theories hold that moral rules exist for our sake, to guide us toward beneficial-to-people and away from harmful-to-people courses of action. In deontological theories, systemic rules come first; in teleological theories, goodness comes first. In Hartman's teleological theory, intrinsic goodness of and for people and other conscious individuals comes first.

Hartman, who aspired to develop a scientific ethics, clearly came down on the side of "the good" and of teleological ethics. He wrote,

In the light of G. E. Moore's analysis, scientific ethics must be based on the nature of good; all ethical terms, including "ought," must be deduced from it. From the point of view of scientific ethics in the Moorean sense, basing axiology on "ought" rather than on "good" is the wrong choice....

The more rationally inclined writers are, the more they will tend toward "good"' the less rationally inclined, the more they will tend toward "ought" (Hartman, 2002, 279, 280).

As previously explained, in Hartmanian axiology, "ought" just means "what is better or best (or least harmful)—so do it." What is better or best is that which is richer or richest in good-making properties. So, the ethical "ought" requires us to act in ways that are likely to have consequences that are richest in good-making properties for ourselves and for others who are affected by what we do.

Ethical theories have traditionally included accounts of A. Moral Rights, B. Moral Rules and Exceptions, C. Moral Virtues, D. Moral Motives and Attitudes, and E. Moral Absolutes. All of these have a bearing on acting in morally correct ways upon ourselves and other unique persons. How would an axiological ethics deal with each of these?

A. Moral Rights

Moral rights received very little direct attention from Hartman himself, though much that he wrote has an indirect bearing upon the topic. Individual moral rights are personal entitlements to be treated ethically as ends by others in certain very fundamental ways. Moral duties and rights are correlative. When individual persons have moral rights, others have moral duties to them—to respect them and act in accord with or to secure those rights.

From an axiological perspective, rights exist to protect and provide for the intrinsic worth of individual persons or conscious beings. They presuppose that conscious individuals have intrinsic worth. They insist that although this inner core of intrinsic worth can be, it should not be, threatened, damaged, or destroyed by the actions of others. Some rights require not merely that harm be avoided but, more positively, that the necessities for living well identified by the corresponding rights be provided or secured. Where children have a moral right to a basic education and everyone has a moral right to basic health care, other people (society, government, churches, charities, etc.) have positive duties to provide these essentials. Individual rights exist to protect the intrinsic worth of individuals from harm by the unwarranted intrusion of others and by natural or social deprivations that others ought to act to alleviate. Moral rights can be enacted into law as legal rights. Legitimate legal rights presuppose moral rights. *We can and do legislate morality.*

No infallible or complete list of human moral rights exists anywhere, but most of us are familiar with those mentioned in the "Declaration of Independence," the

"Bill of Rights" to our Constitution, and the "The Universal Declaration of Human Rights" of the United Nations. We are familiar with the rights:

- to life, liberty, and the pursuit of happiness,
- to equality before and under the law,
- to freedom of speech, thought, and communication,
- to vote,
- to a basic education,
- to basic health care,
- to freedom of conscience,
- to freedom of religion,
- to informed voluntary consent with respect to medical care
- to freedom of movement and assembly,
- to freedom from torture and slavery,
- to freedom from discrimination based on race, sex, age, religion, or sexual preferences,
- to equality of opportunity,
- to own and dispose of property,
- to fair compensation for work, and so on.

From an axiological point of view, these rights exist to protect, to provide for, and for the sake of, the intrinsic worth of individuals. They forbid others to act extrinsically toward and upon us in ways that violate our basic intrinsic worth. They require others to provide needy persons with the basic necessities of human existence. In one brief discussion of human rights, Hartman said that communistic nations fail to provide systemic legal rights (to liberties like those above) whereas capitalistic countries fail to provide social human rights to security (the basic necessities of life, health care, etc.). He continued,

> The extrinsic valuation of man's intrinsic value means to guarantee a person the material benefits due to his human dignity, his right to a dignified nonalienating job and remuneration, to housing and all the other demands of social justice in the intrinsic or moral sense. Here belong all demands for social welfare; "Welfare" supplies the intrinsic dimension to social justice (Hartman, 1976, 140).

Can human rights be ranked axiologically in accord with the Hierarchy of Value? Perhaps so, at least roughly, as follows.

Intrinsic rights are the most basic or fundamental rights of all. They are the rights that most protect intrinsic human worth, including the hard core set of intrinsic human and individuating properties. *The rights to life* and to *the elemental necessities of life* like *basic health care* aim to protect, preserve, or restore the complete human self or person, especially the hard core of a person's total integrated property inventory. With the loss of life, all else is lost, and no other rights matter. The right to life protects individuals from being directly killed by others. Other rights also protect personal dignity, individuality, and intrinsic worth from unwarranted intrusion, damage, or destruction by others. *Rights to freedom of conscience, to freedom of religion, to freedom of thought, to informed voluntary consent, to freedom from torture and slavery, and to freedom from discrimination based on such things as race, sex, age, religion, or sexual preferences* also seem to be rights that protect basic intrinsic worth, the hard core of unique personhood. Some people would add the right *to a "good death"* to this list.

Extrinsic rights come next, though not far behind intrinsic rights. They protect and provide for the extrinsic-action parts of the human self or person. Among such extrinsic rights seem to be the *rights to vote, to freedom of movement and assembly, to equality of opportunity, to own and dispose of property, to fair compensation for work, to dignified work, to equal pay for equal work, etc.* Such rights are not very far removed from intrinsic rights, for loss or lack of them results first in misery and can ultimately result in personal disintegration and/or death.

Systemic rights come third or last. They either provide for and protect the cognitive parts of the human self or person, or else they provide *legal* protections for all basic moral rights. Among these would seem to be the *rights to freedom of speech, thought, and communication,* (overlapping intrinsic rights), *to a basic education, and to equal protection under the law.*

Doubtless, many rights do not fall primarily or neatly into only one dimension of value, and all of the above rights are most effective when taken together as a complete value-combination package. No one is adequately protected without rights in all three value dimensions. Without life itself, extrinsic and systemic rights are pointless, and their significance would probably seem negligible or irrelevant while being tortured. Without the basic necessities of life, no time or energy remains for the "higher things of life" like moral conscience and endeavor, higher education, and religion or spirituality. According to Abraham Maslow's "hierarchy of needs," basic physical needs or necessities must be met first, and only then do higher human needs and interests come into play. Little time or energy is available for the pursuit or exercise of knowledge where there is little or no life and the necessities that sustain it. Yet, without knowledge and the liberty to communicate it, we cannot effectively protect ourselves, the inner cores of our individualities, the people we love, or the institutions, practices, and physical environment that sustain us. In ignorance, we do not know what our rights are or how to claim them; we do not even know how to acquire the basic necessities of life; and being knowers, doers, and lovers, is essential to who we are intrinsically. Rights in all value dimensions inhere in and complement one another.

B. Moral Rules, Exceptions, Conflicts, and Supererogation

Moral Rules also received very little direct attention from Hartman himself. Yet, an ethics based on axiology should have something meaningful to say about them. So what is it? Let's now consider

    i. The value of moral rules

    ii. Making exceptions to moral rules

    iii. Conflicting moral rules, and

    iv. Supererogation: Going beyond the call of duty.

i. The Value of Moral Rules

Moral rules are systemic value-objects; they are not intrinsic or extrinsic value-objects. As such they are the least valuable aspects of morality—less valuable than moral action, and less valuable than people or other conscious beings. Moral rules are not ends in themselves; they are not valuable for their own sake, for they have no "own sake;" that is, they have no consciousness, interests, or values of their own. They are not intrinsic absolutes; people are intrinsic absolutes, though finite. We do not exist for the sake of "the law;" the law exists for our sake. Moral rules are useful general guidelines for doing good and not doing evil, nothing more. They are action-guiding rules expressed in terms of "duty," "ought," "ought not," "right," and "wrong." They are most effective when socially supported, taught, and commended, that is, when they are established institutional or cultural practices.

Though they are not ends in themselves, moral rules can be exceptionally helpful in guiding us toward treating people as ends in themselves, but we should avoid becoming "rule worshipers," and we should try to separate essential and effective rules from those that are unessential, trivial, misinformed, outdated, or even unconscionable. All societies have moral rules of some kind, and, as someone said, they represent "*the funded moral wisdom of the ages*" with respect to doing the morally right or correct thing. At least the best and most defensible of them do this. Yet many socially funded rules may be obsolete or morally objectionable. They cannot simply be taken "as is" without careful critical consideration. We need not only to do what is best but also to find the best guidelines for doing it.

Advising us simply to "Do good" or to "Be good, then do as you please," and nothing more, would resemble Hartman's story about asking someone to go get your car from the parking lot. "Which one?" he asks. "The good one!" you reply. Well, with only that much information, he will never find your car! (Hartman, 1967, 102-103). Similarly with nothing more than "Do good" or "Be good" as supreme moral principles. They are so abstract that they give little guidance; much more information is needed. More specific or concrete moral guidelines, often called "secondary rules," are required for knowing exactly how to go about "doing good" and "being good." Like rights, there is no complete and authoritative list of helpful moral rules, but most of us will recognize the ones identified in what follows—some negative, some positive.

Negatively, we ought not to kill, steal, lie, commit adultery, envy, or harm others in the innumerable ways that this can be done. Positively, we ought to help those in need and distress, to observe, protect, and provide for human rights, to do unto others as we would have them do unto us, to forgive rather than seek revenge, to be virtuous persons—kind, considerate, honest, truthful, loyal, forgiving, compassionate, loving, and so on. More will be said about moral virtues as this discussion progresses.

ii. Making Exceptions to Moral Rules

Moral rules can be formulated in various ways, and axiology ought to help us to form or express them more clearly and efficiently. One of the toughest philosophical problems about expressing and adopting reasonable moral rules has always been *making and legitimizing exceptions.* For example, consider two ways of formulating a moral rule against killing:

1) It is wrong to kill another person, no matter what.
2) It is wrong to kill another person, except
   a. during a defensive or otherwise "just" war,
   b. in self-defense, when no other alternative is available,
   c. in defense of loved-ones, friends, or other immediately endangered persons, when no other realistic alternative is available,
   d. where an informed dying patient voluntarily requests or gives present or advance directives for active or passive euthanasia when in excruciating and unrelievable pain.
   e. where an informed dying patient voluntarily requests or gives advance directives for active or passive euthanasia when irreversibly comatose.
   f. where required for purposes of capital punishment—a very controversial exception.

Exception f. is very controversial, and so are exceptions d. and e.

Systemic absolutists who stand up for "principles" no matter what would be attracted to 1) above. Intrinsic absolutist might be attracted to something like 2) above because these exceptions seem to put real people above abstract principles. The troublesome thing about these exceptions is that they all involve harming people for the sake of helping people. They involve "the lesser of evils," that is, doing something bad for the sake of something good or to avoid something even worse. Can axiology help us to understand and accept this? Can it show us how to justify doing bad for the sake of something good or to avoid something worse? Perhaps so.

Toward the end of his life, Robert S. Hartman wrote an article, published after his death, titled "The Value Structure of Justice." There he conceived of *justice* so broadly that it was almost identical with creating any positive value composition; and *injustice* was practically identical with creating any negative value transposition. In this article he also advanced the narrower notion of *corrective justice*, defined as "the relevant disvaluation of a value transposition," and as "the relevant disvaluation of the injustice" that must "*invert the act of injustice and through this inversion disvalue the injustice*" (Hartman, 1976, 132). He also called it the "relevant disvaluation of disvaluation." Using the "I," "E," and "S" symbolism for each of the three value dimensions, he gave many illustrations such value combinations. He also gave a general axiological formula for corrective justice. In this formula, "U" stands for one value and "V" for a second value, as follows:

> The formula here is $(U_V)_U V$, the correction of an injustice by the corresponding justice, or the correction of the violation of a norm by the corresponding observance of the norm (Hartman, 1976, 145).

Frank G. Forrest points out that all of Hartman's formulas and illustrations on corrective justice are positive, that is, they cover only combating or correcting evil with goodness; but they do not cover combating or correcting evil with evil (Forrest, 2008), which is what we often need in making and justifying exceptions to moral rules. Over the years, Forrest gave much careful consideration to doing bad for the sake of good or to avoid something even worse. In his most recent book, *Ethical Decision Making for the 21st Century,* Forrest calls it "Justifying Wrongs and Badness." He says that it is a matter of "transposing transpositions with transpositions," and, using transfinite math, he shows how to make formal calculations about such things (Forrest, 2001, 60-66). Elsewhere, he explained how to apply transposing transpositions to making exceptions to moral rules (Forrest, 1995, 160-165). The book you are now reading will not attempt to duplicate or explain the details of the creative work that Forrest has done in developing and applying the transfinite axiological calculus to ethical issues. This book is an *introduction* to the *Essentials of Formal Axiology* that will help to prepare you for and point you toward further work, including Forrest's significant contributions to formal axiology. (See the references to Forrest in the "Works Cited" at the end of this book, and see the discussion of "Other Applications" at the end of this chapter).

Of special relevance, "transposing transpositions with transpositions" (combating evil with evil) may be very helpful in identifying legitimate exceptions to general moral rules (like a. through e. above). On your own, consider whether this might help identify reasonable or justified exceptions to other general moral prohibitions of acts like stealing, lying, promise breaking, etc.

The upshot of this is, the disvaluation of a disvalue by a "corresponding" or "relevant" disvalue can result in a positive value, or in avoiding something even worse. You have no doubt heard of "Fighting fire with fire" and that "Two wrongs don't make a right." But maybe two wrongs DO make a right—where the second evil corrects or counterbalances the first—just as a "double negation" in English grammar results in a positive. *Acts that might otherwise be wrong turn out not to be wrong when they properly correct (that is, disvalue) another wrong.* Of course, there must be proper "relevance" or "correspondence," which seems to mean that the second or correcting wrong should not be greater than or out of proportion to the first. The correcting evil must not be greater than the evil being corrected, and no less extreme measures are realistically available or workable in those circumstances.

Consider first exceptions a. through c. above. Killing someone ("the enemy") in a just war does irreparable harm to the enemy; it deprives him or her of life itself, on which all other values and rights depend. Presumably, it is done to prevent the enemy from killing you, your fellow soldiers, your fellow citizens, or other innocent persons. A long tradition expressing the good-making properties of a "just war" is available, though not further explored here, but an axiological analysis of "just war" theory might be very illuminating. The essential point is that in a just war, the enemy is out to kill for unwarranted reasons, and someone has to "fight back," which is to combat evils with lesser evils. Killing unjustly aggressive enemies to save "innocent" lives is doing evil to prevent even worse evil, correcting disvalues with proportional disvalues, transposing transpositions.

The same considerations apply in non-war situations with respect to exceptions like killing in self-defense and to protect loved ones, assuming that no less destructive alternatives are available. In euthanasia situations, cases d. and e., the harm to be rectified is usually being effected by "natural causes," not by human enemies. Yet, extreme and irreversible harm is being done, and self-chosen death may be the least bad alternative. Justified exceptions to moral rules are usually the "lesser of two evils." As for executing murderers, what do you think that accomplishes? Is it the least bad of all of the available alternatives?

Although Hartman did not apply it this way, the idea of counterbalancing evils with proportional or lesser evils might help us to identify legitimate exceptions to moral rules, indeed to include justified exceptions within the rules themselves, as in 2) above. *Where no less extreme alternatives are viable, and killing is the last resort,* can exceptions a. through e. or f. above to "Killing is wrong" be justified because they counterbalance evils with proportional or lesser evils?

Generally speaking, making exceptions to, or including exceptions within, the meaning of moral rules is justified *when not making them would very likely have worse results than making them,* or *when making them would very likely have better results than not making them.* This is simply an application of the basic principle of ethics, *We ought always to identify-with, prefer, choose, and do what is best, that is, what is likely to be richest in good-making properties.* In many moral predicaments, the best available course of action is the one that is least harmful.

iii. Conflicting Moral Rules

Most problems about *conflicting moral rules* can be resolved with the foregoing "lesser of evils" principle. Absolutistic moral rules that allow *no exceptions* often come into conflict. For example, if you know that person A is out to murder person B, and you know where B is hiding, should you tell the truth when A asks you if you know where B is? Or should you lie to save B's life? "Save lives" (with suitable exceptions) is the positive corollary to "Don't kill" (with suitable exceptions). In the present situation, the venerable moral rule of "Save lives" clearly conflicts with "Don't lie." This is actually a conflict of an intrinsic good with a systemic good, so which has priority? Obviously, the intrinsic, so you should try to save the life of B by lying.

Philosophers who like Kant rank systemic values such as "the moral law" highest say that you should tell the truth no matter what. What do you think? What does your carefully considered conscience tell you? Which course of action would likely have the worse results, which the least harmful? Kant thought that we should never consider results or consequences of any kind (like saving lives); we should only consider simplistic rules for their own sake (e.g., "Don't lie"). He refused to consider making exceptions to moral rules because he confused self-serving exceptions with generally beneficial exceptions. Which version of the rule against lying could *you* will to be a universal law, "Don't lie, no matter what," or "Don't lie, unless it will likely save one or more life," or (plus other suitable exceptions)? Your answer will reflect how you rank systemic in relation to intrinsic values.

iv. Supererogation: Going Beyond the Call of Duty

Another age-old problem for ethicists who emphasize good over right is that of *going beyond the call of duty,* or what philosophers call *"supererogation."* Many ethicists suggest that everyone ought to be required to fulfill minimal obligations to one another like respecting one another's rights, but at some point "doing good" exceeds these minimal requirements, ceases to be a moral requirement, and becomes morally optional. We should not moralize the whole of life, they say. Beyond some point of minimal human decency and respect, they say, being motived and acting to maximize goodness go "beyond the call of duty," and doing what is best becomes desirable and voluntary but not morally obligatory. Saintliness or heroism that goes beyond what is minimally required or expected of ordinary people should be encouraged, but it should not be morally compulsory, they claim.

A teleological ethics *requires* people to *maximize* goodness, but critics often suggest that this is ideal is far too demanding for ordinary people. A *minimum* of moral decency and mutual respect can and should be required of everyone, but we should not expect or require everyone to make great heroic or saintly personal sacrifices for the well-being of all.

Axiology may be able to shed a little light on this problem of supererogation. The primary task of axiology is to help us understand goodness in both theory and application.

First, axiology does tell us to try to do what is best. No doubt about that! The best lives we can possibly lead are those that are richest in goodness, not only for ourselves, but also for others who are influenced or affected by our thoughts, attitudes, feelings, and actions. Second, axiology does indeed identify what is obligatory with what is best, for "ought" just means "best, so do it," as earlier noted. What we ought to do is what it would be best for us to do. Getting down to *specifics*, however, we must ask whether it would be morally best to *require* people to do far more than they are normally able and willing to do. The crucial thing here is the distinction between *requiring* and *encouraging* what is best.

What is involved in *moral requiring*? And how does this differ from *moral encouraging*? Both requiring and encouraging involve *identifying* courses of action that would be better or best, as well as *telling others* that certain actions would be better or best. Requiring, however, goes beyond identifying, honoring, and telling (encouraging); it involves *penalties* (evils) for not doing what is best, as John Stuart Mill indicated. The Utilitarian tradition in moral philosophy called these penalties "sanctions." Minimal sanctions include the evils of a guilty conscience and social disapproval (adverse public opinion), but sanctions can extend as far as unwanted fines, imprisonment, and using the police power of the state to enforce the rules. Moral sanctions thus involve externally or socially imposed evils for the sake of individual goodness or well-being, or for the sake of avoiding or preventing greater evils. *Requiring* has a negative price that *encouraging* does not have. Requiring is a value transposition, and the evils thereof must weighed in the balance, but encouraging is only a value composition.

Perhaps the problem of supererogation could be resolved with a consideration like this. *Don't use sanctions to support doing good and avoiding evil when it would be less harmful simply to encourage doing what is best or least harmful.* Up to a certain point, (e.g., with respect to protecting people's basic rights), penalties seem to be worth the price. Evils to combat evils seem justified as long as they are not worse than the evils being combated. Would the evils involved in forcing people to be saints and heroes at all times be like this?

Saints and heroes voluntarily make great personal sacrifices for the sake of the well-being of others or the common good. Extreme personal sacrifices involve voluntarily accepted disvalues—the evils (pains, losses, wounds, even death) of the sacrifices. That's why we call them "sacrifices." In extreme circumstances, saints and heroes will voluntarily "lay down their lives" for others. Unlike externally imposed penalties, saintly and heroic sacrifices are self-chosen and harmonize with their highest self-ideals and their virtuous loving-kindness toward others.

Somewhere between penalizing wrongdoing and making extreme saintly sacrifices for the well being of others, the weight shifts away from harmful penalties for wrongdoing and toward voluntarily accepting disvalues for extreme rightdoing. Up to some point, not socially imposing penalties for wrongdoing would likely have worse consequences than imposing them; but beyond that point, imposing them would be worse than not imposing them. Recall that "worse" formally means "having the most bad-making properties." Should the *extreme* self-chosen harms involved in saintly and heroic rightdoing be imposed by a guilty conscience, by social disapproval, or by the police power of the state with its jails and prisons? Or would the price of penalizing people for not being great saints and heroes at all times be too high? How that question is answered determines one's position on supererogation.

Penalizing people for not being saints and heroes all the time would be a value transposition. Both axiologically, and intuitively to most people, this would be much worse than just *encouraging* people to make such sacrifices, a value composition. Simply allowing saints and heroes to choose the harms of self-sacrifice for themselves with no penalties or disapproval if they don't seems to be the least bad choice. Social penalties or disvalues for not observing basic moral decency like respecting one another's rights seem worth the price, but penalties like guilt, social disapproval, fines, imprisonment, or some kind of police enforcement for not making extreme personal sacrifices (self-chosen evils) do not. An adequate formal calculus of value (toward which others axiologists are working) should be able to make this clear—some day.

Axiology would perhaps draw the line separating basic moral decency from extreme saintly heroism somewhere between systemic and extrinsic values and valuations, on the one hand, and the most profound intrinsic values and valuations, on the other. Understanding and obeying behavioral rules that make for morally decent social orders involve little more than our ordinary systemic and extrinsic capacities and desires. Going far beyond the call of duty, however, involves more than this; it requires extraordinary heroic intrinsic-oriented action and uncommonly intense love, empathy, compassion for, and identification with others. These should be strongly encouraged, but with no penalties for inaction or failure, which precisely is supererogation. Saintliness and heroism involve not just minimal or ordinary but the greatest extraordinary intrinsic moral virtue, which should not be externally demanded or compelled, though it can and should be encouraged, honored, and celebrated in many ways.

You have probably heard it said that "We can't legislate morality." Well, perhaps this is true of exceptionally saintly and heroic morality, but we actually can and do legislate morality at the systemic and extrinsic levels. In fact, we do it quite successfully all the time, and systemic and extrinsic morality is the very thing that we should legislate! All our laws against murder, rape, perjury, discrimination, etc. legislate morality.

C. Ethics in Three Dimensions

As noted, Hartman's definition of ethics as "the application of intrinsic value to individuals" is much too narrow, too one-dimensional. Evaluating individual persons intrinsically is the height or peak of saintly morality, but protecting unique persons from harm and providing for and protecting the basics of human well being must start much lower on the self/others scale. This means that protecting people from harm and providing for the basics of human well being must start at the levels of systemic and extrinsic values and valuations. It means that we need ethics in all three dimensions, not just in the intrinsic dimension, not just at the level of valuing persons intrinsically. To get to the top of anything, we usually have to start at the bottom, and so it is with morality.

An adequate axiological account of morality, one that aims at maximum well-being or value-abundance for all unique conscious beings, not just for oneself, has to be developed at systemic, extrinsic, and intrinsic levels, all three.

1) At the level of *systemic morality*, we find moral rules, guidelines, laws, commandments, and the rational or impartial appreciation and adoption of them. At this level, we actually do constantly legislate morality quite successfully. It is morally wrong to murder people, and we have positive laws prohibiting murder. It is morally wrong to steal people's property, and we have positive laws prohibiting theft. It is morally wrong to violate anyone's basic rights, and we have laws that prohibit rights violations and provide for liberty and justice for all. It is morally wrong not to educate our children, and we have laws requiring people to send their children to school and to pay taxes to provide resources for that. It is morally wrong for medical professionals to impose medical tests, experiments, and treatments upon people without their informed voluntary consent, and we have laws that prohibit such things. It is morally wrong not to provide basic health care for all, and, like most countries in the western world, we in the United States should have laws requiring and providing resources for that. The health care reforms enacted in early 2010 may have changed things for the better. Systemically, we legislate as much morality as we know how to legislate effectively, or at least as much as our politicians have the integrity, wisdom, and courage to enact.

2) At the level of *extrinsic morality*, we *actually do* what basic moral rules, laws, and insights require us to do. Rules are the forms of morality; practical behaviors are the substance of morality. Without being saints and heroes, we do actually live decent everyday lives together, at least most of the time. We do not passionately love everyone, but we *know how to get along*, we normally *want* to get along or live in relative harmony, and *we normally do so*, even without exceptionally well developed (saintly) capacities for intrinsic valuation. We know how to respect both people and the law, or people through the law, and to act accordingly. Practical common sense extrinsic morality tells us how to get along with others and helps us to have the motivation to do it. We do not have to be

exceptionally saintly, loving, empathetic, compassionate people in order to behave ourselves, and to want to behave, in ways that are essential for the preservation and functioning of a decent society that has high and widespread degrees of personal and social flourishing. Extrinsic moral living just requires us to be ordinary, law-abiding, practical people with good common sense, everyday moral virtues, a basic respect for others, and a willingness to live and let live in mutual harmony. Pragmatic extrinsic ethics may never get beyond the self-interested "reciprocal altruism" of the "social contract" (so loved by philosophers)—" You scratch my back, and I'll scratch yours; if you don't harm me, I won't harm you." Socially enforcing this much morality makes perfectly good practical extrinsic sense.

3) *Intrinsic morality* is the tip of the moral iceberg, but it has a deep base in systemic and extrinsic morality. Hartman's definition of "ethics" as "intrinsic valuation applied to individual persons" is much too narrow because it ignores systemic and extrinsic morality. Intrinsic morality is the highest level of morality, but it is not the sum total of ethics. It is based upon and manifests genuine and profound love, empathy, compassion, and self-identification with others. Its requirements go far beyond those of systemic and extrinsic ethics. With increasing degrees of intensity and specification, all three levels of morality orient us toward and are governed by the basic principle of morality—*We ought always to identify, prefer, choose, and do what is best, that is, what is likely to be richest in good-making properties.* The systemic level gives more specific action-guiding moral rules for optimizing moral goodness; the extrinsic level largely lives it but without great passion; the intrinsic level does it best, most thoroughly, and with the most intense, profound, and saintly moral motives and virtues.

D. Moral and Non-moral Virtues

Moral virtues are enduring states of character that internally incorporate systemic, extrinsic, and intrinsic values and regularly result in morally correct extrinsic actions for intrinsic reasons, that is, in doing what we ought to do, which is what is best for ourselves and others, from intrinsic motives. Being or acting morally (in accord with moral rules) because it pays, or to avoid getting in trouble with the law, are not the same as being moral because we are profoundly moral, that is, from love, compassion, and respect for persons as ends in themselves. Axiology makes a place both for an ethics of rules and an ethics of virtue.

Moral virtues have a triple axiological significance. They are integral aspects of our ought-to-be-fulfilled concepts of ourselves, which include how we relate to others. They regularly (though not inevitably) bring about beneficial consequences for ourselves and others. And they predictably enrich our own lives and those of others intrinsically as well as extrinsically and systemically. Moral virtues are not good *in themselves*, but they definitely are good *for us*. The moral virtues are three-dimensional; they involve systemic thinking about self and others, extrinsic acting toward self and others, and intrinsic feelings about and identifying with self and others. The moral virtues consist of self-ideals and guidelines, extrinsic moral behaviors that benefit others, and intrinsic enrichment for self and others.

Moral goodness is not the same thing as general axiological goodness and should not be confused with it. All moral goodness is axiological goodness, but not all axiological goodness is moral goodness. Some personal virtues like being a good flute-player or a good mathematician are morally neutral. People can even be good at moral vices, (e.g., a good "hit man") without being morally good. *Axiologically*, there can be good devils, good crooks, good murderers, good gamblers, good prostitutes, etc., but there cannot be any *morally* good devils, crooks, murderers, gamblers, or prostitutes, as such. Of course, every person so described may have some moral virtues and good-making properties (e.g., the prostitute with "a heart of gold"). No morally bad person is absolutely bad in every conceivable way.

Moral virtues are not the same as specific *social role or work role virtues*, which can be axiologically good without necessarily being in harmony with moral goodness. The many Business Consultants using the Hartman Value Profile know that someone may have very good general HVP scores and yet have very bad work role scores; or *vice versa*. Axiological consultants regularly develop models of *work role goodness or virtues* for specific jobs in particular work environments, and they use the HVP, or some variant of it, to test specific individuals to see if they would be good at fulfilling those roles and manifesting those virtues. Specific work roles may be those of CEOs, Assistant CEOs, Middle Managers, Salespersons, Foremen, Secretaries, Office Managers, Assembly Line Workers, Laborers, or "Hired Hands" of any description. Specific talents, dispositions, attitudes, and behaviors constitute the good-making properties of those roles, and people who manifest them have the relevant work-role virtues. Consultants using the HVP know how to create models of work role accomplishment that can be tested and applied with remarkable success. If they give the HVP to a sufficient number of successful people in a given position, and to a sufficient number of unsuccessful people in that position, they can develop an ideal model or pattern for success and failure in that position that can be used with remarkable effect in hiring, retaining, and promoting. They have learned, however, that ideal models of work role goodness or virtue can vary immensely from one company to another, or even from one part of the country or specific environment to another within the same company. *Specific ideal work role concepts are often a-moral if not downright immoral, though not necessarily so. Work role virtues may be moral vices.*

Morally bad or neutral people may be very good at their work. Though morality requires intrinsic value and valuation dominance, specific business roles may require systemic or extrinsic value and valuation dominance—sometimes at the expense of ethics and moral virtue. A "truly good business" would allow the intrinsic, extrinsic, and systemic to thrive optimally and in harmony; but such a "truly good business" might not be a "money-making business," especially where businesses are not adequately regulated and thereby required to play on a morally level playing field. In the "real world," systemic and extrinsic virtues may be much more desirable and in demand than intrinsic moral virtues.

Unless businesses are required by governments to play in accord with sound moral and fiscal guidelines, they may be more profitable than businesses with moral integrity by not offering "fringe" benefits like retirement plans, medical insurance, profit sharing, decent working hours, and safe working conditions to their employees. Ethics may require one thing, profit-making just the opposite. Axiologically sound governmental regulations would insure that every business offer such person-respecting benefits to all employees so that all businesses would be playing on the same morally level field. International compliance would be enforced by good governmental regulations and penalties applied to imports and exports. Hartman certainly thought that morally good businesses would be more profitable in the long run than non-moral or immoral businesses (Hartman, 1991a, 193-199), but that may depend on the overall business environment within which they operate, including sound versus unsound governmental regulations.

All forms of goodness, whether moral, a-moral, or immoral, involve concept fulfillment. Moral virtues are among the good-making properties of morally good persons, though not necessarily of work roles within profitable businesses. The good-making predicates that belong within the concept of "morally good persons" would be the basic moral virtues, but the concept of "good worker" can be moral, a-moral, or immoral.

Some individuals may not conceive of themselves as morally good persons, or they may have only a dim awareness of their own moral conscience and integrity. Yet, "I am morally good" *ought to be* an integral aspect of everyone's self-concept. Why so? Because it would be best for them and for others if it were so. We should cultivate moral self-concepts and their corresponding virtues or dispositions to "do good," and others should encourage and facilitate our own moral soul-making. The most abundant-in-goodness life that anyone can lead is the moral life, conjoined with the spiritual life. Being disposed to act in morally virtuous and responsible ways is best not only for our own well-being but also for the well-being of others. The moral life is richer in good-making properties, thus richer in goodness.

In explaining "ethics" as "the application of intrinsic valuation to persons or human beings," Hartman regularly used virtue-concepts to illustrate what this means. It means, he wrote, that "Morally good persons are those who fulfill their own concepts of themselves, are what they are ("genuine," "honest," "sincere"), and do not pretend or play roles" (Hartman, 2002, 252). Genuineness, honesty, and sincerity are moral virtues; they are enduring states of intrinsic character that reliably result extrinsically in *doing what is best for everyone*; but they are also *integral aspects of our own personal or intrinsic well-being.* They enrich our own lives, as well as the lives of others. Other moral virtues (e.g., courage, wisdom, truthfulness, kindness, and justice) do the same.

Morally virtuous people live better lives, more virtuous lives, more abundant lives, lives richer in good-making properties, than people who are not morally virtuous. They act in ways that enrich and do not diminish the lives of others as well as themselves. "Virtue is its own reward," we have often heard, but we seldom know what it means. It means that moral virtues are value-enhancing or enriching intrinsic personal properties. Virtuous persons live better lives, lives that are richer in more satisfying and satisfactory good-making properties, than non-virtuous persons.

Aristotle said some interesting things about moral virtues that are well worth considering. He noted that we are not born virtuous, just as we are not born well-educated. That is, we are not born having well-developed enduring moral or rational states of character. We are not born with actual moral or intellectual virtues, though we naturally have the potential for them. Virtues, moral and non-moral, have to be cultivated. Our natural potentialities have to be activated. To do this *we must perform virtuous acts regularly and repeatedly until doing so becomes habitual or "second nature."* Only after acting morally or intellectually become habitual through repetition do we come to have the corresponding enduring moral or intellectual states of character. One good or bad deed will not make us virtuous or vicious, but many of the same kind will create such enduring states of soul.

Becoming morally virtuous is very much like becoming proficient in athletics or musicianship. We are not born as expert ball-players or pianists. We have to practice. The more we practice, the more proficient we become. At first, pitching the ball over the plate, or through the hoop, or playing the piano, or acting in morally virtuous ways, may be very hard; but the more we do it, the easier it becomes. Finally, at the "peak of our game," it becomes "second nature." What is not there in "first nature" can be cultivated and created by practice until it becomes our prevailing "second nature." As William James artfully expressed this Aristotelian insight, "Sow an action, and you reap a habit; sow a habit and you reap a character; sow a character and reap a destiny" (Richardson, 2007, 315).

So, the way to acquire genuineness, honesty, sincerity, etc., as enduring moral states of character, is through practice, through seizing upon and not passing up concrete, day-to-day, moment-by-moment opportunities to act in genuine, honest, sincere, truthful, helpful, kind, considerate, respectful, courageous, and other virtuous ways. In each and every life-situation, just stop being phony, playing phony roles, and acting toward yourself and others in phony ways. Hartman explicitly recognized corresponding moral vices like being "dishonest," "insincere," and "not-genuine" (Hartman, 1967, 306). These can also become habitual through practice.

Traditional ethical theory recognizes many additional moral virtues and their corresponding vices, any of which can become "second nature" through practice. For example, prudence, temperance, courage, justice, and wisdom were principle moral virtues for the Greeks; Christianity added additional virtues that span the morality/spirituality spectrum—faith, hope, and love. Scattered through his writings, Hartman himself refers to almost all of these, plus many additional virtues *and* vices, such as: "honesty, integrity, kindness, generosity, slyness, superiority, humility and similar obviously ethical concepts" (Hartman, 2002, 30). (Note that some items in this list are vices, which can also become habitual.)

Hartman's most detailed discussion of "similar obviously ethical concepts" can be found in an unpublished document titled "The Individual in Management," where he contrasted "Persons of Intrinsic Faith" (Virtue) with "Persons of Intrinsic Fear" (Vice) in twenty different ways, as follows. [The following edited text is abstracted from Hartman, "The Individual in Management," unpublished manuscript, 40-50. Hartman's own wording here was originally cast in the masculine, ("he"); but to avoid "sexist language," it is here re-cast in pluralistic non-sexist language ("they," etc.) that embraces both males and females. A few of the following phrases were added from a similar discussion in Hartman, 1994, 114-116.]

Here is how Hartman distinguished between the virtues and vices of:

Persons of Intrinsic Faith and Persons of Intrinsic Fear

1.

Faith: **Humility** – They do not need defiance; they are cradled within the universe as a child in the arms of his mother. They trust God as does the child. They are "poor in spirit;" they "bend humbly to the spirit." They are the meek, the gentle, who shall inherit the earth. They are the pure in heart who will see God. They are humble in spirit toward God, and gentle toward people.

Fear: **Defiance, Spitefulness, Superiority** – They cannot trust the world. They can only trust themselves. All they have are themselves, their own power. They have to be in command for otherwise everything would go awry. They have and need a feeling of superiority and indispensability for they are the only ones who can make order in the universal chaos. They cannot delegate authority; if they did everything would go wrong; the world itself would fall apart. God was just lucky that they came around.

2.

Faith: **Serenity** – They feel a deep joy at being alive and around. They make everyone around them feel good. Nothing touches them. They are spiritually happy. They are transparent within themselves.

Fear: **Aggressiveness, Defensiveness, Combativeness** – Fearful people are aggressive, defensive, and combative. They have to be because everything depends upon them.

3.

Faith: **Cooperation** – To them, their fellows are helpers in a cooperative world. Everyone is a friend.

Fear: **Competitiveness** – To them everyone is a potential enemy who has to be overcome.

4.

Faith: **Expansive** – Their spirit is as large as the whole world and it takes in everyone. They are continuously in love with the world and with everything in it. As God has his arms around them so they have their arms around everyone and everything.

Faith: **Restrictive, Narrow**– Fearful people are like the fellow in Steig's organ box who is cowering in that box and gasping "People are no damn good." They are narrow. They want to shrink the world; they want to shrink themselves. They want to be nothing, in order not to be touched by anything.

5.

Faith: **Humaneness** – They love people. They help them. They never say a bad word about anyone, no matter who. They give everyone the benefit of the doubt. They always build others up; they always find something good in everyone. They see the human in everything.

Fear: **Cynicism** – They tear down everyone and everything. The word "cynic" comes from the Greek word "*kyon*" or "dog." Fearful people feel themselves to be dogs, and they make a dog out of everyone—although I don't want to offend dogs. They see everything and everyone as evil.

6.

Faith: **Magnanimity** – Since they see the best in everything and everyone, they are magnanimous. They have great souls. They praise with full hearts; every praise is a praise of God's creation and thus of themselves.

Fear: **Sanctimoniousness, Holier-than-thou Attitude** – They pretend at greatness of soul, but their praise is tinged with superiority. They are condescending, talking down to everyone, even when they praise. For them, every building up others means tearing down themselves. Thus, when they praise they have to do so with condescension so that their own merit will not be obscured. They praise rarely since few things or people appear to them praiseworthy. They have the Holier-than-thou attitude of the dogmatic and the fanatic.

7.

Faith: **Generosity** – They can afford to give because they know that when they throw their bread on the waters it will come back to them manifold. Money and indeed all material goods mean little to them; yet, they value them in their place and are not prodigal or wasteful. They respect the economy of the world.

Fear: **Greed** – Unless they take theirs, somebody else will take it from them. They have to keep piling it up, lest they may starve one day.

8.

Faith: **Unpretentiousness** – They don't try to call attention to their appearance. They don't have to try to pretend they are anything but what they are. This is their world, and they belong. They may be a little sloppy, but they will never be dirty. They follow nature in their outward appearance and do not force nature to follow them. Vanity is outward appearance, the ornament of pride; humble persons who are gentle and natural cannot be vain.

Fear: **Vanity** – They have to improve on creation, including their own appearance; thus they have to squeeze themselves into things and tie themselves down to forms that their nature may dislike. They use their handsomeness in order to be effective and beat others who are not similarly endowed. Thus they build up themselves. They look at themselves in the mirror, and their finery makes them feel good.

9.

Faith: **Not Easily Hurt, Self-Possessed** – They never expect anything extra from the world, but they take whatever they receive as grace, as a gift from the bounty of God's goodness, for which they are grateful.

Fear: **Easily Hurt, Touchy** – They're so insecure, and they have great self-pity. They have to struggle so hard, and everything is against them. They're concerned only about their own suffering, not that of others. They are spiritually thin-skinned. They are not overly sensitive generally but only where themselves are concerned. They think the world owes them a living and, more importantly, owes them loving. They are love-starved. Since they did the world a favor in being born, much against their will, the world ought to reciprocate and pamper them. Thus anything that goes against them is exaggerated because it is so unjust, and anything that goes for them they take for granted.

10.

Faith: **Boldness, Courage** – Nothing to them appears impossible, every problem resolvable, every deed achievable, every difficulty superable. They know they are on the right track so they aren't afraid to move ahead. They take everything in stride, never getting overly agitated either in failure or in success.

Fear: **Cowardice** – They are scared in their spirit, thin-skinned. They are born, so to speak, without a spiritual skin against the world, but they are sensitive only about themselves. They are spiritual crybabies; few things appear possible to them. They try to hoard what they have – like the unfaithful servant in the Parable of the Talents.

11.

Faith: **Forgivingness** – With their great hearts, they are forgiving. They know that vengeance is the Lord's. They pity rather than hate the malefactor.

Fear: **Vengefulness** – They will not rest until they have wrought their revenge. Since they are the navel of the universe, anything done against them is done against the world itself; and it is up to them to righten this cosmic evil.

12.

Faith: **Light Touch** – They are blessed with the light touch. They bounce through life, having with them the powers of infinity. They play on the instrument of the world like a virtuoso on a piano, seemingly without effort; yet behind this light-handed and light-footed performance is their effort of acquiring the power of eternity.

Fear: **Heavy Touch** – They are burdened with the heavy touch. Everything is very, very difficult for them. They have to work so hard, harder than anyone else, and nothing comes of it. Hitler always said he worked day and night for the German people and they did not thank him.

13.

Faith: **Uncomplicated, Purity, Innocence, Common Sense** – They have an innocence of spirit and purity of heart that sees through the chaos of a situation to its very core. Such persons are Billy Budd in Melville's novel; St. Bernadette in the novel of Franz Werfel, who winds all the great theologians around her little finger; and such persons are the true scientists, the people of genius who see the simple solution of the complicated. They can see things as they are and not as they would like them to be.

Fear: **Complicated, Lack of Common Sense** – They regard complication as a virtue and a sign of profundity. As they are deficient in spirit, they are also deficient in mind.

14.

Faith: **Relevance, Sense of Proportion** – They are prone to see the relevant. They have a sense of proportion, see things in their true relation to each other. They are able to differentiate. They take the important seriously and value it accordingly, and they take the unimportant not seriously and disvalue it accordingly.

Fear: **Irrelevance, No Sense of Proportion** – They are prone to see the irrelevant. They lack a sense of proportion, make mountains out of mole hills, or *vice versa*. Since they have little direction, they take everything to be equally important. They thus confuse the important with the unimportant, giving importance to the unimportant and no importance to the important. They exaggerate trifles and dismiss weighty matters with a wave of their hand.

15.

Faith: **Rationality** – They use reason in conformance with the structure of the world itself. Therefore, true science, although nothing but a construction of the human mind, can yet account for what is going on in the world.

Fear: **Irrationality** – Fearful people are at bottom irrational. Their defective selves interfere with the clarity of their vision. They use systems in order to bolster themselves.

16.

Faith: **Spontaneity, Flexibility** – They play upon and with systems as a virtuoso with and upon his instrument. They are sovereign above systems; the system is not sovereign over them.

Fear: **Systemicness, Rigidity** – They use systems as a crutch and are lost without them – as was Adolf Eichman. The system is sovereign over them.

17.

Faith: **Relaxed Dynamic** – They are relaxed; their dynamics is quite like that of a noiseless Cadillac and therefore much stronger than that of the bustling busybody who sputters like a scooter and takes extrinsic activity for intrinsic dynamics.

Fear: **Tense, or Frantic, Business** – They exhibit bustling busyness. Their activity is like that of children squirting water pistols.

18.

Faith: **Perseverance, Patience** – They know they're on the right road and if they persist, they will reach their goal. They feel within themselves the strength of the universe. They never stop for a moment on their way, but they are never obtrusive. They are the still waters that run deep.

Fear: **Inconstancy, Hesitancy, Impatience** – They lack enough faith and inner strength to move toward their objectives consistently. They may seem persistent, but they have a certain deep hesitation about their actions and their work. Since they do not have enough faith and enough strength for the whole universe, they only go up to a certain point and then stop, looking for another direction.

19.

Faith: **Awareness, Vision, Warmth, Wisdom** – They have complete awareness, wide vision, warmth and wisdom. They are wide awake to everything that the world offers them. The world is right, and God is in His Heaven watching it. They are cosmic optimists. There are many bad things in the world, but they are flaws of the design, or the execution of the world, but they are not its essence. They belong to the realm of contingency, and this realm is a small part—a statistically calculable small part—of the grand design. The pessimist does not see the whole for the parts, and thus ... is a little crazy.

Fear: **Non-awareness, Myopia, Dullness, Coldness, Trifling Acuteness, Fastidiousness** – Since they lack complete awareness, they have a certain dullness of vision and of feeling, a coldness of heart which, coupled with their trifling acuteness and fastidiousness, their attention to detail without seeing the great line, makes them deadly bores. Lacking vision, they must exaggerate the small and denigrate the big. Their dullness, coldness, and fastidiousness are consequences of the irrelevancy of their actions. They do not have faith in either God or the world.

20.

Faith: **Compassion** – Compassion is their deepest trait. They suffer with the sufferers. Every suffering is their own suffering. They manifest within themselves the intrinsic oneness of all creation. Compassion, as we said, is the touchstone of morality; this is the most important difference between moral types.

Fear: **Indifference, Callousness** – They are indifferent toward what really counts, especially toward the infinite greatness of human beings. Since they are weak inside and hate to be touched by anything unpleasant, they are indifferent to suffering.

Did you find yourself anywhere in this discourse? What are your virtues and vices?

E. Moral Virtues, Motives, and Attitudes

Moral virtues, motives, and attitudes require a three-dimensional analysis. Minimal moral virtues, motives, and attitudes would be those associated with the functioning of *systemic moral consciousness*—a cognitive awareness of the requirements of "the moral law" (moral rules) and an objective, dispassionate acceptance of them.

Extrinsic moral virtues, motives, and attitudes would move us beyond dispassionate acceptance and toward a practical or common sense *extrinsic moral consciousness* that actually does what morality minimally requires of us. It both "talks the talk" and "walks the walk." Extrinsic moral virtues, motives, and deeds would engage the normal desires, feelings, emotions, attitudes, customs, manners, and moral habits and practices of everyday life, civilized harmonious social interactions, and basic human decency. Extrinsic moral virtues, motives, and attitudes are the practical moral glue that prevents societies from falling apart and degenerating into what Thomas Hobbes called the "state of nature," where life would be "solitary, poor, nasty, brutal, and short." Extrinsic moral consciousness is largely a matter of "reciprocal altruism," "tit for tat," the "social contract," "I'll scratch your back if you will scratch mine."

Intrinsic moral consciousness manifests virtues, attitudes, and motives that go beyond systemic and extrinsic morality. Hartman repeatedly emphasized the genuinely unselfish virtues/motives of profound love, empathy, and compassion. He called compassion "the touchstone of morality." These belong to the very core of well-developed moral personhood. Intrinsically moral people have distinctive good-making properties, specifically these, that people who are merely systemically or extrinsically moral do not have. Thus, they live more abundantly.

At this point, we now have fairly well developed and explained concepts of "morally good persons." The opposite, "morally bad persons" would both lack the above good-making properties and manifest their contraries, namely, immoral vices, attitudes, and motives. The richest possible concept of "morally good persons" includes the systemic, extrinsic, and intrinsic moral virtues. *Systemically*, morally virtuous persons know and dispassionately accept the difference between good and evil, right and wrong. *Extrinsically*, morally virtuous persons act and live in ways that make for morally decent and mutually beneficial social orders. *Intrinsically*, morally virtuous persons go far beyond the call of systemic and extrinsic duty; they are loving, empathetic, and compassionate, and they fully identify with others, not just occasionally, but regularly and dependably. Fulfilling this rich three-dimensional concept of a "morally good person" has to be done by each unique individual in her or his own distinctive way, concrete life situation, and personal circumstances. Fulfilling this rich concept of moral goodness within ourselves in the way we think, act, and feel is the best way to enrich our own lives and the lives of others with good-making properties. It is the best way, the most effective way, to live abundantly oneself and to contribute to the common good.

As often noted and emphasized by Hartman and many others, we cannot love others at all unless we first love ourselves; certainly it would be pointless to love others *as* we love ourselves if we don't love ourselves. Comprehensive intrinsic evaluation includes knowing and appreciating ourselves, seeing ourselves as others see us, and seeing others as they see themselves. It also includes thinking, feeling, and acting as they would think, feel, and act if we were "in their shoes." *Empathy and compassion* are the key affective/cognitive virtues, attitudes, and motives of intrinsic valuation and intrinsic moral goodness. To be truly intrinsic, these moral affections must be truly intense; they cannot be felt at sporadic, trivial, or ordinarily weak levels. In profound intrinsic virtue, these feelings are keen, powerful, dominant, and enduring. To be truly virtuous, these moral attitudes and motives must be relatively constant, habitual, dependable. We are not born that way, not born either "good" or "bad." We are born with the potentials for each and for conflicts between them. Getting there takes a lot of time and effort. We succeed in being morally good persons only by degrees and through serious efforts.

Empathy is the general ability to identify with another. *Compassion* is the more specific ability to identify with another's pains and sufferings. Both involve concepts as well as potent feelings. They include conceiving of, feeling for, and acting to help others. Empathy and compassion are principle components of love, along with commitment, loyalty, faithfulness, and concentration.

In his essay on "The Nature of Valuation," Hartman gave an excellent description of the ethical affective/motivational aspects of intrinsic evaluation. The quote below selects and emphasizes these features of what he said.

> In intrinsic valuation, the class in question consists of only one member ... There
> is pure experience between me and the one thing; I experience the thing in its

whole fullness without any thought of anything else....Intrinsic good is love or sympathy; it is *agape*, loving concern, translated often by "charity."

In axiological terms it means that since I do not abstract in intrinsic valuation, I concentrate on the thing as it is, I am fully concentrated on this one thing. For this reason, intrinsic valuation when applied to things brings about aesthetic valuation; the artist is fully concentrated on the thing he creates. He and the thing are empathetically related; they form one unit. Applied to persons this valuation is ethical; it is complete involvement of one person with another, complete concentration of one person on another; the persons are sympathetically related and form one unit. We may call this relationship between persons Community (Hartman, 1991b, 22-23).

Intrinsic evaluation has an extrinsic-action component as well as systemic-cognitive and intrinsic-affective components. Every form of valuation is taken up into complete intrinsic valuation. Love, empathy, and compassion involve much more than mere thoughts and mere feelings; they involve doing as well. They are three-dimensional ethical concepts. We cannot really love other persons without understanding them or thinking about them. We do not really believe something unless we are willing to act on it. We do not really love someone unless we are willing to do those works of love unto them that we would have them do unto us. Real compassion is more than just *knowing about* or *feeling* the suffering and distress of other; real compassion knows what suffering is and *acts* to relieve it.

Where intrinsic evaluation is not accompanied by extrinsic action, hypocrisy results. Secular as well as spiritual intrinsic evaluators can be hypocrites. Have you ever noticed that many absolutely devoted American patriots are willing to do anything for America except pay for it? Hence all the griping about paying taxes! Some discontent about taxation is justified where there is governmental waste and "pork barrel" spending. Most of it, however, just wants to enjoy all the legitimate benefits of government without having to pay for them. Yes, literally pay. Lip-service patriotism is one thing, but real patriotism is three-dimensional! Does the same sort of passion without action, or preaching without practice, manifest itself in other human organizations, e.g., in universities or churches?

This discussion of intrinsic moral consciousness must end with a final word of caution. Just as we are not capable of infinite thinking and acting, even so, we are not capable of infinite love, empathy, compassion, and self-identification-with-others. We must acknowledge and remember our finitude, even with respect to intrinsic valuation. Caretakers of children, elderly, frail, or incapacitated loved ones learn this lesson of their own finitude the hard way, especially when such responsibilities are prolonged and unrelieved. *You* can learn it the easy way by taking heed. *We are capable of burning out on love, empathy, compassion, and self-identification, just as we can with anything else like philosophizing, plumbing, philandering, or plowing.*

After we have done our finite best, there is nothing immoral about compassion-fatigue. This is just "human nature." We are not gods or God; we are finite creatures trying to be good but always falling short of moral perfection. Nature and Nature's God have designed us for thinking, acting, loving, etc; but they have not designed us for infinite thinking, acting, loving, compassion, or self-identification. Kant argued that, "Ought implies can," which logically implies "Cannot implies no ought, no duty." Even those finite but saintly and heroic human beings who go far beyond the call of duty cannot think an infinite number of thoughts, do an infinite number of loving and heroic deeds, or be infinitely loving, empathetic, and compassionate toward an infinite number of others. We can do and be only what we can do and be. We are only human, not divine.

F. Moral Absolutes

Are there any moral absolutes? Chapter One showed that the Form of the Good is absolute in theory but relative or subjective in application. So, are all moral values merely relative? Are any moral values not "subjective"? The answer depends largely on what we mean by "subjective" and its opposite, "objective."

Ethical relativists, who claim that there are no objective values and that all human values are merely subjective, mean by this that no values are universally human. That is, no human values are affirmed by all (or most) people in all cultures, times, and places. Their obvious evidence for this is the vast diversity of values and practices present in the many different cultures of the world. Human values differ drastically from culture to culture, they say, and that proves that there are no absolute or objective values, moral or otherwise.

What would it take to refute this central claim of ethical relativists? The existing evidence for value relativism is at best "anecdotal," as social scientists would say. This means that the commonplace claim of universal value relativity is not based on methodologically sound scientific studies. Until recently, neither was the claim of value-objectivists, who think that there are at least a few universally valid and shared human values. Anecdotal evidence for value relativity does not prove that no universal human values exist. A few universal human values and valuations might be hidden deeply within the conspicuous axiological diversity of the world's cultures. There may or may not be universal human values, depending on the outcome of truly scientific studies of the problem area.

Until recently, there have been no *truly empirical scientific studies* that could even provide relevant evidence for, much less settle, the moral subjectivism/ objectives debate. This is because *no validated scientific instrument was available to employ in such a study*. Fortunately, Hartmanian formal axiology now provides such an instrument, the Hartman Value Profile!

Furthermore, this instrument has now been deployed in significant cross-cultural or multi-cultural studies. The relevant work was done on his own time and at his own expense by long-time member and the former President of the Robert S. Hartman Institute, Dr. Leon Pomeroy. His most definitive results are reported in

Chapters Sixteen and Seventeen of his 2005 book, *The New Science of Axiological Psychology*. There he gives the results of cross-cultural studies with the HVP in the United States, Mexico, Indonesia, Japan, and Russia. He recognizes that his results need to be replicated by additional and more extensive or expansive multi-cultural studies using the HVP, but his preliminary results do indeed seem to identify some universal human values hidden with all the apparent cultural diversity. Summarizing his results, Pomeroy writes,

> Axiological perspectives and contexts reveal core patterns of axiological absolutes as well as patterns of axiological relativity. The Hartman Value Profile records both culture-bound (nation-bound) axiological patterns and culture-free (nation-free) *axiological* universals. It reveals a universe of commonality among the deeply held evaluative habits that make us all human (Pomeroy, 2005, 224).

So what values are at least tentatively proved to be universally human by such methodologically sound empirical studies? Primarily, the Hierarchy of Value! *People are more valuable than things, and things are more valuable than ideas of things or people.* In their cool, calm, reflective moments, people in all cultures studied thus far affirm this well over 90 percent of the time! The "reflective moments" qualification is very important here. In reality, people do not always live up to their most carefully considered value affirmations and potentials. HVP results show that people everywhere have realistic potentials for being better than they often are and for living better than they actually do. They at least know what is best, even if they do not always do it.

Also, given morally undeveloped human nature, the Hierarchy of Value may be applied contextually only to "insiders" but not to "outsiders." These distinctions are always drawn according to local and individual beliefs, customs, and prejudices.

Yet, there it is! Scientific studies, not just anecdotal evidence, shows that some basic human values are affirmed almost universally. People (if only insiders) have more worth than things, and things have more worth than mere words for or ideas of people and things. Scientific studies definitely seem to refute value relativism, which says that there are no universal human values at all. Of course more than ninety percent agreement is not 100 percent agreement, but this is about as good as empirical evidence for any empirical claim ever gets, especially those of a social nature. Most philosophers would agree that if an overwhelming majority of thoughtful people affirm certain values in their moments of careful consideration, those values are universally valid. We must conclude that *axiological studies actually refute value relativism and affirm value-objectivity.* In every human culture, knowledgeable and thoughtful people are highly valued; in every culture, practical people are highly valued; in every culture loving and compassionate people are highly valued. These are universal human values. In their more reflective moments, most people in every culture judge that people are more valuable than mere things, and things are more valuable than mere ideas of them or of people.

What kind of an ethics correlates with the objectively valid Hierarchy of Value? Precisely the ethics developed in this chapter! Applied to ethics, the Hierarchy of Value generates or correlates with such moral rules or guidelines as:

1) We ought to value people more than things, and things more than ideas.

2) We ought to develop ourselves, and to help others develop themselves, systemically, extrinsically, and intrinsically.

3) We ought to value all persons and conscious beings, including ourselves, intrinsically, and never *merely* extrinsically or merely systemically.

4) In all possible value dimensions, we ought to choose courses of action that sustain or increase value and avoid actions that decrease value for ourselves and others who are affected by what we do.

5) Thus, *we ought always to identify-with, prefer, choose, and do what is best, that is, what is likely to be richest in good-making properties.*

Items 1) through 4) are the ethical absolutes that tell us how to do this. The preceding sections of this chapter make these basic moral principles more understandable, more specific, and more readily applicable to daily living.

Finally, what kind of persons would correlate most fully with the axiological Hierarchy of Value? When Hartman described saints, it was clear that he saw ethics merging into profound spirituality, with no clear separation between them. The basic axiological capacities of ethical persons, primarily for intrinsic valuation, are the same as those of moral/spiritual saints. The differences between saints and ordinary moral persons are only in degree and scope, with no sharp dividing line between them. Saints are at the pinnacle of moral/spiritual growth; people who are merely moral are just lesser saints. Consider Hartman's description of saints:

> Indeed, geniuses in axiology may well be saints, "saint" being defined as an axiological genius both in knowledge and action. To be a saint is a profession, like any other; it is the identification of self with every self.
>
> The more intelligent a person is the better he or she will know how to value, for the more and wider concepts he or she considers; the most intelligent sees all *sub species aeternitas*. The narrower one is, seeing more and more of less and less, as does the specialized scientist ... the less will one be able to value. The saint is the genius of intrinsic valuation, of ethics, applied to people.
>
> Only saints can fully live [the] infinite range of the self. A saint is a person who puts his whole power, all the resources of himself, into his own goodness, a man who has discovered his oneness with all creation, all men, all animals, even all things. He lives within the depth of everybody and everything. He is a man of infinite compassion. The deepest intrinsic goodness is to live so deeply and transparently within ourselves that we live deeply and compassionately with every human being, indeed every living being—indeed, every being. As St. Francis said to Brother Leo when he tried to extinguish the fire on St. Francis' coat: "Brother Leo, be careful with Brother Fire." Or as Albert Schweitzer, who felt pain at having to kill the bacteria when he did an operation. Compassion is one touchstone of moral value (Hartman, 1995d, 86).

5. Aesthetics, Religion, Psychology, and Other Applications

In his "Summary and Outlook" at the very end of *The Structure of Value* (303-311), Hartman predicted how the three value dimensions of formal axiology would be developed and applied in the future. After several pages of explanation, he summarized his predictions in the following table, given on his page 311.

APPLICATION TO	INTRINSIC VALUE	EXTRINSIC VALUE	SYSTEMIC VALUE
Individual Persons	Ethics	Psychology	Physiology, Jurisprudence of "Person"
Groups of Persons	Political Science, Social Ethics	Sociology	Law of Persons and Institutions
Individual Things	Aesthetics	Economics	Technology
Groups of Things	Science of Civilization	Ecology	Industrial Technology, Civil Engineering, Games, Law of Property, Ritual
Concepts	Metaphysics	Epistemology	Logic
Words	Poetry, Literary Criticism	Rhetoric, Semantics, Linguistic Analysis	Grammar, Theory of Communication

Immediately following this table, Hartman wrote,

> The application of axiology to actual situations through the applied axiological sciences is a task for new generations of pure and applied axiologists, pure and applied social and moral scientists, and finally, the mechanics and craftsmen of social and moral situations.... The achievements of the moral scientists of the future, analyzing moral situations in terms of formal axiology, will lead to the building of a new society with new people, living on higher levels of awareness and possessing undreamed of insights into the subtleties and depths of moral reality (Hartman, 1967, 311).

So ended his book. Hartman realized in 1967 that axiology had not yet been applied to the disciplines mentioned in his table. That this was to be a "task for new generations." This was more prophetic than he realized, for at the time he did not anticipate his own premature death in 1973. When he wrote this, he did not know that he would have so little opportunity to apply his axiology to these and other disciplines. We have already noted his unfulfilled plan to write a book applying axiology to ethics and aesthetics. This chapter begins the process of applying axiology to ethics—just one little rectangle in his table. Members and friends of the Robert S. Hartman Institute, organized in 1976, and actualized with its first meeting in 1977, have begun to fulfill his prophesy, but a world of work remains to be done.

This book on *The Essentials of Formal Axiology* is only an *introduction*. It will conclude with a brief account of progress, or lack thereof, in applying axiology to a variety of disciplines. The following brief summary will indicate where readers might go next to further their knowledge of axiology and its applications. For a fuller account, go to the sources mentioned in what follows. For more information about the publications mentioned below, go to the "Books and Publications" page of the website of the Hartman Institute, http://www.hartmaninstitute.org.

A. Axiology and Aesthetics

No one has yet attempted to write a serious and comprehensive account of how axiology might illuminate aesthetic theory. As in the preceding table, Hartman defined aesthetics as the application of intrinsic value to individual things, in contrast to ethics, the application of axiology to individual persons. By "application" he seems to have meant the intrinsic evaluation of things in aesthetics and of people in ethics. We now understand that his limiting of ethics to intrinsically evaluating people was much too narrow. Ethics requires a three dimensional axiological analysis. An adequate theory of aesthetics would also likely involve systemic and extrinsic as well as intrinsic considerations, insights, values, and evaluations.

Hartman seemed interested only in the rather narrow topic of how creative artists incubate their projects, then concentrate intensely upon and identify themselves with the art objects they are creating. This was what he meant by the intrinsic valuation of individual things. Several preceding quotes illustrate this.

Note carefully, however, that intrinsically evaluating art objects (or beauty in inanimate natural objects) does not convert them into intrinsically valuable beings in their own right. That is, even though objects of art like paintings and statues are unique, they are still not conscious beings having concepts or ideals of themselves to be fulfilled or frustrated. No painting, sculpture, or any other work of art can be so described. Art objects don't have "souls." Art objects are valuable to us, but they are not ends to, for, and in themselves. They are not intrinsic value-objects proper, thought they can be intrinsically evaluated. Strictly speaking, it is improper to speak of them as "intrinsic values," though Hartman and others sometimes talk(ed) that way. Both artists and spectators can value art objects intrinsically, but art objects are still just "things," not unique consciously valuing beings in their own right.

Aesthetics involves the intrinsic valuation of *things,* which really are just things; ethics involves the intrinsic valuation of *people,* who truly are ends in themselves.

Concentrating (as Hartman did) almost exclusively on how people intrinsically evaluate and create art objects, even when extended to beauty in nature, still leaves untouched many topics usually included in aesthetics. It still leaves the systemic and extrinsic aspects of aesthetics untouched. A truly adequate application of axiology to aesthetics would also have to show how axiology applies to and illuminates many aesthetic issues that range far beyond intrinsically valuing things. For example, how does axiology apply to or help illuminate the following?

– defining "art," distinguishing art objects from aesthetic objects that occur naturally, and differentiating between good art and not-so-good art,

– explaining the differences between particular arts like painting, sculpture, architecture, drama, opera, music, dance, literature, poetry, etc.,

– defining many key concepts in aesthetics such as "beautiful," "ugly," "sublime," "comic," "tragic," "style," "criticism," "imitation," "imagination," "creativity," etc., and

– any additional issues in traditional and present-day aesthetics.

Hartman wrote much about the meaning of "good" but almost nothing about "beauty," other than that it meant "aesthetic 'good'" (Hartman, 1967, 180). He did not explain this and did almost nothing with it or other key concepts in aesthetics.

The closest that Hartman himself came to applying axiology to aesthetics was his article on "The Value Structure of Creativity," that appeared in *The Journal of Value Inquiry,* 6: 1972, 243-279; and, except for creativity, most of that article has little to do with aesthetics as usually understood. Doctoral student at The University of Tennessee, Steve Byrum, wrote his dissertation in 1976 on *Intrinsic Value and Play,* and Cynthia Chance, wrote her dissertation in 1978 on *A Hartmanian Aesthetic: The Value Structure of Poetry.* These were of limited scope and were never commercially published, but they are available in the University of Tennessee library. Obviously, the process of applying axiology to aesthetics has hardly begun. We still await the appearance of an axiological aesthetic genius!

B. Axiology and Religion

Significant progress has been made in applying axiology to religion. Hartman's own reflections on God and other spiritual or religious themes are scattered throughout his published and unpublished writings, but he never wrote an axiology of religion. Steven C. Byrum pulled many of these themes together in his book, *The Value Structure of Theology,* published by The University Press of America in 1978. Steve further explores axiology and spirituality in the book he co-authored with Leland Kaiser, *Spirit for Greatness,* Tapestry Press, 2004, especially Section Four.

Rem B. Edwards used the Hierarchy of Value to identify and explore in depth the spiritual types of worldliness, ideology (dogmatism), and saintliness in his

Religious Values and Valuations, published by Paidia Press in 2000. Hopefully, an extensively revised and expanded version of this book will be republished soon as *Spiritual Values and Valuations*.

In recent years, a general monotheistic "Religious Value Profile," and a more specific "Christian Value Profile," based on the eighteen formulas underlying the Hartman Value Profile, but with specifically religious or Christian items, were developed by Rem B. Edwards, David Mefford, and Vera Mefford. These were published in 2005 by Xlibris Press in their accompanying handbook of spiritual reflections and exercises titled *Developing Your Spiritual Potentials.* A website for taking and interpreting these profiles was available for several years, during which time it had around six thousand visitors, but it is no longer functional, and this book is no longer available. The book has now been extensively improved and revised, as has the Christian Value Profile. It is now available as an e-book titled *Developing Your Christian Values.* The new website for the much improved CVP and for obtaining the e-book is: http://www.christianvalueprofile.com. Edwards further applied axiology to religion in his forthcoming *John Wesley's Values, and Ours.*

C. Axiology and Psychology

By far the most successful and widespread application of axiology to any discipline thus far has been to psychology. Specifically, Hartman's own "Hartman Value Profile" (HVP) is now widely used in business consulting, psychological counseling, and other related areas. Parallel forms and speciality forms that deviate from Hartman's wording but retain his underlying formulas are now being used by many consultants, and the Board of Directors of the Robert S. Hartman Institute has produced the modernized "Hartman Institute Value Profile," which is currently being validated and will be made available eventually to Axiological Service Providers. For more information, go to the official website of the Robert S. Hartman Institute, http://www.hartmaninstitute.org, and click on the relevant buttons.

Two books dealing with the Hartman Value Profile are now available. First, Hartman's own *Manual of Interpretation, Second Edition*, 2006, is available from the Hartman Institute. It is sold only to dues-paying members of the Institute. For more information, go to the above website, click on the "Books and Publications" button, and scroll down to this item.

Second, a major contribution to validating the Hartman Value Profile and creating a new empirical science of behavioral psychology has now been written and published by Leon Pomeroy as *The New Science of Axiological Psychology.* For more information on this highly recommended book, go to the "Books and Publications" page of the Hartman Institute website, and scroll down to this item. To learn more about distributors and consultants now using the Hartman Value Profile, please go to the Hartman Institute website and click on the "Axiological Service Providers" button in the left hand column.

D. Developing an Axiological Calculus

Formal axiology aspires to advance an axiological calculus that could express all axiological issues in terms of relations that can be formalized and calculated. Frank G. Forrest developed Hartman's proposed axiological calculus far beyond the point where Hartman left it. Further developing Hartman's unrefined suggestions, Forrest uses the transfinite math that was criticized and rejected in Chapter Two as philosophically ungrounded and seriously misleading in some cases.

The Hartman/Forrest axiological calculus should not be dismissed completely or taken lightly. While criticizing it, it was also noted that remarkable things can be done with it. Forrest's work on this is available in his *Valuemetrics^N: The Science of Personal and Professional Ethics.* Amsterdam - Atlanta: Editions Rodopi, 1994; in his "A Reply to 'Ten Unanswered Questions'" published in Rem B. Edwards, ed., *Formal Axiology and its Critics.* Amsterdam - Atlanta: Editions Rodopi, 1995, 153-170; in his self-published *Ethical Decision Making for the 21st Century,* 2001; and in his "Is Killing to Save Lives Justifiable?," *Journal of Formal Axiology: Theory and Practice,* 1:2008, 161-176. For more information about publications, go to the website of the Hartman Institute, http://www.hartmaninstitute.org.

Despite postulating infinite numbers of good-making systemic, extrinsic, and intrinsic properties (that do not exist), the transfinite axiological calculus can still be very helpful because it captures and tells us how to make calculations based upon the following powerful moral intuition, specifically: *Intrinsically good, extrinsically good, and systemically good entities have incommensurable hierarchical worth.* This may need more careful examination, but it tells us that no quantity of extrinsically good things can ever add up to the value of a unique human being (e.g., so many barrels of oil for an American or Iraqi soldier); and no quantity of thoughts can ever add up to the value of a real thing or a real person (e.g. so many "barrel of oil thoughts" for a real barrel or oil). No number of thoughts about "Joe Hussein" will ever equal the worth of the living Joe Hussein.

The Hartman/Forrest transfinite-based calculus must be used with great care because it may occasionally give unconscionable results, as earlier explained. More often than not, because it captures the incommensurability of the value dimensions, it gives the right results, i.e., results that cool and careful conscientiousness *would approve or confirm even without assuming any infinities.* The real moral work is being done by enlightened conscience, but the calculus can be a significant aid in developing, uncovering, unfolding, understanding, and enlightening conscience!

There are at least two kinds of transfinite mathematics, cardinal and ordinal. The cardinal variety used by Hartman and Forrest assumes the actuality of infinite sets of good-making properties and focuses on literal applications of numbers like "n," "$\aleph_0$," and "$\aleph_1$." The ordinal variety assumes only that transfinite numbers cannot be reduced to one another and that they are ordered in "greater than" or "less than" relations. It allows for not taking them literally. The ordinal "metaphorical-in-application" approach would probably be the most fruitful for an axiological calculus, though it might have the counterintuitive applications indicated earlier. Better mathematical systems are currently being sought, and serious work on this is being done. Stay tuned! Read future issues of the *Journal of Formal Axiology*!

An alternative finitistic calculus based on quantum wave theory mathematics was offered by Mark A. Moore in his "A Quantum Wave Model of Value Theory," in Rem B. Edwards, ed., *Formal Axiology and Its Critics*. Amsterdam - Atlanta: Editions Rodopi, 1991, 171-215. See also his "Mathematical Models and the Science of Values," in Rem B. Edwards and John W. Davis., eds., *Forms of Value and Valuation: Theory and Applications*. Lanham, MD: University Press of America, 1995, 171-192. His latest essay is "Killing to Prevent Murders and Save Lives" in *Journal of Formal Axiology: Theory and Practice*, 2008, 1, 177-185.

A serious critique of Forrest and Moore by Ted Richards, "Killing One to Save Five: A Test of Two Hartman-style Value Calculuses," was in the *Journal of Formal Axiology: Theory and Practice*, 1:2008, 187-205. Ted is now trying to find a more adequate mathematics for an axiological calculus. See his "The Difficulties of a Hartmanesque Value Calculus," in the 2010 issue.

E. Sports Axiology

David and Vera Mefford, together with several prominent persons in athletics, are developing the new field of sports axiology. Their work includes a new sports axiology profile, the "Pro-Sports Profile" and related profiles for specific sports. For more information, see their article on "Sports Axiology" in the *Journal of Formal Axiology: Theory and Practice*, 1:2008, 21-46. Go also to their websites, http://www.innertactics.com or http://www.thevaluesourcegroup.com

F. Future Applications

Today, we have only begun to apply axiology to the disciplines Hartman identified in 1967 at the end of *The Structure of Value*, as well as to medical ethics, business ethics, professional ethics, ethics and animals, etc. Today, we still must say that applying axiology is "a task for new generations." Hartman's dream of "building of a new society with new people, living on higher levels of awareness and possessing undreamed of insights into the subtleties and depths of moral reality" (Hartman, 1967, 311) is yet unrealized, but progress has been made.

APPENDIX: AXIOLOGICAL GLOSSARY

axiology: value theory, or the general theory of value, which deals with questions of good and evil, right and wrong, beauty and ugliness, reasonableness and unreasonableness, correctness and incorrectness, etc..

axioms: one or more fundamental organizing principles of a belief system, whether scientific, philosophical, theological, or whatever.

axiom of axiology: the "Form of the Good," which is, "Good is concept (or standard) fulfillment."

axiom of ethics: We ought always to identify-with, prefer, choose, and do what is best, that is, what is likely to be richest in good-making properties.

best: having more good-making properties than anything else in its class of comparison.

better: having more good-making properties than something else in its class of comparison.

composition: a combination of two or more value-objects that sustains or increases value.

concept: a mental content having both intensional and extensional properties.

conscience: the aspect of the self that sets and identifies standards for distinguishing between moral right and wrong, good and evil; more broadly, any standard-setting and identifying aspect of the self, moral or otherwise.

consciousness: being actively awake or alert, as distinct from being asleep or otherwise unconscious. Semi-consciousness seems to involve being awake, but with no capacity for processing or acting upon or with what is being experienced.

definitional properties: qualities or relations that anything must have in order to be a member of some class.

denumerably infinite: capable of being correlated one by one with each of the endless set of whole numbers.

disinterested: objective or fair-minded interestedness uncorrupted by prejudices or feelings that would interfere with the unbiased search for truth; being distinterested should not be confused with being uninterested or indifferent.

disvalues: things that are bad, evil, wrong, worthless, ugly, hurtful, irrational, tasteless, etc. Formally, disvalues are things that are inherently bad, or things that completely fail to manifest the good-making properties that they are supposed to manifest, or value combinations that diminish or destroy goodness.

end in itself: good or valuable for its own sake and not merely for the sake of something else; worthwhile in and of itself; valuable to, for, and in itself.

ethics: 1) defined by Hartman as "the application of intrinsic value to individual persons." 2) A more adequate or inclusive definition would be, "the value discipline that aims at maximum well-being or value-abundance for all unique conscious beings, not just for oneself, in all three value dimensions, systemic, extrinsic, and intrinsic. (See "axiom of ethics.")

expositional properties: everything must have its definitional properties just to be what it is or to belong to it classification, but beyond its defnitional properties, its expositional properties are the qualities and/or relations in terms of which anything's goodness, or degrees thereof, are assessed.

extensions, or extensional meanings: the entities or realities to which words or ideas refer. Extensions are referents, denotations, or denotative meanings.

extrinsic valuation: valuing anything for its usefulness with ordinary everyday practical emotional involvement, with commonplace emotions, desires, and interests; valuing anything as fulfilling extrinsic value standards.

extrinsic values: means to ends; useful things, objects, processes, and actions; public space-time objects, processes, and activities accessible through ordinary sense experience; members of empirical classes; examples: houses, cars, cash, food, tools, machines, moral actions, etc.

formal axiology: the study of the general or formal patterns involved in what we value (value-objects) and how we value (valuations).

form of the good: the general logical pattern inherent in all uses of "good"; the basic axiom of formal axiology, "Good is concept fulfillment."

good: concept or standard fulfillment. A good X is one that has all the good-making properties that it is supposed to have, one whose properties match the good-making predicates within its standard or concept.

good-making predicate: a conceptual element or criterion within a mental concept or standard of goodness; for example, "gas-efficient" is a good-making predicate of "cars."

good-making property: a property that an actual value-object must have in order to fulfil its concept; a quality, relation or feature toward which someone has pro-attitudes after careful consideration; a feature of an actual value-object that exemplifies a good-making predicate; for example, actual gas-efficiency in a real car.

hierarchy of value: a ranking of the three basic kinds of value, according to which intrinsic value-objects have the most worth, extrinsic value-objects the next worth, and systemic value-objects the least worth. The hierarchy of values thus affirms that intrinsic values are better than extrinsic values, which are better than systemic values; each increasingly valuable dimension has more good-making properties than the preceding dimension. In application, this means that people are more valuable than things, and things are more valuable than mere ideas of people or things.

identification with: being or becoming one with another valuationally and psychologically, so that even though they still exist, differences no longer matter; the most complete and intense manifestation of intrinsic valuation.

indifferent: completely lacking all interest, whether positive or negative; totally uninvolved; not valuing in any way.

intensions, or intensional concepts or meanings: ideas as such, as distinct from the enitities or realities to which they refer (their extensional meanings or referents); intensions are connotative meanings, ideas (word-meanings) that just mean themselves, or they are words that define or explain other words.

intentional concepts: ideas that require objects as an integral feature of their meanings; for example, "desires" are usually *for something*, "love" is usually *for someone, or some thing, or some idea.* Though intentional concepts usually have objects, a few are merely "free floating," seeking objects.

intrinsic values: ends in themselves; entities valuable to, for, and in themselves; examples: unique (one of a kind) conscious subjects of value and valuation like people, God, and animals.

intrinsic valuation: valuing anything with total personal identification; valuing anything with intense love, empathy, compassion, and concentration; valuing anything as fulfilling intrinsic value standards.

means to ends: useful in getting or achieving values beyond itself.

metaphors: in axiology, all figurative or non-literal words, phrases, and language forms such as similes, analogies, poetry, parables, myths, allegories, and the like.

morality: see "ethics."

moral virtues: enduring states of character that internally incorporate systemic, extrinsic, and intrinsic values and regularly result in morally correct extrinsic behaviors for intrinsic reasons, that is, in doing what we ought to do, what is best for ourselves and others, from intrinsic motives.

non-denumerably infinite: so vast as to exceed the endless set of whole numbers; an infinity of infinities.

objective: valid for or acceptable to any rational person or any disinterested being whatsoever; universally valid, accepted by most thoughtful people in all cultures.

ought: defined by Hartman as meaning "better than." A slightly more refined and inclusive definition would say that "We ought to do X" means "Doing X is the best thing we could do, so do it."

science: the combination or synthesis of an isomorphous formal axiom or system with its given subject matter or phenomenal field.

set: a group or collection of thoughts or objects.

systemic valuation: valuing anything with minimal emotional involvement; valuing disinterestedly or objectively, but not indifferently; valuing anything as fulfilling systemic value standards.

systemic values: concepts, ideas, thoughts, beliefs; examples: conceptual constructs, definitions, laws, rules, rituals, formalities, systems of belief, mathematics, logic, philosophy, theology, and the natural sciences.

transposing a transposition: disvaluing a value combination that diminishes or destroys value in such a way as to produce positive value, as does negating a negation in grammar or logic.

transposition: a combination of two or more value-objects that diminishes or destroys their value, as in crashing a good Ford into a good Buick.

uninterested: see "indifferent."

unique: Hartman offered three not easily reconcilable definitions. Unique things: 1. have all the properties that they have; 2. have properties or configurations of properties that nothing else has; 3. have a non-denumerable infinity of properties.

universal property: a quality or relation that can occur or be instantiated more than once.

value: 1. sometimes synonymous with "good,"—anything that fulfills conceptual standards or criteria; anything with which we are involved in any way. 2. sometimes not synonymous with "good,"—our most inclusive value word that covers all other value words that identify value similarities, words like "good," "bad," "valuable," "disvaluable, "fair," "average," "poor," "no good," etc.

valuation: how we value; the ways we attach value to something or anything; the process or activity of conscious cognitive, active, and affective involvement with value-objects; conscious personal involvement, by degrees.

WORKS CITED

Davis, John W. (1991). "Extrinsic Value and Valuation." In Rem B. Edwards and John W. Davis, eds., *Forms of Value and Valuation: Theory and Applications*. Lanham, MD: University Press of America, 59-80.

Dicken, Thomas M. and Edwards, Rem B. (2001). *Dialogues on Values and Centers of Value*. Amsterdam - New York: Editions Rodopi.

Edwards, Jonathan (1830). "The Justice of God in the Damnation of Sinners," *The Works of President Edwards*. New York: G. & C. & H. Carvill, 1830), Vol. 5.

Edwards, Rem B. (1973). "The Value of Man in the Hartman Value System," *The Journal of Value Inquiry*, 7, 141-47.

_____ (1979a). "Intrinsic and Extrinsic Value and Valuation," *The Journal of Value Inquiry*, 13: 133-43.

_____ (1979b). *Pleasures and Pains: A Theory of Qualitative Hedonism*. Ithaca, NY: Cornell University Press.

_____ (1991). "Universals, Individuals, and Intrinsic Good." In Rem B. Edwards and John W Davis, eds. *Forms of Value and Valuation: Theory and Applications*. Lanham, MD: University Press of America, 81-104.

_____ (1995). "Some Spurious Proofs for the Pure Ego." In Rem B. Edwards, ed. *Formal Axiology and Its Critics*. Amsterdam - Atlanta: Editions Rodopi, 41-50.

_____ (2000). *Religious Values and Valuations*. Chattanooga, TN: Paidia Press.

Forrest, Frank G. (1994). *Valuemetrics^N: The Science of Personal and Professional Ethics*. Amsterdam - Atlanta: Editions Rodopi.

_____ (1995). "A Reply to 'Ten Unanswered Questions.'" In Rem B. Edwards, ed., *Formal Axiology and its Critics*. Amsterdam - Atlanta: Editions Rodopi, 153-70.

_____ (2001). *Ethical Decision Making for the 21st Century*. Self-published.

_____ (2008). Two e-mail letters sent to Rem B. Edwards in October.

Hartman, Robert S. "Fundamental Terms in Ethics," perhaps unpublished, though scheduled for publication in the *Encyclopedia of Relevant Knowledge*, which may never have been published.

_____ "The Science of Value: Five Lectures on Formal Axiology," unpublished, 63 pages.

_____ (1952) "Research in the Logic of Value." *The Graduate School Record.* Ohio State University, 3:4, 6-8.

_____ (1957). "Value Propositions." In Ray Lepley, ed., *The Language of Value.* New York: Columbia University Press, 197-231.

_____ (1960). "Sputnik's Moral Challenge." *The Texas Quarterly,* 3: 9-23.

_____ (1961). "The Logic of Value." *The Review of Metaphysics,* 14:3, 389-432.

_____ (1962a) "The Individual in Management," an unpublished manuscript.

_____ (1962b). "The Self in Kierkegaard." *Journal of Existential Psychiatry,* 8: 409-36.

_____ (1964). "Four Axiological Proofs of the Infinite Value of Man." *Kant-Studien,* 54:4, 428-38.

_____ (1967). *The Structure of Value.* Carbondale, Ill.: Southern Illinois University Press.

_____ (1968). "Singular and Particular." *Critica,* 2: 15-51.

_____ (1970). "The Revolution Against War." In Robert Ginsberg, ed., *The Critique of War.* Chicago: Henry Regnery, Co.

_____ (1972). "The Value Structure of Creativity." *The Journal of Value Inquiry,* 6: 243-79.

_____ (1974). "The Value Structure of Intrinsic Value." *The Journal of Value Inquiry,* 8:2, 81-101.

_____ (1976). "The Value Structure of Justice." In Eugene Freeman, ed., *The Abdication of Philosophy: Philosophy and the Public Good: Essays in Honor of Paul Arthur Schilpp.* LaSalle, IL: Open Court Publishing Company, 129-56.

_____ (1991a). "Applications of the Science of Axiology." In Rem B. Edwards and John W. Davis, eds., *Forms of Value and Valuation: Theory and Applications.* Lanham, MD: University Press of America, 193-209.

_____ (1991b). "The Nature of Valuation." In Rem B. Edwards and John W. Davis, eds., *Forms of Value and Valuation: Theory and Applications.* Lanham, MD: University Press of America, 9-35.

_____ (1994). *Freedom to Live: The Robert Hartman Story.* Amsterdam - Atlanta: Editions Rodopi.

_____ (1995a). "Reply to Charles Hartshorne, 1965, 1967." In Rem B. Edwards, ed., *Formal Axiology and its Critics.* Amsterdam - Atlanta: Editions Rodopi, 56-61.

_____ (1995b). "Reply to Gordon Welty, 1970." In Rem B. Edwards, ed., *Formal Axiology and its Critics.* Amsterdam - Atlanta: Editions Rodopi, 94-104.

_____ (1995c). "Reply to Rem B. Edwards, 1968." In Rem B. Edwards, ed., *Formal Axiology and its Critics.* Amsterdam - Atlanta: Editions Rodopi, 61-5.

_____ (1995d). "Reply to Rem B. Edwards, 1973." In Rem B. Edwards, ed., *Formal Axiology and its Critics.* Amsterdam - Atlanta: Editions Rodopi, 111-17.

_____ (1995e). "Reply to Robert W. Mueller, 1969." In Rem B. Edwards, ed., *Formal Axiology and Its Critics* (Amsterdam - Atlanta: Editions Rodopi, 1995), 81-94.

_____ (2002). *The Knowledge of Good: Critique of Axiological Reason.* Amsterdam - New York: Editions Rodopi.

_____ (2006). *The Hartman Value Profile (HVP) Manual of Interpretation, 2nd Edition.* Knoxville, TN: The Robert S. Hartman Institute.

James, William (1890). *The Principles of Psychology, Vol. I.* New York: Dover Publications, Inc.

Kant, Immanuel (1949). *Fundamental Principles of the Metaphysics of Morals.* New York: Liberal Arts Press.

_____ (1956). *Critique of Practical Reason.* New York: The Liberal Arts Press.

Mayo, Bernard (1942). *Jefferson Himself.* Charlottesville: University Press of Virginia.

Moore, G. E. (1903). *Principia Ethica.* Cambridge, England: Cambridge University Press.

Moore, Mark A. (1991). "Mathematical Models and the Science of Values." In Rem B. Edwards and John W. Davis., eds., *Forms of Value and Valuation: Theory and Applications.* Lanham, MD: University Press of America, 171-92.

_____ (1995)."A Quantum Wave Model of Value Theory." In Rem B. Edwards, ed., *Formal Axiology and Its Critics.* Amsterdam - Atlanta: Editions Rodopi, 171-215.

Niebuhr, Reinhold (1956). *An Interpretation of Christian Ethics.* New York, Meridian Books.

Pomeroy, Leon (2005). *The New Science of Axiological Psychology.* Amsterdam -New York: Editions Rodopi.

Richards, Ted (2008). "Killing One to Save Five: A Test of Two Hartman-style Value Calculuses." *Journal of Formal Axiology: Theory and Practice*, 1, 187-205.

Richardson, Robert D. (2007). *William James: In the Maelstrom of American Modernism.* Boston: Houghton Mifflin Company.

Steinhart, Eric (2008). E-mail communication to Rem B. Edwards, Nov. 2008.

Suber, Peter (1998). "A Crash Course in the Mathematics of Infinite Sets." *The Saint John's Review*, 44:2, 35-59. Available online at:
http://www.earlham.edu/~peters/writing/infapp.htm.

Taylor, Jill Bolte (2006). *My Stroke of Insight: A Brain Scientist's Personal Journey.* New York: Viking.

Whitehead, Alfred North (1953). *Science and the Modern World.* New York: The Free Press.

_____ (1971). *The Concept of Nature.* Cambridge: The University Press.

INDEX

ABOUT THE AUTHOR

REM B. EDWARDS, Ph.D., received his A.B. degree from Emory University in 1956, where he was elected to Phi Beta Kappa. While in graduate school, he was a Danforth Graduate Fellow. He received a B.D. degree from Yale University Divinity School in 1959 and a Ph.D. in Philosophy from Emory University in 1962. He taught for four years at Jacksonville University in Florida, moved from there to the University of Tennessee in 1966, and retired from there partly in 1997 and partly in 1998. He kept an office on the University campus until the end of May, 2000. He was a U. T. Chancellor's Research Scholar in 1985 and a Lindsay Young Professor from 1987-1998. He continues to be professionally active.

His areas of specialization are Philosophy of Religion, American Philosophy, Medical Ethics, and Ethical Theory, with a special focus on Mental Health Care Ethics, Ethics and Animals, and Formal Axiology.

He is the author or editor of twenty other books including *Reason and Religion* (New York: Harcourt, 1972 and Lanham, MD: University Press of America, 1979); *Pleasures and Pains: A Theory of Qualitative Hedonism* (Ithaca: Cornell University Press, 1979); with Glenn Graber, *BioEthics* (San Diego: Harcourt, 1988); with John W. Davis, *Forms of Value and Valuation: Theory and Applications* (Lanham, MD: University Press of America, 1991); *Formal Axiology and Its Critics* (Amsterdam - Atlanta: Editions Rodopi, 1995); *Violence, Neglect, and the Elderly*, co-edited with Roy Cebik, Glenn Graber, and Frank H. Marsh (Greenwich, CT: JAI Press, 1996); *New Essays on Abortion and Bioethics*, (Greenwich, CT: JAI Press, 1997); *Ethics of Psychiatry: Insanity, Rational Autonomy, and Mental Health Care*, (Buffalo, NY: Prometheus Books, 1997); *Values, Ethics, and Alcoholism*, co-edited with Wayne Shelton, (Greenwich, CT: JAI Press, 1997); *Bioethics for Medical Education*, co-edited with Dr. Edward Bittar, (Stamford, CT: JAI Press, 1999); *Dialogues on Values and Centers of Value* (Amsterdam - New York: Editions Rodopi, 2001), co-authored with Thomas M. Dicken; and *What Caused the Big Bang?* (Amsterdam - New York: Editions Rodopi, 2001). *What Caused the Big*

Bang received the "Best Book of 2001" award from the Editors of the Value Inquiry Book Series. Forthcoming are several books dealing with values and religion. Edwards has also authored over eighty articles and reviews.

He is an Associate Editor with the Value Inquiry Book Series, published by Editions Rodopi, where he has been responsible for the Hartman Institute Axiological Studies special series. For a number of years he was co-editor of the Advances in Bioethics book series published by JAI Press. He did significant editorial work on the following books published in Rodopi's Hartman Institute Axiological Studies: Frank G. Forrest, *Valuemetrics^N: The Science of Personal and Professional Ethics*, 1994; Robert S. Hartman, *Freedom to Live: The Robert Hartman Story*, 1994; Armando Molina, *Our Ways: Values and Character*, 1997; Gary Acquaviva, *Violence, Values, and Our Future*, 2000; Robert S. Hartman, *The Knowledge of Good*, 2002, co-edited with Arthur Ellis; Leon Pomeroy, *The New Science of Axiological Psychology*, 2005; Gary Gallopin, *Beyond Perestroika: Axiology and the New Russian Entrepreneurs*, 2009. In 2008, Edwards became the senior editor of the new *Journal of Formal Axiology: Theory and Practice*.

Edwards has been the President of the Tennessee Philosophical Association (1973-74), the Society for Philosophy of Religion (1981-82), and the Southern Society for Philosophy and Psychology, (1984-85). He is a Charter Member and Fellow of the Robert S. Hartman Institute for Formal and Applied Axiology and has served on its Board of Directors since 1987. In 1989 he became its Secretary/ Treasurer; after October of 2007 he continued as its Secretary until October, 2009. He is the Webmaster for the website of the Robert S. Hartman Institute at: http://www.hartmaninstitute.org. He is a lifelong Methodist.

CPSIA information can be obtained
at www.ICGtesting.com
Printed in the USA
LVHW092230200321
682006LV00027B/210